FAST FOOD/SLOW FOOD

SOCIETY FOR ECONOMIC ANTHROPOLOGY (SEA) MONOGRAPHS

Deborah Winslow, University of New Hampshire
General Editor, Society for Economic Anthropology

Monographs for the Society for Economic Anthropology contain original essays that explore the connections between economics and social life. Each year's volume focuses on a different theme in economic anthropology. Earlier volumes were published with the University Press of America, Inc. (#1–15, 17), Rowman & Littlefield, Inc. (#16). The monographs are now published jointly by AltaMira Press and the Society for Economic Anthropology (http://nautarch.tamu.edu/anth/SEA/).

No. 1. Sutti Ortiz, ed., *Economic Anthropology: Topics and Theories.*
No. 2. Sidney M. Greenfield and Arnold Strickon, eds, *Entrepreneurship and Social Change.*
No. 3. Morgan D. Maclachlan, ed., *Household Economies and their Transformation.*
No. 4. Stuart Plattner, ed., *Market and Marketing.*
No. 5. John W. Bennett and John R. Brown, eds, *Production and Autonomy: Anthropological Studies and Critiques of Development.*
No. 6. Henry J. Rutz and Benjamin S. Orlove, eds, *The Social Economy of Consumption.*
No. 7. Christina Gladwin and Kathleen Truman, eds, *Food and Farm: Current Debates and Policies.*
No. 8. M. Estellie Smith, ed., *Perspectives on the Informal Economy.*
No. 9. Hill Gates and Alice Littlefield, eds, *Marxist Trends in Economic Anthropology.*
No. 10. Sutti Ortiz and Susan Lees, eds, *Understanding Economic Process.*
No. 11. Elizabeth M. Brumfiel, ed., *The Economic Anthropology of the State.*
No. 12. James M. Acheson, ed., *Anthropology and Institutional Economics.*
No. 13. Richard E. Blanton, Peter N. Peregrine, Deborah Winslow and Thomas D. Hall, eds, *Economic Analysis Beyond the Local System.*
No. 14. Robert C. Hunt and Antonio Gilman, eds, *Property in Economic Context.*
No. 15. David B. Small and Nicola Tannenbaum, eds, *At the Interface: The Household and Beyond.*
No. 16. Angelique Haugerud, M. Priscilla Stone, and Peter D. Little, eds, *Commodities and Globalization: Anthropological Perspectives.*
No. 17. Martha W. Rees and Josephine Smart, eds, *Plural Globalities in Multiple Localities: New World Border.*
No. 18. Jean Ensminger, ed, *Theory in Economic Anthropology.*
No. 19. Jeffrey H. Cohen and Norbert Dannhaeuser, eds, *Economic Development: An Anthropological Approach.*
No. 20. Gracia Clark, ed, *Gender at Work in Economic Life.*
No. 21. Cynthia Werner and Duran Bell, eds, *Values and Valuables: From the Sacred to the Symbolic*
No. 22. Lillian Trager, ed, *Migration and Economy: Global and Local Dynamics*
No. 23. E. Paul Durrenberger and Judith Martí, eds, *Labor in Cross-Cultural Perspective*
No. 24. Richard Wilk, ed, *Fast Food/Slow Food: The Cultural Economy of the Global Food System*

FAST FOOD/SLOW FOOD

The Cultural Economy of the Global Food System

EDITED BY
RICHARD WILK

ALTAMIRA PRESS
A Division of Rowman & Littlefield Publishers, Inc.
Lanham • New York • Toronto • Plymouth, UK

ALTAMIRA PRESS
A division of Rowman & Littlefield Publishers, Inc.
A wholly owned subsidiary of The Rowman & Littlefield Publishing Group, Inc.
4501 Forbes Boulevard, Suite 200
Lanham, MD 20706
www.altamirapress.com

Estover Road, Plymouth PL6 7PY, United Kingdom

Copyright © 2006 by Society for Economic Anthropology (SEA)

British Library Cataloguing in Publication Information Available

Library of Congress Cataloging-in-Publication Data

Fast food/slow food : the cultural economy of the global food system / edited by Richard Wilk.
    p.   cm. — (Society for Economic Anthropology monographs ; v. 24)
    A collection of papers presented at a conference.
    Includes bibliographical references and index.
    ISBN-13: 978-0-7591-0914-8 (cloth : alk. paper)
    ISBN-10: 0-7591-0914-1 (cloth : alk. paper)
    ISBN-13: 978-0-7591-0915-5 (pbk. : alk. paper)
    ISBN-10: 0-7591-0915-X (pbk. : alk. paper)
    1. Food industry and trade—Social aspects–Congresses.   2. Convenience foods—Social aspects—Congresses.   3. Cookery—Social aspects—Congresses.   4. Food habits—Social aspects—Congresses.   5. International economic integration—Social aspects—Congresses. I. Wilk, Richard R.   II. Title: Cultural economy of the global food system.   III. Series.
HD9000.5.F29 2006
338.4′7664—dc22

2006010813

Printed in the United States of America

Contents

Part I: Introduction

CHAPTER 1

Food at Moderate Speeds   SIDNEY MINTZ   3

CHAPTER 2

From Wild Weeds to Artisanal Cheese   RICHARD WILK   13

Part II: Whole Food Economies: Breaking Down Dichotomies

CHAPTER 3

Building Lives with Food: Production, Circulation, and Consumption
of Food in Yap   JAMES A. EGAN, MICHAEL L. BURTON, AND KAREN L. NERO   31

CHAPTER 4

Food for the Malian Middle Class: An Invisible Cuisine   DOLORES KOENIG   49

CHAPTER 5

Taco Bell, Maseca, and Slow Food: A Postmodern Apocalypse for Mexico's Peasant
Cuisine?   JEFFREY M. PILCHER   69

CHAPTER 6

From Hunger Foods to Heritage Foods: Challenges to Food Localization
in Lao PDR   PENNY VAN ESTERIK   83

CHAPTER 7

Tasting the Worlds of Yesterday and Today: Culinary Tourism and Nostalgia
Foods in Post-Soviet Russia   MELISSA L. CALDWELL   97

Part III: The Contradictions of Industrial Food

CHAPTER 8

Kaiten-zushi and *Konbini*: Japanese Food Culture in the Age of Mechanical
Reproduction   THEODORE C. BESTOR   115

CHAPTER 9

Rice Ball Rivalries: Japanese Convenience Stores and the Appetite of Late Capitalism
GAVIN HAMILTON WHITELAW   131

CHAPTER 10

Global Tastes, Local Contexts: An Ethnographic Account of Fast Food Expansion
in San Fernando City, the Philippines   TY MATEJOWSKY   145

Part IV: Transforming Markets and Reconnecting with Consumers

CHAPTER 11

From the Bottom Up: The Global Expansion of Chinese Vegetable Trade for
New York City Markets   VALERIE IMBRUCE   163

CHAPTER 12

The Role of Ideology in New Mexico's CSA (Community Supported
Agriculture) Organizations: Conflicting Visions between
Growers and Members   LOIS STANFORD   181

CHAPTER 13

Artisanal Cheese and Economies of Sentiment in New England
HEATHER PAXSON   201

CHAPTER 14

Fast and Slow Food in the Fast Lane: Automobility and the Australian Diet
CATHY BANWELL, JANE DIXON, SARAH HINDE, AND HEATHER MCINTYRE   219

CHAPTER 15

Just Java: Roasting Fair Trade Coffee   SARAH LYON   241

Index   259

About the Contributors   265

INTRODUCTION I

Speak Out
TCF

Food at Moderate Speeds ⅠI

SIDNEY MINTZ

THE THEME OF THE CONFERENCE where these essays were first presented considers where the history of food has led us Americans, particularly in the course of the last fifty years. In accord with that goal, I wish to offer a comment on food and on food studies, as I think an anthropologist of my generation might view them. It seems to me that, in the case of the American food system, an impasse has been created for us by the forces of what's called "progress," and so far, no one has found a way to escape it. Yet I must also wonder whether we, who like to think that we care greatly—both about what we eat, and about the health and environmental consequences of our food system—have thought seriously enough about what it is that we confront. Perhaps we need to know more than we do about the history and sociology of our own food practices. In our daily life we meet the enemy all the time, and indeed he probably is us. To "think out loud" about our problem, permit me to look back briefly in time.

For much the greater part of human existence, no large mass of people ever lived on basic foods that came from more than perhaps a dozen miles away. Until the rise of ancient empires, probably the only human food that ever traveled very far was salt. For millennia after the rise of such empires, most of the world's peoples in most places continued to live mainly on food from nearby. In the exceptional cases about which much is known, such as the Graeco-Roman world, basic food, especially wheat, did indeed travel far, to supplement local production. But Peter Garnsey (1988) has shown with what difficulty such regimens were instituted and maintained. Rome was more successful than Greece, but neither Greece nor Rome ever rested easy in regard to any long-distance food supply.

The far-flung ancient empires of which we read today were not, in fact, very far flung. Alexandria, Egypt, is about as far from Rome, Italy, as Atlanta, Georgia is from Albany, New York. For Rome, that was an immense distance. Accordingly, the Egyptian wheat exported to Greece and to Rome was unusual. Such grain was food for commoners, shipped to supplement local production; to everyone's thinking, it had traveled exceedingly far. Luxuries and rarities, of course, traveled much farther. But I am thinking here of basic foods, staples, consumed by large masses of "ordinary" people.

This obvious comment about distance and our food history has to be grasped firmly, in order to put in perspective the quickening of change in recent centuries. Over the centuries, foods continued to be moved great distances only with considerable difficulty. Nearly a millennium after the fall of Rome, when Henry III wanted sugar for the royal table, he was moved to ask the mayor of Winchester, that famous site of international fairs, for "three pounds of Alexandrine sugar, if so much can be had at one time" (Mintz 1985:82). That is not quite the tone we expect British kings to adopt when dealing with mayors—even in 1226.

Nor did this relative immobility of food systems decline rapidly. It is worth keeping in mind that until the very end of the fifteenth century, the world contained no *planetary*—that is, transoceanic—states. Not more than two centuries later, however, the European discovery of the New World had led to great changes in the world distribution of foods. Except for sweet potatoes (*Ipomoea batatas*), and unresolved debates as to the pre-Columbian presence of chickens in South America or maize (*Zea mays*) in Asia, there *were* no New World foods in the Old World—or vice versa—until the sixteenth century. As late as 1650, hardly any foods but spices traveled far, or fast, or were eaten by large numbers of people remote from their locus of production. Hence the dawn of a time when the foods of commoners might travel vast distances, to be consumed matter-of-factly each day by them, and possibly even more than once a day, was epochal in its significance.

I date the shift somewhat arbitrarily from the stabilization of sweetened tea as the common drink of the people of the United Kingdom. Those two alien substances, sugar and tea, had first been carried to Europe from the ends of the earth to tickle the fancy of the wealthy and powerful; yet within a mere century they had become a daily necessity of the European laboring masses.

Unlike the monarch's ermine and purple, his dolphins and swans, no sumptuary laws ever held back the consumption of such substances as sugar and tea. These intensely desired foods of the common man swiftly became favorites of the state, not because *nobody* could buy them, but because *anybody* could buy them. That was a crucial transformation of the state's rules for the regulation of consumption, including food consumption. It marked what appears to have been an absolutely irreversible alteration in a world system of provisioning. Thus in its time it seems that the only force more powerful than the sumptuary laws of royalty was the market. By itself that datum tells us something of what was happening to the market—and to the power of kings.

I use the plebeian consumption of sugar and tea in Europe and soon enough, in her overseas settlement colonies, merely as an indicator of a new day dawning:

capitalism had turned some sort of important corner. Later stages in the history of food can be marked off by such mileposts as the success of canning, particularly of meat; the start of the steamship era; the entry of Anglophone colonies such as Australia and Canada and New Zealand (and some might add, not entirely tongue-in-cheek, Argentina) into the British Empire (Friedmann 1978); the perfection of the internal combustion engine as an agricultural power tool; and so on. There seems no doubt that the era of the Industrial Revolution, which corresponded to basic changes in the depth and breadth of world capitalism, was also one of transformations in the nature of food production, distribution, and consumption.

Many would claim that the last few decades have seen yet another fundamental change. Certainly the volume of food traded over continental distances has risen swiftly, while the variety of food available worldwide has also risen. Even great peasant nations such as China, India, and Indonesia, as well as smaller ones such as Vietnam, Haiti, and Jamaica, are now drawn into skeins of international food trade as never before. Those nations that were thrust into the global system by plantation development centuries earlier, as were many of the Caribbean islands, have now become consumers of Florida orange juice, even as their inhabitants move to London, Amsterdam, and Paris in continuing waves of settlement.

The expansion of scale, the increased velocity of the market mechanism, and the ongoing migrations are of course coefficients of changes in production, in the division of labor, and accordingly, in eating habits, over large portions of the earth's surface. Gainful employment in global agriculture has actually declined, as agricultural productivity has risen. Every day more and more people eat more and more food that has been grown, processed, or cooked for them by fewer and fewer others.

Because I mean to make some assessment of how we eat, this brings me to cuisine. Unless we mean by *cuisine* merely *diet*, we need to say how we know a cuisine when we see (or eat) one. Its meaning inheres first of all in regularity. Cuisine has to begin with one person—in the history of our species, usually a female—preparing food for others. Those foods were made familiar by being made often, and in approximately the same way. The concept of cuisine is tied to regularity, to familiarity, to kin groups, and to the social use of local resources to meet the need for food. We humans have been cooking animals at least since the Upper Paleolithic, and possibly for far longer than that (Wrangham et al. 1999). We can infer from this that the relationship between the food that people customarily eat, and the place where that food is produced, was for much of the human record quite specific.

In accord with Revel (1982), I believe that, historically, a genuine cuisine can only begin as a local or regional manifestation. It takes shape within a definable ecological framework; it involves cooks who are drawing upon the same culinary repertory. It involves eaters who were aware of others like them, eating the same things, prepared in the same ways. Thus described, local or regional cuisine implies access to particular food resources, linked to specific local conditions. In turn, those resources imply seasons, the year's round; customs within local culture that form part of the structure of eating habits; and locally distinctive food processing and cooking techniques.

In any such region, many fish, fowl, and other feral animal resources are not available at all times. They have their seasons as well, revealed reproductively and, in the case of mammals, in the nurture of the young. Anadromous fish, such as the salmon and shad, exhibit dramatically what seasonality means. Nor do domestic plants and animals circumvent seasons: cows freshen and bear; lambing time is particular; most plants, including fruit-bearing trees, must be planted and harvested seasonally. Thus the ensemble of resources upon which a cuisine is erected are the local foundation, the raw materials, for that cuisine, along with its processing, preserving, and storage techniques.

And so local or regional cuisine refers to a specific set of raw foods; particular cooking and processing techniques; integration within local culture—a social group or community whose members cook known dishes regularly and seasonally; and consumers from the same region who know the cuisine and feel competent to discuss it. Even the lexicon is affected when chefs and eaters belong to the same culture, many of them competent enough to trade places as chefs and eaters. Hence even their food idioms become distinctive.

What, then, has been happening to such local cuisines, over time? The progressive emergence of a global system has worn away at local culinary systems of this sort, even as it has provided certain benefits. In the West, local or regional cuisines have been modified—occasionally even eliminated in large measure—by freezers, new processing and preservation techniques such as irradiation, packaged foods, improved transport, and the like. Similar changes are rapidly unfolding in the non-Western world as well.

Modernization is tremendously important because it has served to surmount the constraints of time and place. But some of those same constraints were once perceived simply as limiting conditions, as challenges; ingenious local solutions to the problems they posed were what gave those cuisines-in-place a lot of their flair and distinctiveness. Yet it is not surprising that in this era of rapid change, local people have sometimes chosen the immediately apparent benefits of modernization, unaware that among those features of their lives that they would eventually give up in exchange were such things as the smell of fresh-baked bread, the flavor of freshly picked berries, the taste of homemade pickles, and the sense of satisfaction to be found in one's own competence.

Many of the big technical additions, such as the invention and diffusion of canning, refrigeration, and freeze-drying, were extremely broad in their effects.

Indeed, at an earlier stage, many were highly beneficial in terms of sanitation and storage. Some were basically medical, such as pasteurization; some were technical, such as the invention of oleomargarine by the French chemist Mège Mouriès or Appert's invention of canning.

These changes frequently brought worldwide benefit. In their widest effects, they might be compared to such innovations as the hand-operated Singer sewing machine, possibly even to the spread of electrification. For my part, I do not believe that devices like the Bron Mandoline, the Cuisinart, or the pressure cooker should be damned, simply because they are modern. Indeed, in particular situations—where, for example, the labor demands upon women were absolutely excessive—such inventions actually made the perpetuation of traditional foods easier. I stress these considerations because, in our hope of retaining or recapturing what we may be losing, we must not forget that some technical advances have brought real benefits.

Still, so far as diversity in *local* foods, in processing, and in distinctive techniques and tastes are concerned, I fear that the aggregate effect of such changes overall has been erosive of difference—a settling for the mediocre—flattening variation, dissolving subtlety. The cumulative, selective process of modernity in action—whether of food, cooking method, cooking medium, plant variety, animal breed, or taste—has repeatedly picked as criteria such things as standardization, efficiency, preservability, convenience of packing and shipping, and underlying it all, the desire for profit.

Although it is not always crystal clear which criterion of success is at the top of that list, it is difficult not to conclude that taste always seems to be at the bottom: giving us wonderfully fragrant fruit that lacks taste, and meat that is tender but bland. Tomatoes and celery are my favorite examples of organoleptic reduction to the least common denominator; you may have others. It is certainly not that modern food often tastes bad. It is, rather, that if a novel food meets some of these other criteria (such as shipping well or maintaining a long shelf life), it is likely to be pushed on the consumer even if it is only minimally tasty. Hence there are grounds for a growing conviction that such advances will eventually destroy local taste and cooking, rather than sustain or improve it—by first establishing and then maintaining what can become, in effect, a global baseline of mediocrity. It usually involves over time the elimination of local production, and among the reasons given for doing so are convenience, time saving, reduction in manual labor, and "becoming modern." None of these reasons is intrinsically "bad"—as those who tout them are quick to remind us.

Since the end of World War II, many of the changes that we have witnessed in the so-called developed world have been unfolding elsewhere, as well. More income in what used to be called the Third World seems to result in similarities of preference that transcend cultural differences: increased consumption of cereals instead of tubers, bread instead of porridge, more animal protein and less vegetable protein, more food eaten outside the home, and so on. This may be a global pattern, surfacing in many poor countries. Starting from a purely caloric orientation, people replace tubers with cereals, and when cereal consumption has peaked, they begin to add animal protein. This sequence implies rising affluence, and a downward flow of income (and food). One need hardly add what everyone knows already. In the developed countries, obesity, heart and circulatory problems, and many other ills are laid at the door of a particular diet. That diet is eerily similar to that which the upwardly mobile struggle to achieve in the developing countries—only then to be followed by their own poor.

That there are also substantial exceptions to these inclinations, based on religious and ideological barriers, does not seem to invalidate what look like general global trends. In this way the world food picture appears somewhat to mirror the environmental picture: developed nations tell poor nations not to eat up their environments, while poor nations struggle for the right to be just as prodigal as their erstwhile colonial masters. The difference is that local agriculture is likely to decline, while forests disappear to make room for beef cattle for export. None of it bodes well.

The incongruity is made more dramatic when we recognize that relative prosperity in the West lies behind much of the culinary development of the past several decades. The artificially low cost of fossil fuel, water, and agricultural land—especially in the United States—is not indefinitely sustainable. Meanwhile, some of the upscale features of contemporary world food distribution, even if they are maintainable for another few decades, are clearly destructive from an ecological and, I would say, ethical perspective. In the future more and more people are likely to begin asking whether such features make any sense at all.

A trend in the direction of locally sustainable agricultures and food patterns appears now to be gathering momentum, if only at a snail's pace; the reasons for this trend are not altogether based on environmental concerns. Perhaps a growing anxiety about our future and the future of our children is leading people to think back with some longing to the order and predictability once provided in daily life by *constraints* of time and space—before an emerging world system began gradually to block out these facts of life as wasteful and unnecessary, and to replace them by making available food that was cheap, quickly prepared and eaten, and not very good.

The social role of food in daily life has figured importantly in this revaluation process. We eat every day, and often; we bring up our children at table; we celebrate their growth, and every holiday, personal and public, by eating together; we once thought it appropriate to grow herbs and fresh vegetables in the backyard, and to cook our own food, most of the time. Good food, consumed unhurriedly, in good company, was taken for granted. As with so much in life, we thought unthinkingly that it would go on forever.

I have argued elsewhere that what is given up that is most important when food supplies are no longer integrated with kin groups, communities, and regions concerns the loss of that rich texture of daily social interaction that underlies and sustains the production, processing, local distribution, and consumption of food. Now and then, people seem to be saying to each other, "*That's* what's missing." And if this is so—if *that* is what matters most to people who reject the global food system—then organizations such as Slow Food have much to give us.

To be sure, the signs of this concern are neither clear nor unequivocal. Even as many people bemoan the loss of a rich, highly personal culinary past, many *other* people celebrate their seeming *freedom*, and this is not fantasy. They celebrate freedom from the kitchen, from dishwashing, from provincial life, from the backyard, and so on. Somehow unsurprisingly, there is also celebration of the freedom from intimacy. Relatives can be a blessing, but not always; having one's babysitters living upstairs is a blessing, but not always. There is, then, hardly any unanimity, and I think we need to listen carefully. Listen, for example, to the writer who asks why the recipe for the bread made by his grandmother was not passed on to any of her eighteen descendants:

> How, after all, did my grandmother acquire her culinary magic? It required an elder not just willing but determined to share her powers with a neophyte. And it required an upstart who craved to follow the path treaded by forebears. Is it possible that as much as my grandmother's eighteen progeny revered her, that none of them wanted to *be* her? (Steinberg 1998:296)

How convenient to admire from a distance those wonderful home chefs whom we miss but do not really wish to be like! Becoming modern, it turns out, is not simply adding on new items of behavior, and when societies change, they rarely instruct those who are changing about the things they may be losing. Indeed, "societies" do not do the changing monolithically; the people in such societies do not always *know* what they are giving up. And then, too, not everybody laments the losses as losses but welcomes them as gains.

Yet there are those of us who do see these losses as losses, and we, too, are many. As we succeed in freeing ourselves, we also discover that among the things we have freed ourselves *from* are things we might, on second thought, really want to *keep*: a year punctuated by planting and harvest, especially if we're not doing all of the work ourselves; by first fruits and the end of seasons; by a sense of the year's round, connected with particular foods *and* with people—a feeling for time and place that has *not* been overwhelmed by technology. More and more of us wonder whether such things should be brought back, not only for ecology's sake, but also for the renewed meaning they can provide, in giving us, in addition to the recognition of our own mortality, a measurable human existence. If this is so, then a cuisine for the future will be as diverse as the world's peoples are: a cuisine that respects locality and distinctiveness, that does not make the erasure of cultural difference, the obliteration of time and space, and the mass production of satisfaction the best measures that we've got of human progress.

Trying to bring such changes about, however, compels us to confront difficult choices. Population growth, endangered water supplies, the need for alternative energy, the risks of endangered species and environments—all challenge an attempt to make plentiful, healthful, diverse, and delicious food available locally for more and more people. Even many worthy and intelligent programs designed to cope with one or another such problem may enjoy only limited appeal, either because there are too many competing worthy causes, or the message is not convincing to a broad crossclass audience, or "the other side" in each case has far greater resources and much wealthier protagonists. Of course, it is exactly because the promoters of "the other side" are so powerful that Slow Food, Chefs Collaborative, and other such programs are important. But we need also to acknowledge that those programs reach a limited number of people, most of them in the West, most of them educated people of some means. In practice, we have not yet gotten to that fork in the road where individuals who decide to live differently become parts of popular movements that can translate individual choices into politically significant group actions.

Often enough the choices—for example, fast food versus slow food—are painted in stark terms. At times they even contain an element of nostalgia that does not, of itself, make the problems any clearer. It is worth pondering whether we should invest all of our energies in restoring food to its former importance without tying our hope for better food to programs that raise ethical questions about labor practices, the expansion of cattle herding into crop-poor countries, the dredging of the sea, the overuse of water and fossil fuels, and much else. In other words—and of course I write this down only for myself—if we can formulate a food program worth supporting, it must have to do with far more than the foods themselves, where they come from, and how we prepare and eat them.

It was in thinking about those wider aspects to our hopes for better food for the world that I decided to make this a chapter not about fast food, nor even about slow food, but about what I call here *food of moderate speeds*. I do not think that we can legislate fast food away, and I doubt whether we can bring slow food to more than a modest fraction of the world's people. In that case, why not make our goal good and healthy food, produced locally, for everybody? Perhaps that would be food at moderate speeds. What are the steps to be taken; how can we formulate those necessary steps? One can hope that good and healthy food for more and more people is a reasonable goal, and that such foods can be made available fast enough—and more important, prepared at slow enough speeds—for all of us.

References

Friedmann, H. 1978. World Market, State and Family Farm: Social Bases of Household Production in the Era of Wage-labor. Comparative Studies in Society and History 20(4):545–86.

Garnsey, P. 1988. Famine and Food Supply in the Graeco-Roman World. Cambridge: Cambridge University Press.

Mintz, S. 1985. Sweetness and Power. New York: Viking-Penguin.

Revel, Jean. 1982. Culture and Cuisine. Garden City, NY: Doubleday.

Steinberg, S. 1998. Bubbie's Challah. In Eating Culture. Ron Scapp and Brian Seitz, eds. Pp. 295–97. Albany, NY: SUNY Press.

Wrangham, R. W., J. H. Jones, G. Laden, D. Pilbeam, and N. Conklin-Brittain. 1999. The Raw and the Stolen. Current Anthropology 40(5):567–79.

From Wild Weeds to Artisanal Cheese   2

RICHARD WILK

IN CHAPTER 1, SIDNEY MINTZ provides a magisterial view of global changes in food systems over the last millennium. Instead of sudden points of rupture or watersheds, he identifies a slow and uneven process of transition. Food systems in which the majority of every person's diet came from the immediate local environment and through the efforts of neighbors and kin have gradually been replaced, supplanted, or perhaps just augmented by systems of trade that move food as a commodity between anonymous producers and consumers.

I can see this contrast every Saturday morning in my home town. On my way to the thriving downtown farmer's market, I pass lines of cars stacked up at the take-out windows of McDonalds, Taco Bell, and Burger King. While I am buying organic peaches grown less than ten miles from my house and loading up my cooler chest with grass-fed lamb chops from an Amish farmer, others are on the way to the supermarket for grapes grown in Chile and frozen lamb from New Zealand. In our county some people live on a diet that is substantially homegrown or traded with friends and kin, who know where every bite came from, while many other families eat meals whose every ingredient has been processed in distant factories by strangers. Some families eat a home-cooked dinner around the table every night, while others eat microwaved frozen meals in front of the TV or sacks of take-out in the car.

Contrasts like these reveal the incredible variety and heterogeneity of the food system in the developed world, its protean creativity and unpredictable trends. But at the beginning of a semester when I ask students in my Food and Culture class about the future, this complexity and diversity suddenly disappears. They tell me that local food is dying, fast food is completely taking over, and the future will bring more and more artificial, industrially processed food, until we are all eating chemicals and protein grown in vats. And this is before they have begun to read their first assignment, Schlosser's (2001) *Fast Food Nation*.

My students see the stark contrast between the farmers' market and McDonalds, and like many other people, they jump to the conclusion that we are in the midst of an epic world-changing transition from one kind of food economy to another. The futuristic vision of a world of food pills and automated kitchens still has a grip on their imaginations (Belasco 2000). They have been brought up with an essentially linear understanding of history as *progress*. Even in their short lives they have seen new waves of fashions and technologies constantly driving old things out of the market. Many of them also come from very strong Christian backgrounds, so they have a lifelong acquaintance with biblical morality tales about the rise and fall of civilizations, including the original fall from grace (see Sahlins 1996). They have been ideologically prepared to think of the world as a sequence of states marked by radical transitions, where the old traditional world disappears under the weight of the new. This prepares them to look at the mixed food systems around them and extract a linear evolutionary story. They only disagree on the moral valences—some think the death of local and homemade foods is a tragedy that should be prevented if possible, while others see it as an inevitable sign of progress, or even as a great convenience that liberates people. After all, most of my undergraduates eat fewer than four sit-down meals a week; the rest of the time they swallow sandwiches and pizza in a process they have poetically termed "squat and gobble."

I never cease to be amazed that at the beginning of the semester, without having read a page or listened to a single lecture, my students seem capable of arriving at exactly the same conclusions as the well-informed scholars who wrote the books and articles on the syllabus. The students even come up with some of the same solutions. Even before they have started to read Petrini's (2001) *Slow Food*, they guess that the spread of modern gourmet tastes can support a "revived" or "resuscitated" form of traditional old-time cuisine. Some come from rural parts of Indiana where people still raise and butcher their own pigs and chickens, where old-fashioned roadside farm stands and rural shops sell high-quality local produce, and where home-canning on the farm is still widespread. Most have been to farmers' markets and green markets and are already far too familiar with the revival of artisanal beers, since our small town supports two micro-breweries. They intuitively understand what people are talking about when they contrast local slow foods with industrialized fast food, and they find it easy to arrange things in evolutionary phases that fit the sequence of premodern → modern → postmodern.

My students, like many of those writing about food for a popular audience, have fallen into a fundamental paradox of globalization and culture change, which most anthropologists will recognize immediately. In the long term, and at a very general scale, we can indeed discern major epochal evolutionary changes, what Mintz identifies as the "expansion of scale, the increased velocity of the market mechanism, and the ongoing migrations" that have so fundamentally changed world food systems (this volume: 5). Five thousand years ago most people were self-provisioning hunter-gatherers or small village farmers, and today most people in rich countries are eating processed foods bought in markets or stores, which are connected to global infrastructure, finance, and commodity flows.

The paradox is that when we look at any particular place or group of people, we find their food system works at a variety of scales. Part of their diet may be grown far away but processed at home, while another part is bought already cooked from street vendors who grow the ingredients or barter or buy them through an informal economy. Even the most "modern" urban people may relish a hybrid food like a microwaved imported frozen pizza topped with mushrooms gathered on a weekend hike in the woods. Food is everywhere *cooked*, which usually means being mixed, processed, and prepared in ways that combine ingredients of different origins. In one bite you may have slow grains and fast oil. The smaller the scale, the closer you look, the harder it is to use large-scale evolutionary generalizations to understand what you are seeing. This is one of the most important and central points made by the contributors to this collection, an issue that came up repeatedly at the conference where these essays were originally presented. The extremes of slow and fast, local and global, artisanal and industrial, are ideal types; at some level they may be good intellectual tools, but all the real action takes place *in between*, in the complex and interconnected highways where Mintz's "food of moderate speed" is traveling.

Each chapter in this book faces the general fact that, over time, industrial food systems that are more concerned with convenience, consistent delivery, and profit than flavor, individuality, or health, have flourished, often tearing away at the intricate webs of relationships that protect and sustain the poor and preserve local environments. As Mintz points out, we have good reason to worry about a future in which the whole world eats as wastefully and as unhealthfully as do the majority of North Americans and increasingly Europeans today. Many excellent studies show just how destructive industrial food systems can be, especially when they are abetted by political and economic policies that aim to steamroller the systems that support more than a billion rural farmers under the wheels of "free trade," "efficient markets," and "improved technology" (e.g., Goodman and Redclift 1991; Goodman and Watts 1997; Andrae and Beckman 1985; Madely 2000; Barndt 1999, 2002). The commodity foods spewed out by an increasingly centralized agro-industrial complex provoke justified fears of contamination, cultural homogenization, and exploitation. They are arguably responsible for an epidemic of obesity and have certainly dished out death and illness through *e. coli*, BSE (mad cow), and other forms of adulteration. A recent collection on the politics of food explores a whole range of important cultural and social issues raised for both producers and consumers by the globalization and industrialization of food

(Lien and Nerlich 2004, see also Bonanno et al. 1994). The paradox is that this same industrial food system is also feeding a huge global population of unprecedented size, without the sweeping famines which have been predicted by generations of Malthusians.

The authors in this volume generally share a sense of alarm at the direction of the industrial food system and are deeply aware of the complex politics of food. Each one shows the inadequacy of terms like *slow* and *fast*, or *traditional* and *modern*, to understand how people really eat, in settings as far apart as Yap and Mali. From a global scale, what looks like a linear long-term trend begins to resolve into processes that are full of contradictions, the contingencies of culture and human agency, and unexpected cycles, rehearsals, reversals, and reprises.

I have found exactly this degree of complexity in my research over the last fifteen years on the history and development of diet and cuisine in Belize (Wilk 1999, 2001, 2004, 2006). As in the rest of the Caribbean and many other parts of the world, industrial mass-produced food was part of the diet of the very first European settlers of the area. Buccaneers and pirates, masters and slaves, all ate large amounts of salted meat and fish, dried peas, biscuits and bread, wines, beer, and liquors, which were produced by proto-industries in Europe and North America. Producing, processing, and exporting this early industrial "fast food" diet was a major force in the economic rise of the North American colonies. Historically, the imported "industrial" diet has changed and developed alongside and completely intermingled with local subsistence economies, production for local markets, and an export economy. Brown sugar produced in Belize was exported to England and processed into white sugar, which was then re-exported back to Belize and other colonies, where it was considered far "superior" in quality to raw and local sugars and sweeteners. Coffee, cocoa, tobacco, and even curry powder followed similar long and complex pathways from colonies to the metropolis, and then back out to the colonies.

My point is that in Belize, what appears today as "local" and "traditional" cuisine incorporates earlier phases of industrial food. In the current phase of globalization driven by migration and tourism, new mixtures and interpretations of Belizean cuisine are appearing in places like Los Angeles, coastal tourist resorts, and among street vendors in Belize City. To be sure, you can visit a brand-new Subway store in Belize and order a sandwich made almost entirely from ingredients imported by the container-load each week—only the tomatoes and green peppers are local (the very idea of importing jalapeño peppers to Belize has comic potential). But Subway alone has very little significance for understanding the process of change in Belizean foodways. While it attracts rhetorical attention as the symbol of American fast food imperialism, more complex and important changes are taking place in farms, markets, and everyday domestic kitchens.

More telling is what I learned when I recently spoke to the owner of a restaurant in western Belize that serves Cambodian and Vietnamese dishes alongside standard Belizean fare. She explained that when she lived in Los Angeles, she learned the cuisine when visiting Asian markets, which were the best place to find the tropical root crops and vegetables she needed to make Belizean food for her sons, to teach them "what home tasted like." Now she can buy some of those same Oriental vegetables from Chinese immigrants who have taken up truck farming around cities and towns in Belize. Learning new cuisines has only sharpened her sense of Belizean food, even as she introduces a whole range of new foods to the neighborhood. You could ask for no clearer example of the intricate ways that processes of globalization affect food of *all* speeds, often in unexpected ways that resist being slotted into a grand narrative of progress or destruction. Mixing is constant, but somehow ideas of "tradition," "authenticity," and "home" which are essential elements of locality and social affiliation persist, and even thrive and flourish. How can we make theoretical sense out of the simultaneous processes of mixing and ordering?

Midtwentieth-century theorists of economic development tried to understand the complexity of poor countries with a concept of the "dual economy" (Boeke 1942; Furnivall 1948; Ranis 1977). Within each developing country you would find at the same time a "modern sector" that should be encouraged to grow and a "traditional sector" that would be pushed aside or allowed to wither away. Even at that time many economic anthropologists knew better, and they recognized that so-called primitive or traditional people had long historical engagements with the world economy, that urbanism and trade were ancient parts of economic life in many corners of the world.[1]

Part II of this book, beginning after this chapter, carries on this tradition of empirical holism. The chapters take an open-minded empirical approach to understanding how food systems are changing, rather than using evolutionary categories to predetermine the areas for analysis. They show how Yapese households combine food from many different sources in their daily meals (Egan et al.), how famine foods and gourmet treats from Laos are unexpectedly juxtaposed through connections to North American markets (Van Esterik), and that capitalist development and the appreciation of food heritage have become compatible in Moscow (Caldwell). In a comprehensive and holistic discussion of cuisine in Oaxaca, Pilcher shows how slow food tamales, culinary tourism, mass migration, and industrial tortillas combine in a setting that is simultaneously thoroughly global and completely local.

Koenig's chapter on the complexity of modern food systems in Mali suggests that the "invisibility" of a large part of the food system has allowed modernization theory and functional dualism to play a game of economic make-believe. A major portion of the food system is run by women in a sector economists typically dub "domestic" or "informal" and leave entirely out of their statistics. This is part of a general trend within economics, particularly macroeconomics, that devalues or obliterates the work of women, so that cooking a meal in a restaurant kitchen is counted as part of gross domestic product, while the same person cooking the same meal for the same person in a home kitchen is left out (see Ferber and Nelson 1993). Only industrial food traded in formal markets counts, in this worldview, and everything else is relegated to the traditional "subsistence" sector of the economy. Following this logic in a city where formal public institutions and legal trade have ceased to exist, like Kinshasa, would make the entire food economy invisible (Trefon 2004)!

More fundamentally, the chapters in this part of the book suggest that linear narratives of evolutionary change fail to describe contemporary food systems because they cannot grapple with the noncorporate nature of food culture itself. Food is by nature mobile, mixable, unfettered, and reflexively self-referential. A linear story about change requires stable characters—people or species or individual organisms. Conventional stories about the evolution of food require a similarly fixed object, a culture with a stable repertoire of tradition and custom, which includes a set menu of ingredients and recipes that can be passed down between generations.[2] One can certainly argue (and many have) that there is no element of culture that meets this definition, but food and cuisine fit the bill particularly poorly.

Recipes vary from kitchen to kitchen, and like ingredients, they tend to move freely across even the most substantial cultural boundaries. Cultures may temporarily fix or freeze a particular food or ingredient, like the American Thanksgiving roasted turkey, in a ritual context that defines important ideas of identity and cultural membership, but even iconic dishes are always changing in subtle ways (Wallendorf and Arnould 1991). Rather than being a random assortment of cultural elements like Lowie's "shreds and patches," however, food culture is always incorporating and rearranging new elements according to tastes, habits, and recipes that have an underlying logic, one aspect of which was eloquently described by Mary Douglas in her classic essay on the British meal (1971). Each of the chapters in part II tracks a part of the cross-cultural and international traffic in ingredients, recipes, and dishes, while simultaneously reporting on the processes of localization and re-incorporation of cuisine in a particular setting.

Contradictions and Counter-Currents

If the local food histories of places like Laos and Belize are not so easily separated into slow and fast categories, what about the centers of global industrial food like the United States and Canada, or the far-flung fast food empires of McDonalds and the Kentucky Colonel? Every time I go to a supermarket it looks like more and more of the shelf space belongs to fewer and fewer agribusinesses and food processing conglomerates. In my local market, "choice" of chicken means Perdue or Tyson, and a close look at labels shows that the frozen birds have all been injected with "broth" solutions full of salt and preservatives, comprising up to 10 percent of their weight.

Once again, however, the closer you get to the monolith of the food industry, the more it resolves into a complex mix of contradictions and contingencies. Recently anthropologists like Miller (1997) and Blim (2000) have urged us to think not of a single unitary capitalism, but about *capitalisms* in the plural, and to use the same ethnographic tools to understand the local particularities of capitalism that we have always used to analyze other kinds of economies.[3] Part III of this volume takes up this task, showing how the global/industrial food system includes simultaneous movements toward generification, homogeneity, and mass production, and new kinds of localization, creolization, and hybridization. Building on the work of theorists like Ritzer (1998, 2000), these chapters explore the contradictory tendencies within industrial food systems, which can be seen as the manifestation of the "creative destruction" Schumpeter saw as inherent in industrial capitalism (1975).

The authors in this book identify several different kinds of contradictions in the food industry. At the most intimate level, while producers and retailers continually strive to standardize and regularize their products, making food into just another commodity, consumers are fickle, and the dimensions of taste and preference continually elude the efforts of food science to reduce everything to measurable stimulus and response.

As scholars of consumption, particularly those in cultural studies, have gone to great lengths to show, consumers are often creative agents who subvert and bend mass-market commodities to their own ends (e.g., Mackay 1997). This is especially so in food consumption, which is never a passive activity and often involves processing, preparation, presentation, and other creative processes. De Certeau uses the particularly apt metaphor of "poaching" to describe the way consumers use commodities in ways their producers never expect (1984), as when young Canadians transform a cheap convenience food like Kraft macaroni and cheese into a nostalgic symbol of childhood and comfort (Rock 2004). As Whitelaw shows in chapter 9, this can lead retailers and consumers into a perpetual cat-and-mouse game where vendors have to stay agile in constant pursuit of the very food fashions they have promoted.

Even the largest behemoths of the food industry have to deal with the resistance and indifference of consumers, and the inherent contradictions of their tastes and demands, wanting for example both high-speed convenience and home-cooked flavor, or lots of fat but no calories. Consumers want food produced by hand which also meets industrial standards of quality, has no additives, and comes from happy animals and farmers. Diners want to find the same food in every outlet of a chain, but they also want a memorable meal, and to be welcomed and treated as individuals. In the long term this has led not to the much-anticipated flattening out of a McDonaldized world of uniform burgers and franchises but to a continual diversification and localization of the fast food industry, as shown by Matejowsky's contribution to this book. Matejowsky shows how the extension of fast food franchising into the Philippines has drawn on local capital, built on local knowledge, and catered to local taste, creating hybrid forms that are neither completely local, national, or global.

The chapters by Bestor and Whitelaw show that the tools of mass production offer considerable gains in convenience and profits, but all such efforts must eventually cope with the ineffable qualities of taste and continually changing ideas about health and well-being that are often expressed through food preference. As shown by their dogged efforts to force genetically modified and irradiated products onto markets around the world, agribusiness has been reluctant to cope with the cultural significance of food and recognize that it connects directly to very deeply rooted ideals about the healthy body, so it is never going to be an industrial feedstock like gasoline or other fuels. Even as simple a substance as water is so full of cultural meaning that the international trade in bottled water is now a $2 billion a year business.

This brings us to a central contradiction in mass food capitalism that appears in many of the book's chapters. While business seeks to turn food into a substitutable generic commodity, people as consumers constantly find ways to *decommodify* food, to make it personal, meaningful, cultural, and social. Family recipes and local food traditions can be seen as archetypical examples of what Weiner (1992) called *inalienable wealth*, property so thoroughly decommodified that it cannot be bought or sold, only gifted in ways that maintain its social identity and meaning. The very point of many food consumption rituals, from family meals to ceremonial feasts, is to transform sometimes anonymous raw materials into meaningful social relations. One paradox of the marketplace, however, is that the very acts that decommodify— identifying a food as a part of an inalienable *heritage*, to use Van Esterik's and Pilcher's examples in this book—give them higher value as *commodities* to high-end gourmets and cultural tourists. This ability of food to instantly change from commodity to noncommodity and back is why the traditional division of the food economy into *cash crop* and *subsistence* sectors is so useless and misleading, as Egan et al. and Koenig show in their chapters in part II.

These contradictions combine to account for the failure of grand evolutionary narratives to describe both what is happening today and what can potentially happen in the future. In thinking about the inequities and failures of mass-produced industrial food, a long-term historical and anthropological perspective has a great deal to offer. Davis (2001), for example, shows how global "free trade" in food commodities is hardly a new concept. He argues that late Victorian free trade policies led to famine and desolation in many parts of the British Empire, a possibility echoed by critics of today's emerging global food trade system (Oxfam 2002).

Davis and others working on Chinese and Japanese history suggest that different areas have been through many cycles of commodification and decommodification of food, with continual patterns of boom and bust in the production and long-distance trade of specific crops. These studies also show that the history of food industrialization has been contingent and unpredictable, connected to the history of colonialism, trade, and warfare in unexpected ways. Davis, for example, shows how those pursuing the free trade agenda really believed it would benefit Indian farmers. Like innumerable trade and agricultural bureaucrats before and since, they completely failed to understand how farming and food consumption were deeply rooted in culture, in existing socioeconomic structures, and in local human-environmental relationships that are complex and sensitive. As Lansing (1991) and Netting (1993) have persuasively argued, governments' uninformed meddling with these culturally grounded agroecosystems often leads to catastrophe. Local systems that are superbly suited to deal with environmental variability can be completely undercut by global trade and assistance policies, with terrible human consequences.

Making New Connections

Mintz ends his chapter on an optimistic tone, suggesting that somewhere between the pure ideal types of slow and fast food there is room to find a moderate pace where healthy and meaningful food is available to everyone. This is a realist vision that accepts that fast food is never going away, but that farmers' markets, home-cooked meals, and a passion for fresh, nonindustrial tomatoes that actually have taste and texture are never going to disappear either. This perspective moves us away from the idea that we are on the edge of a millennial precipice, watching the dying moments of a world of "real" food. There are many causes for concern and an urgent need for activism, but in many ways we are better off without the tinge of inevitability, the sense of fighting against a leviathan, that comes from simplistic evolutionary thinking. Instead, Mintz's realism prompts us to ask, what can be done to find that moderate pace and improve the kinds of choices and options open to producers and consumers who want quality and variety? The fourth part of this book addresses both the strengths and limitations of food activism and the growth of new connections between producers and consumers that promise something more than a flow of generic industrial commodities.

Food has long been a focus for political and social movements in many parts of the world; food is a potent symbol of what ails society, a way of making abstract issues like class or exploitation into a material, visceral reality. Slow Food is only one of many activist communities concerned with diet; one could also point to political vegetarians, animal rights activists, biolocalists, simple living and neorural groups, world trade opponents, public health advocates, the anti-GMO movement, and various other kinds of environmentalists and conservationists. The range of groups involved in food activism covers the entire spectrum from left to right and can create unlikely alliances between conservative religious groups and Marxists. Each of these activist and policy communities is itself culturally constituted and amenable to study using all the tools of economic anthropology.

Three chapters in part IV (Stanford, Paxson, and Banwell et al.) critically examine the economic networks centered around farmers' markets and specialist gourmet "boutique" food production, asking if they are really achieving their goals. After all, the Slow Food movement has been widely criticized as elitist, and it is easy to see it as just another example of the power of consumerist capitalism to commodify everything, even your opposition to commodification (see Frank and Weiland 1997; Labelle 2005; Chrzan 2005; Gaytán 2005). The authors in this section show, however, that the fundamental issue for those seeking alternatives to industrial farming is finding ways to make new connections between producers and consumers. There are plenty of small farmers willing to produce high-quality food and an abundance of consumers looking for healthy alternatives to supermarket fare, but in most rich countries the national infrastructures of agribusiness and large food processors has completely supplanted the local economic networks that once connected retailers with producers. The case discussed by Imbruce is particularly important in this light, showing how new market connections are being forged to serve the Asian community in the New York area through the actions of individuals working "from the ground up," rather than by large corporations or well-intentioned nongovernmental organizations (NGOs).

All the chapters in this last section of the book show that rebuilding connections between producers and consumers is a challenging and difficult task. The multinational food industry is highly mobile and flexible, allowing it to easily move capital and production to exploit cheap labor and resources wherever they are available. The food industry uses sophisticated information technology to track and predict production and manipulate markets for their own ends. Small farmers, cooperatives, and alternative food networks are going to have to use some of the same tools to get information moving between scattered producers, marketers, and consumers, so they can find and expand new niches. Even with the best intentions, as in the fair trade coffee networks discussed by Lyon in the last chapter of the book, we are likely to end up with a system that is what she calls a "combination of both the oppositional characteristics of slow food and the market-driven strategies of fast food" (this volume: 256).

Paxson's chapter on artisanal cheese producers explains just why the middle ground is so hard to find and occupy. The few producers who are trying to make high-quality cheese that is actually affordable, rather than a gourmet treat, have to cope with competition at both extremes. They have the most difficulty finding market outlets that reach their target consumers. Her chapter invites creative thinking about what food of moderate pace could actually look like, and how it could be produced, promoted, and purchased. Her analysis suggests that the retail system, now dominated in the United States by Wal-Mart and other giants, may be the greatest obstacle to a mass market for affordable, high-quality food. On the other hand, the nimble capitalist businesses that survive in a highly competitive market may simply respond to market demand for higher-quality food by applying the same methods of mass production and rationalization to gourmet products, organic food, and fair trade goods. Wal-Mart, for example, recently announced its intention to become the largest seller of organic food and gourmet wine in the United States in the next ten years (Cantisano 2005). How will this affect the world of alternative production described so well by Paxson?

Lyon's concluding chapter integrates many of the themes of the whole book, delving into the complex moral terrain created by attempts to create a food system that is "fair" to producers while still delivering a high-quality cup of coffee to consumers at a reasonable price. The idea that an economy incorporates moral values as well as utilitarian motives is at the very center of the discipline of economic anthropology. People have been struggling to make markets serve purposes other than simple provisioning and pecuniary gain since the institution was first invented, and there is no sign that people will ever stop infusing markets with cultural meaning. In an era when governments, largely under the influence of U.S. foreign policy, are retreating from their role in protecting consumers and producers and regulating the quality of food, voluntary and private efforts to make markets more moral are often the only option left. As Lyon shows, making new kinds of long-term connections between widely separated producers and consumers is requiring new sorts of agencies and agents, who face formidable problems.

To conclude, even though I have used the terms *fast* and *slow food* in this book's title, in practice they are deceptive categories that obscure more than they illuminate. It is comforting to be on the side of the valiant, small local producers and home-cooked meals, fighting the beast of industrial capitalism, but like it or not, most of us already work for the beast, and those who do not are eager to join up. The real world is far more interesting than any binary opposition or simple evolutionary sequence, and while simple terms may make for good propaganda, they prove woefully inadequate as tools for understanding the processes of change in food systems, and they are misleading and useless for anyone who is seriously interested in making safe, quality food of moderate pace available, not just to gourmets and food activists, but to everyone.

The contributors to this book, and the others who presented papers and posters at the annual meeting of the Society for Economic Anthropology (SEA) in Atlanta in April 2004, showed that economic anthropology has already made a substantial contribution to our understanding of global food systems. They reminded us that we have a vital tradition of scholarship which offers inspiration and practical tools for solving whatever new problems and issues appear on the menu.

Notes

Acknowledgments. The Society for Economic Anthropology has been my intellectual "home" community for many years, and I am grateful for the privilege of organizing an annual meeting on my own theme. When the call for papers went out in 2003, I was surprised and very happy with the response—sixty-one abstracts were submitted. I had the hair-pulling task of choosing just fifteen for the conference plenary session, and the rest were invited to give poster presentations. There were so many excellent abstracts that it was really excruciating to have to leave so many out of the plenary.

The conference itself was a great pleasure, with local arrangements beautifully arranged by Peggy Barlett and Sarah Lyon, with events sponsored by Agnes Scott College, Georgia State University, and Emory University, wonderful traditional southern food served in the very appropriate setting of the Decatur First Baptist Church, and a sumptuous closing banquet at the Eurasia Restaurant. The whole meeting was capped off with a guided tour of the De Kalb farmers' market on Sunday morning. The conference made the most of the opportunity the SEA annual meetings offer for a sustained and focused intellectual conversation. The sum of the meeting was far greater than the total of the parts. This kind of experience has become regrettably rare in academia, which makes it all the more valuable. I thank all the participants, and especially Peggy and Sarah for many kinds of support and help.

I wish I could have included all eighteen of the conference presentations in this book, but space limitations forced me into difficult choices having more to do with the thematic organization than the quality of the papers, which was uniformly high. I also asked Penny Van Esterik to expand her poster presentation from the conference into a full chapter for the volume, and Sidney Mintz kindly took time to adapt his keynote speech into an introductory chapter. I want to thank the three readers of the first draft of the book, who helped me make tough choices and assisted in getting comments to the authors to use in their revisions. My greatest editorial debt is to Deborah Winslow, who has been the SEA series editor since the office was created and has done a superb job getting the series organized and keeping the volumes on track. She is directly responsible for the consistently high intellectual quality of the books in this series, and she gave me excellent advice at every stage of this project.

My own intellectual debts in food studies are far too numerous to list here. I have to mention Marianne Lien, Warren Belasco, and especially Anne Murcott as my generous intellectual guides as I entered what was for me a new scholarly field. I also thank Anne Pyburn, who has shared my journey into the world of food, eating the same meals and often thinking the same thoughts. Nobody could ask for a better partner.

1. This is not the place for a history of early economic anthropology; one can find many examples of early economic anthropologists who included both subsistence and cash crop production in their holistic studies. Manning Nash's (1958) *Machine Age Maya* is a good example.

2. These are the familiar essentialized Weberian cultural entities that have been so thoroughly debunked by the last generation of critical scholarship in anthropology.

3. To a large extent the ethnographic study of capitalism was prefigured in Geertz's work in Java and Bali (1963); economic historians like Kirzner (1979) and more recently Storr (2004) have argued for a cultural approach to the varieties of capitalist enterprise.

References

Andrae, Guinea, and Born Beckman. 1985. The Wheat Trap: Bread and Underdevelopment in Nigeria. London: Zed Books.

Barndt, Deborah. 2002. Tangled Routes: Women, Work, and Globalization on the Tomato Trail. Boulder, CO: Westview Press.

Barndt, Deborah, ed. 1999. Women Working the NAFTA Food Chain: Women, Food and Globalization. Toronto: Second Story Press.

Belasco, Warren. 2000. Future Notes: The Meal-in-a-Pill. Food and Foodways 8(4): 253–71.

Blim, Michael. 2000. Capitalisms in Late Modernity. Annual Review of Anthropology 29:25–38.

Boeke, J. H. 1942. The Structure of the Netherlands Indies Economy. Washington, DC: Institute for Pacific Relations.

Bonanno, Alessandro, Lawrence Busch, William Friedland, Lourdes Gouveia, and Enzo Mingione, eds. 1994. From Columbus to ConAgra: The Globalization of Agriculture and Food. Lawrence: University of Kansas Press.

Cantisano, Amigo. 2005. Wal-Mart Plans to Move More Aggressively into Organics, Now Its Fastest Growing Category. Ag News You Can Use #70, June 17, 2005. Accessed online at http://www.organicconsumers.org/organic/walmart.cfm

Chrzan, Janet. 2005. Slow Food: What, Why, and to Where? Food, Culture and Society 7(2):117–32.

Davis, Mike. 2001. Late Victorian Holocausts: El Niño Famines and the Making of the Third World. London: Verso.

de Certeau, Michel. 1984. The Practice of Everyday Life. Berkeley: University of California Press.

Douglas, Mary. 1971. Deciphering a Meal. *In* Myth, Symbol and Culture. Clifford Geertz, ed. Pp. 61–82. New York: Norton.

Ferber, Marianne, and Julie Nelson, eds. 1993. Beyond Economic Man: Feminist Theory and Economics. Chicago: University of Chicago Press.

Frank, T., and M. Weiland, eds. 1997. Commodify Your Discontent. New York: W. W. Norton.

Furnivall, J. S. 1948. Colonial Policy and Practice. Cambridge: Cambridge University Press.

Gaytán, Marie Sarita. 2005. Globalizing Resistance: Slow Food and New Local Imaginaries. Food, Culture and Society 7(2):97–116.

Geertz, Clifford. 1963. Peddlers and Princes: Social Development and Economic Change in Two Indonesian Towns. Chicago: University of Chicago Press.

Goodman, David, and Michael Redclift. 1991. Refashioning Nature: Food, Ecology and Culture. London and New York: Routledge.

Goodman, David, and Michael Watts, eds. 1997. Globalizing Food, Agrarian Questions and Global Restructuring. New York: Routledge.

Kirzner, Israel. 1979. Perception, Opportunity and Profit: Studies in the Theory of Entrepreneurship. Chicago: University of Chicago Press.

Labelle, Julie. 2005. A Recipe for Connectedness: Bridging Production and Consumption with Slow Food. Food, Culture and Society 7(2):81–96.

Lansing, Stephen. 1991. Priests and Programmers. Princeton: Princeton University Press.

Lien, Marianne, and Brigitte Nerlich, eds. 2004. The Politics of Food. Oxford: Berg.

Mackay, Hugh. 1997. Consumption and Everyday Life. London: Sage Publications.

Madely, John. 2000. Hungry for Trade: How the Poor Pay for Free Trade. London and New York: Zed Books.

Miller, Daniel. 1997. Capitalism: An Ethnographic Approach. Oxford: Berg.

Nash, Manning. 1958. Machine Age Maya. Glencoe: Free Press.

Netting, Robert Mc. 1993. Smallholders, Householders: Farm Families and the Ecology of Intensive, Sustainable Agriculture. Tucson: University of Arizona Press.

Oxfam. 2002. Rigged Rules and Double Standards: Trade, Globalization and the Fight against Poverty. London: Oxfam International.

Petrini, Carlo. 2001. Slow Food: The Case for Taste. William McCuaig, trans. New York: Columbia University Press.

Ranis, Gustav. 1977. Development Theory at Three-Quarters Century. In Essays on Economic Development and Social Change in Honor of Bert F. Hoselitz. Manning Nash, ed. Pp. 269–325. Chicago: University of Chicago Press.

Ritzer, George. 1998. The McDonaldization Thesis. London: Sage Publications.

———. 2000. The McDonaldization of Society. Thousand Oaks, CA: Pine Forge Press.

Rock, Melanie. 2004. Consumption, Social Distinctions and Embodying Inequalities: Kraft Dinner in Montréal. Paper presented at the annual meeting of the Society for Economic Anthropology, Atlanta, April 22–25.

Sahlins, Marshall. 1996. The Sadness of Sweetness. Current Anthropology 17(1):395–428.

Schlosser, Eric. 2001. Fast Food Nation. Boston: Houghton Mifflin.

Schumpeter, Joseph A. 1975. [1942] Capitalism, Socialism and Democracy. New York: Harper.

Storr, Virgil. 2004. Enterprising Slaves and Master Pirates: Understanding Economic Life in the Bahamas. New York: Peter Lang.

Trefon, Theodore, ed. 2004. Reinventing Order in the Congo: How People Respond to State Failure in Kinshasa. London: Zed Books.

Wallendorf, Melanie, and Eric Arnould. 1991. "We Gather Together": Consumption Rituals of Thanksgiving Day. Journal of Consumer Research 18(1):13–31.

Weiner, Annette. 1992. Inalienable Possessions. Berkeley: University of California Press.

Wilk, Richard. 1999. "Real Belizean Food": Building Local Identity in the Transnational Caribbean. American Anthropologist 101(2):244–55.

———. 2001. Food and Nationalism: The Origins of Belizean Food. In Food Nations: Selling Taste in Consumer Societies. Warren Bellasco and Philip Scranton, eds. Pp. 67–89. Routledge: New York.

———. 2004. The Binge in the Food Economy of Nineteenth-Century Belize. In Changing Tastes: Food Culture and the Processes of Industrialization. Patricia Lysaght, ed. Pp. 110–20. Basel: Verlag der Schweizerischen Gesellschaft für Volkskunde.

———. 2006. Home Cooking in the Global Village: Caribbean Food from Buccaneers to Ecotourists. Oxford: Berg.

WHOLE FOOD ECONOMIES: BREAKING DOWN DICHOTOMIES II

Building Lives with Food: Production, Circulation, and Consumption of Food in Yap 3

JAMES A. EGAN, MICHAEL L. BURTON, AND KAREN L. NERO

FOOD IS EVERYWHERE RICHLY cultural. This is certainly so in the island complex of Yap in the Federated States of Micronesia, where local cultigens and fish have long played central roles in cultural reproduction. Yet food systems in Yap, like so many of the world's indigenous food systems, are threatened today by global processes that have led to transformations in the ecological and social contexts in which foods are produced, circulated, and consumed. One manifestation of these changes has been a general decline in local food production coupled with increased consumption of imported food. The broader social, economic, and political issues associated with these changes are numerous and include, among other things, important cultural disruptions. Local foods frequently express local cultural values in the ways that they bind people and land together in ecologically sustainable relationships. The diminished importance of these local foods in so many settings throughout the world speaks not only to reduced biodiversity in the earth's food supply, but also to new challenges to cultural diversity. Yet the transformations underway in Yap and elsewhere are not of a unitary nature. Nor are their outcomes foretold by simple evolutionary models that posit the replacement of the traditional by the modern, or even of "slow" foods by "fast" foods. Rather, interpretation of these changes in local settings requires careful attention to processes through which new relations and local-global interconnections are socially negotiated, possibly with unexpected results.

In this chapter we discuss a specific ethnographic case in which both local and imported foods are used in routine expressions of sociality that keep localized cultural distinctions alive in contexts that are becoming increasingly globalized. Within the Micronesian island complex of Yap, "slow" and "fast" foods are at the heart of pressing concerns for both economic self-sufficiency and cultural identity. Food is perhaps the quintessential means through which Yapese express important cultural values. Women's production of core starch foods (primarily taro and yams), balanced by male production of fish and other protein foods, has long underpinned the Yapese political economy. These locally produced and culturally elaborated foodstuffs continue to play central roles in cultural reproduction. But during the past forty years, an expanding wage economy has led to economic and social transformations in nearly all aspects of Yapese life. Contemporary standards of living include widespread consumption of food imports. Today over half of the Yapese diet is composed of imported foods, of which rice, canned meats and fish, and frozen chickens and turkey tails are central.

The quandaries presented by these economic circumstances are numerous. They include economic dependency accompanying outrageously high import/export ratios. Consumption of imported foods has negative nutritional consequences resulting in health problems such as diabetes, obesity, and hypertension (Schoeffel 1992; Shell 2001; Zimmet 1982). Equally important are perceptions of cultural loss. The very relevance of *yalen nu wa'ab*—customary Yapese ways—within the Yapese' own constructions of modernity is frequently evaluated in the terms of food eaten in Yapese households. As imports are eaten with greater regularity, Yapese express tremendous concern over the declining importance of locally produced foodstuffs that embody core cultural relations.

This concern is to some extent addressed through widespread and near-daily sharing of food resources between households. We have deliberately avoided the anthropological term *exchange* that is generally used to categorize routine daily, as well as occasional ceremonial, transfers of food between actors. While all households ensure that ceremonial transfers between kin groups and villages are relatively balanced over time according to the particular cultural norm, the daily transfers a family food producer makes to neighbors, workmates, and specific kin are more generally categorized as "help" (*ayuw*) and are not as strictly accounted. It is these daily individual, familial, and localized group decisions that constantly negotiate local meanings and values within changing economic circumstances. A farmer or fisher decides on a daily basis how to balance between feeding the family, sharing with neighbors or mates, transferring foods to kin or for community ceremonial use, or selling on the market.

Economic models often fail to include these micro-level processes that mediate between what analysts have labeled "subsistence," "exchange," and market spheres of activity. Statistics generally capture only the market transactions, failing to identify the substantial production and distribution of local foods within Pacific Island societies. Moreover, as Koenig (this volume) notes, the emphasis on cash crops and basic cereal grains leads analysts to overlook "secondary" food crops, such as fruits and vegetables. In much of the Pacific this problem is even more extreme because many crops that are neither cash crops nor basic grains are in fact the *primary* food sources—crops such as taro and breadfruit. Their production tends not to be measured in national income accounting, and these Pacific cultigens are understudied relative to the major market crops of the world. When considered at all, these foodstuffs are relegated to the generally unanalyzed sector of "subsistence" production, defined as production by the domestic unit for its own consumption. Yet, in Yap, the different foodstuffs—taro, yams, breadfruit, bananas, reef fish, and others—have many uses and destinations.

A case from our ethnographic records is typical. "H" is a middle-aged man and head of his household who held a full-time government job, working for the Yap Public Utilities and Contracts Division. His wife was employed at a foreign-owned and -operated garment factory located in the same municipality as their home. One Saturday, H and an adolescent son netted a large catch of fish. While they were loading their harvest into H's pickup truck at the shore, a fellow villager happened by to collect betel and was given a few fish. H and his son completed loading the truck with gear and fish. After a brief stop at home, they brought two stringers of fish to H's elderly father and mother who lived nearby in a neighboring village. H and his son then drove to town with a portion of their catch and sold it to a local store (which in turn sold it to store patrons with only a modest mark-up in price). Meanwhile, H's wife and eldest daughter fried some of the fish, which were eaten by household members later that evening. The remaining fish were placed in the home freezer to be prepared for meals over the course of the next few days.

What we found so striking in these many activities was their seamless fluidity. Allocation decisions were relatively spontaneous, handling at each turn the exigencies of the moment without suggesting any conceptual shift in strategy. To be sure, H recognized cultural obligations and common Yapese expressions of sociality in his distribution of fish, such as in sharing some of his catch with unexpected visitors at the shore and, especially, in providing fish to his parents. Yet different circumstances would have entailed different results: a smaller harvest would not have led to the sale at the local store; a relative's unanticipated request for help in preparing a dish for an office party at his or her place of employment might have suddenly emptied H's freezer. Yapese regularly integrate food production activities, wage labor, and transfers of foodstuffs to people of other households. Fish, betel, and drinking coconuts may end up in the market for sale; be given to relatives, neighbors, and friends; be presented at funerals or at intervillage feasting events; or be consumed by household members. While other kinds of local produce like taro and yams rarely ever found their way into local markets, their routine transfer *between* households and across domestic units, along with their use as forms of wealth at the ceremonial level, play important roles in cultural reproduction. The many social practices governing the ways food in Yap is produced, circulated, and consumed do far more than cover "subsistence"—Yapese use food both within and beyond the household to build their social world. Nor are imports excluded from such a role. Sacks of rice, tinned fish, beer, and other goods are not only presented alongside local foodstuffs as wealth in ceremonial feasting events, but they too are used in routine expressions of sociality that build and strengthen culturally ordered personal networks.

The Yapese Economy in the Global System

Yap is one of the four states of the Federated States of Micronesia (FSM). Part of the United States Trust Territory of the Pacific Islands after World War II, the FSM received independence in 1986 with approval of a Compact of Free Association with the United States, which maintained numerous interlinkages with the United States, including free entry of FSM citizens into the United States and FSM eligibility for many U.S. grants and educational programs. The compact also specified subsidies to the FSM which have totaled approximately 1.4 billion dollars over a fifteen-year period.

FSM reliance on external transfer payments is typical of most of today's Pacific microstates. When we conducted this research on Yap in 1991–1993, foreign transfer payments, mainly through the Compact of Free Association, elevated the standard of living for people throughout the FSM and fueled high import/export ratios. In 1989 imports to the FSM amounted to $72.7 million, of which $24.7 million were for food, beverages, and tobacco. In contrast, exports amounted to only $7.1 million (FSM 1991), including revenues from a garment factory in Yap that mainly employed young foreign contract workers (formerly from Sri Lanka, now from China). Transfer payments provided the primary source of funding for both national and state governments, most jobs were in the public sector, and wage employment was widespread.

Recent economic models of Pacific nations emphasize the role of foreign subsidies along with remittances from family members abroad in keeping national economies afloat, while subsistence production is limited to ensuring a basal standard of living to island populations (Bertram and Watters 1985, 1986; Poirine 1998; Bertram 1999). Although remittances were relatively minor in Yap in the early 1990s, the importance of foreign aid through the Compact of Free Association is clear. Still, we find in Yap that continued production of local foodstuffs is a source of economic strength, regularly making available desirable local food to all Yapese. In this connection, the term *subsistence* that refers to household production of foodstuffs that are consumed by household members is seriously flawed. More than just an "insurance floor" (Bertram 1999), these very foods through their production, circulation, and consumption embody the social and are used to define who Yapese are in a globalized world. Local foods and imports are integrated in the Yapese cultural economy through the ways that Yapese use them to mediate market, wage labor, external subsidies, and identities and relations culturally organized around idioms of land and clan. We further demonstrate that integration between the many components of Yap's economy is achieved through the fluidity of diverse practices conducted on a daily basis. We argue that the emphasis on "subsistence" and atomistic domestic units ignores vitally important social practices that achieve integration, namely everyday transfers of both local and imported foodstuffs between people of different households.

Households and Yapese Cultural Idioms of Land

Domestic production in Yap operates within a cultural context of social relations mediated by the idiom of land. Yapese believe that land is imbued with power and has both the potential for productivity to nourish people and the capacity to order relations among people. Individuals, although born with ties to fellow members of their respective matriclans, become fully social persons only by developing ties to land. Links to land make a person an extension of the land itself and, thereby, of its power and productivity. Moreover, by becoming an actual part of the land, the individual has also become part of the many other people who also have ties to this land, and they a part of him or her. Through land, they have all become one people.

The most basic landed unit to which an individual belongs is the estate—the *tabinaw*, with many *tabinaw* collectively comprising the village (*binaw*). Each *tabinaw* consists of, on the one hand, dispersed parcels of land containing one or more homestead compounds, taro patches, yam gardens, and betel and coconut orchards, and on the other hand, the people who collectively hold rights to these resources and who see themselves as extensions of the very land upon which they live. Yapese use the word *tabinaw* to refer to varying levels of membership in this landed unit. The residents of a *tabinaw* may collectively consist of a set of related households: that of an elderly man and woman, and those of their adult sons with their respective wives and children, although, as we see below, not all such households are nuclear. The spiritual center of this unit is the *def*, the stone foundation of the central dwelling of the elder estate head. But Yapese also refer to each of the constituent households associated with this *def* as a *tabinaw*, for each may reside in its own homestead compound, each is allocated specific resources of the broader estate for its own use, and each cares for its own livestock (pigs and chickens), arranges its own purchase of appliances, pays its own utility bills, and prepares its own meals. We have considered each of the latter specific residential units to be a "household" in our study because each enjoys considerable independence in routine economic decision-making and practice, particularly with respect to the provision, preparation, and consumption of food. Our selection of this level of *def*-based household as our unit of analysis is practical but must not be taken to imply that it is a concrete and discrete entity, as there is significant movement of individuals as well as products among related households, as we will demonstrate.

Still, many important resources are accessed and deployed through membership in higher-order corporate groups that are conceived in terms of land. A man of a "household" may purchase pigs with his own earnings and one day sell them, keeping the money for himself and his wife to use as they choose. He and his wife feed the pigs, however, with coconuts harvested from orchards shared by all the many "households" linked to the same *def.* He may catch fish off the coast of his own village to give as a prestation at the funeral of one of his wife's relatives, or, more likely, he may purchase large tuna in town with his own earnings for the occasion. Yet the fish will join those of the many people of his *def* and be presented in bulk as a contribution from the people of the *def* as a whole. Individuals access and use other resources as members of villages, intervillage alliance networks, and municipalities. While we have highlighted the household as our analytical category, we must emphasize that individuals participate in a variety of other kinds of relationships that produce linkages among households and their members.

We conducted a survey of thirty-five Yapese households in 1992. Here we report on the findings from these surveys, placed within the context of ethnography of the Yapese cultural economy of food. Our sample was divided between twenty-four households in "rural" villages of the municipalities of Dalipebinaw and Weloy, and eleven "urban" households in the vicinity of the port town of Colonia. Our characterization of residences in the vicinity of Colonia as "urban," however, does require qualification. The low population density and prevalent agricultural resources of the Colonia area make it atypical of urban settings in the Pacific region. Moreover, Colonia is centrally located within Yap and well connected to many distant points of the island complex by paved roads. Many people employed in Colonia commute to work each day from their home villages via automobile or the public bus system.

We conducted a household census and an inventory of household resources for each of our sample households. During four seasons we visited the households for seven consecutive days and collected recall data about four categories of activities that had occurred over the previous day. Sample household members reported upon all food production tasks undertaken, and by whom; all food consumption; and all food items entering or leaving the household. We did not weigh food items or assess their nutritional content. The unit of food consumption was in terms of incidence, for example, a thirty-eight-year-old male eating a particular variety of reef fish.

Production within the Yapese Cultural Economy of Food

Marine resources like fish and sea turtle and cultigens like taro and yams are not only staple Yapese foods, they play critical roles in cultural reproduction because of their capacity to encode the very social relations and cultural logics that organize

Yapese production and, in turn, hierarchy. The strategies Yapese people employ to ensure a materially and meaningfully viable existence employ food in ways that negotiate received systems of cultural meaning with the exigencies of new economic and sociopolitical circumstances, namely with wage income and new frames of reference for identity that accompany the forms of globalism present in Yap.

Virtually all of the households in our sample produced local foods. Thirty-two out of thirty-five households reported time spent farming, and nineteen of the thirty-five households reported time spent fishing. The households in the study had a mean of 19.79 hours of local food production per household per week. This included an average of 9.82 hours per week of farming and 2.73 hours per week of fishing. The most basic cultural principle expressed in staple foods is that of gendered complementarity. Yapese production has long been characterized by a division of labor in which men fish to provide protein foods of the culinary category *thumag*, while women farm to produce starchy staples that are collectively called *ggaan*. In our survey men did 85.3 percent of the fishing and women did 75.9 percent of the farming. Women tend irrigated taro patches to grow varieties of taro (chiefly *Cyrtosperma*). Yams, bananas, and other crops are harvested in swiddens. The other main food production task, care of pigs and chickens, is shared equally between males and females. Gendered complementarity in production thus organizes specific obligations among members of Yapese households. Men as husbands recognize obligations to provide fish to wives and young children, as they also are expected to provide fish to aged parents. Men take considerable pride in their reputations as fishermen, and those who rarely make trips to the shore are frequently subject to teasing, which, although conducted in a playful manner, is met with some embarrassment.

While fishing is a quintessentially male obligation, agricultural production has an even more profound association with female identity and the very membership of a wife within the estate of her husband (see Labby 1976; Egan 2004). A wife relocates to the home of her husband and his people upon marriage, where she is expected to demonstrate her worthiness through regular support to his *tabinaw* and village. Integral to this support is her agricultural production. Work in the taro patch is especially significant in this regard, for the taro patch is an agricultural resource maintained over potentially countless generations. The taro patch thereby embodies the labor of generations of women who have married into a particular estate. A woman's labor solidifies both her claim and that of her children (who are members of her matriclan) to positions within her husband's estate. To this end, the worst of all accusations one can make of a woman is to call her lazy (*mal mal*).

The life cycle of the household is an especially important predictor of local food production. Yapese acknowledge that agricultural production is especially challenging for young mothers. Within newly formed households, young mothers are unable to devote much energy to taro patch and swidden. As children age, however, they require less supervision and add to the household pool of labor. Not only are older children charged with the care of younger siblings, thereby freeing mother for agricultural work, but they participate in food production activities themselves. In our survey, girls aged ten to nineteen logged more farming hours than women aged twenty to twenty-nine or women aged thirty to thirty-nine.

However, middle-aged women are the primary agricultural producers in Yap. Yapese identify middle-aged women as the backbone of village support, referring to them as *gelngin e binaw* (the strength of the village). Women between forty and forty-nine years of age spent the most time in agricultural production. Overall, 40.3 percent of the time invested in farming was by women aged forty and over, and an additional 10.4 percent was by men over the age of forty. Similarly, male fishing is done mainly in two age categories: males from ten to nineteen years of age (24.9 percent of all hours reported) and men over forty years (51.5 percent). Younger men with regular cash incomes are able to substitute imported protein and purchased fish for their own fishing production. Most of the men retire by their early fifties and become able to intensify their own productive efforts with more frequent fishing trips (often with their adolescent sons) and some agricultural work.

Critical to these processes is the availability of workers of the appropriate age and gender for the tasks at hand. Larger Yapese households have more workers, especially the older men and women and the adolescent girls, as Yapese tend to live in three-generation households (Burton, Nero, and Egan 2002). Household size is correlated with the distinction between three-generation households and nuclear households ($r = .45$, $p = .007$), and three-generation households spent an average of 33.2 hours per week on food production, whereas other households (mainly nuclear) spent only 15.1 hours per week on food production ($p < .01$).

A second process that appears to be linked with local food production is access to electricity, which allows people to own refrigerators, freezers, and electric stoves. Access to electricity has a strong negative correlation with local food production ($r = -.72$, $p < .001$). Although we have few households in our sample that lack electricity, ethnographic observations support the finding that households without electricity engage in greater amounts of local food production. On the other hand, levels of wage labor had no effect on time devoted to food production.

The Cultural Economy of Food Consumption

Acts of food consumption stabilize and make visible the many local distinctions that organize Yapese production and hierarchy. The gendered complementarity so central to Yapese food production is consummated at meals; to truly eat, one should enjoy the cultural, taste, and nutritional balance achieved by eating foods from both of the basic paired Yapese culinary categories—*ggaan* (the female-produced starches) and *thumag* (male-produced protein). To eat one without the other is not to eat at all. Yapese also hold that an item of food becomes imbued with essences that derive from the land upon which it was grown, from the methods used to harvest it, and from the status of people who procured and prepared it. These essences in turn limit who can safely eat the food item. An elderly man of a *tabinaw* of high status who has been initiated into one of the famed Yapese eating classes (*yogum*) should eat taro harvested only from a high (*tabugul*) taro patch. Moreover, this taro should be prepared only by himself, his wife, or someone of like status, and only in special pots that are kept separate from those used by junior members of the *tabinaw* (possibly in an entirely separate kitchen or cook house). Food consumption thereby affirms one's connection to land and the developed state of order that land represents while, at the same time, ritually differentiating both lands and persons within a hierarchy.

Yapese have been incorporating imported foodstuffs into the diet for well over a century. Reliance upon imported food, however, dramatically increased in the later half of the twentieth century with the advent of large U.S. subsidies to Micronesia. Today, Yapese consume both imported and local foods on a regular basis: members of all thirty-five of our sample households had access to both local and imported foods throughout the year. Individuals reported eating at least some imported starch in 76 percent and local starch in 75 percent of all days sampled, and at least some imported protein in 68 percent of the days and local protein in 57 percent. Hence, although there are variations across household in levels of consumption of imported and local foods, blending of the two is ubiquitous.

Imported foods have to an extent become indigenized so that they embody Yapese cultural distinctions. As we note above, a man who has been initiated into one of the Yapese eating classes might maintain a kitchen separate from that of the common household, complete with its own stove and refrigerator. Condiments like soy sauce, ketchup, and mayonnaise may be purchased to stock each kitchen, thus establishing a conceptual distinction between individual bottles of condiments. Even more important, imported foods, like the local, are conceived in terms of the two gendered Yapese culinary categories. Canned meats and fish, frozen chickens and turkey tails, hot dogs, and other protein foodstuffs are considered *thumag*. This designation goes beyond a simple categorization of nutritional content—imported protein is gendered male. Yapese men, who are culturally obligated to provide *thumag* to wives, to parents, and to wives' relatives in the event of a funeral, regularly meet expectations with selected imported proteins as well as local. Conversely, imported starches (including rice that is now eaten almost every day in most households) are considered *ggaan*. Should a husband's *tabinaw* be hosting a funeral, a wife will expect her own parents, her brothers, and others of her natal *tabinaw* to help her support her husband's *tabinaw* with *ggaan*. Her supporters will answer with sacks of rice just as readily as with baskets of taro. Both are regarded as appropriately female contributions. As in many parts of the Pacific, rice—the quintessential "fast food"—is being indigenized and considered a core staple in both dietary and prestige terms.

Substitutions of imports for local foodstuffs are, however, not without tension. We have often heard Yapese gossip about a fellow villager whose wife and children ate "only mackerel" (meaning canned mackerel). Even worse are rumors that a wife feeds her family "only rice." Such a woman is spoken of as being *mal mal* (lazy), an accusation that strikes at the very core of a woman's being. Her investment in the estate of her husband and in her own children is thereby questioned. Clearly, there are limits as to how well imported foodstuffs can be made to carry the symbolic load of Yapese gender relations. Imported foods invoke very different relations of production and ultimately require either direct participation in Yap's subsidized wage economy or an indirect connection to it through dependable personal networks. They do not denote a wife's care of the *tabinaw* land nor establish as direct a link between people and land through consumption as do local cultigens.

Households throughout Yap regularly prepare both local and imported foods, not infrequently serving foods of both origins in the same day. Dietary variety is positively valued. Among households participating in our survey, it was most often the case that both rice and one or more local starch would be prepared in the morning and made available to household members throughout the day. In contrast, only one protein dish would usually be prepared for the day's meals. Yet it was not uncommon to be given reports of reef fish or a tuna steak being fried in one skillet (with imported vegetable oil), while Australian canned corned beef, onions, and local greens were fried in another. A hungry son might open a can of mackerel for a quick snack, but at the end of the day he might make a major meal of the land crab that his mother had earlier boiled in coconut cream.

Although all Yapese households blend imported and local foods into their diet, we have been able to identify three important correlates of the levels of consumption of these two food categories. The first of these is the level of local food production, which has a positive effect on local food consumption ($r = .64$, $p < .001$) and a negative effect on imported food consumption ($r = -.46$, $p < .01$). However, the absence of farming or fishing did not entail the complete absence of the associated local foods. The three households with no farming managed a mean per capita consumption rate of .73 items of local starch per day, and the sixteen households with no fishing had a mean per capita daily consumption rate of .38 items of local protein. These households would have obtained their local starches through interhousehold transfers.

The second factor associated with food consumption was the life cycle of the household. Households with older heads consumed higher levels of local foods ($r = .43$, $p < .01$) and lower levels of imported foods ($r = -.51$, $p < .005$). Third, access to electricity had a positive correlation with consumption of imported foods ($r = .36$, $p < .05$). Nonetheless, we must reiterate that, despite these contrasts, all households regularly consumed both local and imported foodstuffs. Nor did consumption of local and imported foods vary significantly with the number of wage workers in the household. In order to better appreciate how this could be so, we now turn to interhousehold food transfers.

Food Transfers in the Cultural Economy of Food

Yap has long been famous for its grand ceremonial exchange events known as *mitmit* as well as for some of the special forms of wealth that circulate within these contexts, notably the huge "stone money" disks called *rai* and shell valuables called *yar*. Foods are also forms of wealth that are presented in these same events, and, like traditional valuables, foods express underlying cultural relations through their transfer (Egan 1998, 2004). We have already mentioned the gendered obligations to provide *ggaan* (female starches) and *thumag* (male protein) to funeral hosts. Imported foods have been incorporated into these food categories and now are also given in special public events. Rice and, to a lesser extent, bread join taro and yams as prestige *ggaan*, while canned fish and meats now are presented along with locally caught fish as *thumag*. Marked by the high stakes involved in using these many items to make status claims, ceremonial gifting contexts transform common things of value that are quantitatively commensurate with other common things into items of wealth of qualitatively distinct kinds (Roth 2002; Egan 2004). This is an important process of recontextualization that incorporates imported foodstuffs into Yapese cultural categories.

Although large public gifting events like *mitmit*, *moka*, and potlatch have drawn the attention of anthropologists for nearly one hundred years, what too often is overlooked are *routine* transfers of things between persons of different small domestic units. Far less dramatic and lacking much ceremony, these mundane practices nonetheless may be integral to broader economic and sociopolitical strategies and to the integration of domestic units within entire regional economies. In Yap, frequent sharing of resources between people of different households distributes resources, making local foods available to those who do not produce them and imported foods available to those with limited means to buy them. Routine food transfers also constitute a social practice that binds together people and households that are linked by land or by affinal ties in ways that enable them to tap and distribute wealth within this economy, while to some degree keeping alive landed cultural distinctions and the social relations they support.

The sheer scale of nonmonetized local transfers revealed in our data was enormous. Nearly 40 percent of the local starch and local protein entering households in our yearlong study came from food transfers. Our sample households acquired 38.3 percent of all their local starches through sharing with kin, neighbors, and friends. Transfers of local protein (accounting for 39.4 percent of all local proteins entering sample households) were nearly as important as household production (accounting for 46.1 percent). Furthermore, imported foods also circulated through these same practices. Transfers accounted for 21.8 percent of all imported starches and 17.4 percent of all imported protein obtained by sample households over the year.

Monetized sale of local foods was far rarer than incidents of food sharing. Only 14.5 percent of local proteins was purchased, although nearly 20 percent of all fish entered households via purchase. Numerous small stores operate in the vicinity of Colonia selling batteries, cooking oil, beer, rice, tinned meats, and other imports. Many of these establishments also regularly buy fish directly from local fishermen (at 90 cents a pound in 1992) and offer it to patrons with only a modest markup in price (95 cents a pound). Yet most of the fish purchased by Yapese were acquired from the Yap Fishing Authority, a Yap state–subsidized, commercial export fishing venture that operates a number of boats equipped for long line fishing of tuna. Our survey turned up only two cases of the sale of fish caught by participants in our study to local stores, although we are aware that, in the previous year, the head of one of our sample households regularly sold portions of his catch of fish during a spell of unemployment. Individuals like this young man were important sources of fish for local stores, although, as we noted previously in the case of "H," men did spontaneously sell some of their harvest when it was especially large or when suddenly presented with special needs. In contrast, we had not even one report of the purchase or sale of local starch over the course of the year outside of a couple items purchased at a village fundraiser (transactions that Yapese viewed as contributions to the village and thus qualitatively distinct from market purchase). In 1992, local prestige starches like taro and yams were accessible only through the very land-clan relations that played such a critical role in giving Yapese women political presence in *tabinaw* and village affairs (Egan 1998).

Our emphasis on the smallest level of the Yapese "household" unit in systematic data collection worked well for consumption data, since this "household" is the very unit in which food is prepared and eaten. It has also sufficed for production, although many important resources available to the "household" are accessed through membership in more inclusive landed units. Circulation of food items, however, requires more careful consideration because the practices associated with transferring food items often involve specific relationships which, although conceived in the cultural terms of land, are not easily reducible to "household."

Consider the case of a young woman, living with her husband, who recently had given birth to their first child. Throughout the child's first year, the woman's mother frequently visited, and she rarely came without bringing a basket of taro or occasionally sweet potatoes (which were cooked and mashed to feed to the baby) (see Weiner 1988 for a comparable Trobriand example). Although our statistical analyses treat these events as transfers from one household to another, this interpretation does not well match local conceptions. Here a mother, and not her household, has given starches to her daughter and grandchild, not to another household. The mother's support has materially confirmed that she, daughter, and grandchild all form a matriline within a clan, and are therefore all *part of one another*. The basket of taro or sweet potato so given is deployed within social relationships, and its disposal establishes or affirms an enchainment of persons (see Strathern 1988). This same daughter later needed prestige starch to prepare a dish for an office party at her husband's place of employment. Not yet assigned a taro patch by her husband's elders, she went to her mother's village and harvested yams out of her mother's swidden. Given the logic of Yapese land tenure, swidden and taro patch are cultural products of mother's labor that has made mother and her progeny members of the mother's husband's estate. The swidden as both a tangible and symbolically rich object thus mediates the relationship between mother and daughter by making the daughter a part of her mother, and the daughter felt entitled to use her mother's swidden.

A second anecdote makes clear one more important dimension of the process of enchainment. Things received may be given again, establishing *chains of enchainment*. This vignette concerns the transfer of fish between three wives, all married to brothers of the same *tabinaw*. The first wife (A) and her husband and children live in town in their own home next to the house of the husband's parents. The second wife (B) and her husband and children have their own homestead compound back in the village. The third wife (C) and her husband and children also have their own home back in this same village near B. A's husband returned from a fishing venture with fish and gave them to A, who cut the heads from two especially large fish, and when B and her children were visiting the elderly parents the next day, A gave B the two large fish heads (a most highly valued part of the fish to Yapese). B later returned home to the village and promptly visited C to give her one of the heads, while keeping one for herself. B and C independently later prepared these fish heads to be eaten by themselves and their respective husbands and children in their own homes.

Food transfers in Yap express sociality in ways that build personal networks, and thus they become strategic. B and C above were both young mothers who were unable to do much agricultural work and who frequently depended upon each other for resources. Frequent "re-gifting" enables everyone to participate in these forms of sociality with all kinds of food items, both locally produced and imported, whether or not they are devoting time and energy to local production or are active participants in wage labor. Both the individual's and the particular household's developmental cycle position must be taken into account in the analyses. According to Yapese cultural logic, expectations vary accordingly and it is anticipated that individuals and households will normally progress through the expected cycle.

In our data, food transfers showed systematic relationships with the life cycle of the household. Households with older heads gave out more local food ($r = .36$, $p < .05$), received more imported food ($r = .57$, $p < .001$), and obtained a smaller percentage of food items from stores ($r = -.51$, $p < .005$). In addition, households with electricity received lower levels of imported foods ($r = -.36$, $p < .05$) and gave out less local foods ($r = -.37$, $p < .05$). Yet wage labor and hours spent in local production had no significant correlations with transfers of imported foods. While subtle differences did exist between households, sharing of foodstuffs was universal.

Our data on food transfers point to the importance of interhousehold linkages in mediating economic strategies. Persons and households are not isolated, independent units. Life instead involves connections, which persons must actively forge. By placing oneself within these networks of relationships, one is in a position to tap the many things flowing through them, including both local and imported foods. Some households may have greater access than others to particular foods (imported or local) that are fed into networks of food transfers. Others might draw certain resources from these supporting networks now (such as a young family), and in years to come become important contributors, such as the older heads of large households with many developed agricultural resources. The Yapese landed hierarchy provides a cultural framework for developing connections. The many people of a *tabinaw* who are linked by common association to its *def* may maintain different households and pursue very different lives, but they are all of one people, united by land. The daughter whose place in land has been established by the labor of her mother may now reside with her husband on his land, where she labors to earn a foothold for her own children. But she has not lost all claims to the land of her mother and its people. Idioms of land and the relations they define obtain relevancy in the subsidized wage economy because they continue to organize production of important foodstuffs while also organizing people into networks that establish conduits for the flow of local and imported resources.

Conclusion

Yapese modernity, like everywhere, is experienced in part through taste. Carry-out pizzas freshly made from imported ingredients at local stores are served at children's birthday parties. Family outings are planned at the beach, with friends and relatives taking a break from a volleyball game to sit down at picnic tables draped with checkered tablecloths and eat macaroni salads and barbequed hot dogs and chicken. Special occasions may call for a trip to one of the local restaurants owned and operated by American expatriates that offers "real American" cuisine. Yap has yet to see its first McDonalds franchise, but some might ask if the ever-expanding reach of the global economy is not working its homogenizing effects in Pacific islands famous for the persistence of their cultural traditions.

Today, anthropological analyses note the fluidity of "tradition" and the creative forging of identity. Errington and Gewertz (1996) have likened local systems of cultural meaning and action to "collectively maintained force fields" that each offer a sanctuary of locally controlled distinctions in a world increasingly dominated by global capital and the agendas of the state. We might ask, however, if changing consumption patterns have compromised that autonomy. Contemplating these issues as they are faced by Sepik River peoples like the Chambri of Papua New Guinea, these authors further suggest that limited autonomy, even if obtainable, is linked to the continued vitality of the subsistence economy (Gewertz and Errington 1991; Errington and Gewertz 1996).

Yapese are confronted with similar issues. The recent and heavily moralized discussions among Yapese over those who have forgotten "who they are" and become "customless" attest to the tensions experienced in current construction of modernist identities. Yet the Yapese situation differs in important respects from that of Sepik River peoples and others in Papua New Guinea. The broader economy within which Yapese persons live their lives is of a very different order. Like so many other small island nations in the Pacific basin, geopolitical issues, lack of a strong export commodity, and current political relations that establish adequate integration with a wealthy and powerful donor nation give the economy of the Federated States of Micronesia a very different flavor (see Bertram 1999).

In this context Yapese have developed strategies to meet their needs. Central is the continued relevance of local food production in Yapese lives that are just as touched by active participation in the U.S.-subsidized wage economy. Although it is surely the case that the local food economy absorbs many of the costs of reproducing labor, the production, circulation, and consumption of local foods makes available alternative and locally controlled systems of meaning for building identities, even as these identities also incorporate regular consumption of imported media, foodstuffs, and other commodities. Production and consumption of local foodstuffs vary with the developmental stage and size of the household and with its access to electricity. Yet all Yapese—regardless of employment status and household composition—have access to these foods and participate in social practices that distribute them. Routine transfers of both imported and local foodstuffs, as well as the fluidity of economic practices linking market, interhousehold transfers, and consumption, incorporate local production into Yapese lives in ways that cannot be apprehended simply as "subsistence." Just as important, the networks through which these many items flow are themselves organized by the idioms of land that structure Yapese production, gendered complementarity, and hierarchy. The systems of meaning embodied in land are no doubt transformed in the process, and new tensions arise as changes are socially negotiated. But it appears that the market forces and pushes and pulls of the "modern" world will ensure the persistence of localized Yapese culinary tastes for some time to come.

Note

Acknowledgment. Research for this chapter was funded by a grant from the U.S. National Science Foundation and by a gift from Dr. Robert Gumbiner.

References

Bertram, Geoff. 1999. The MIRAB Model Twelve Years On. The Contemporary Pacific 11(1):105–138.

Bertram, Geoffrey, and Ray F. Watters. 1985. The MIRAB Economy in Pacific Microstates. Pacific Viewpoint 26(3):497–519.

———. 1986. The MIRAB Process: Some Earlier Analysis and Context. Pacific Viewpoint 27(1):47–57.

Burton, Michael L., Karen L. Nero, and James A. Egan. 2002. The Circulation of Children through Households in Yap and Kosrae. Ethos 29(3):329–56.

Egan, James A. 1998. Taro, Fish and Funerals: Transformations in the Yapese Cultural Topography of Wealth. PhD dissertation, University of California, Irvine.

———. 2004. Value, Hierarchy, and the Inalienable in Yap. *In* Values and Valuables: From the Sacred to the Symbolic. Cynthia Werner and Duran Bell, eds. Pp. 21–48. Walnut Creek, CA: Altamira Press.

Errington, Frederick, and Deborah Gewertz. 1996. The Individuation of Tradition in a Papua New Guinean Modernity. American Anthropologist 98:114–26.

Gewertz, Deborah, and Frederick Errington. 1991. Twisted Histories, Altered Contexts: Representing Chambri in a World System. Cambridge: Cambridge University Press.

Koenig, Dolores. 2006. Food for the Malian Middle Class: An Invisible Cuisine. This volume.

Labby, David. 1976. The Demystification of Yap: Dialectics of Culture on a Micronesian Island. Chicago and London: University of Chicago Press.

Poirine, Bernard. 1994. Rent, Emigration and Unemployment in Small Islands: The MIRAB Model and the French Overseas Departments and Territories. World Development 22(12):1997–2010.

———. 1998. Should We Hate or Love MIRAB? The Contemporary Pacific 10(1): 65–105.

Roth, Christopher. 2002. Goods, Names, and Selves: Rethinking the Tshishian Potlatch. American Ethnologist 29(1):123–50.

Schoeffel, Penelope. 1992. Food, Health and Development in the Pacific Islands: Policy Implications for Micronesia. ISLA 1(2):223–50.

Shell, Ellen R. 2001. New World Syndrome. The Atlantic Monthly.

Strathern, Marilyn. 1988. The Gender of the Gift. Berkeley: University of California Press.

Weiner, Annette. 1988. The Trobrianders of Papua New Guinea. New York: Holt, Rinehart and Winston.

Zimmet, Paul. 1982. The Medical Effects of Lifestyle Change in Pacific Populations. Journal of Food and Nutrition 39(1):23–27.

Food for the Malian Middle Class: An Invisible Cuisine

4

DOLORES KOENIG

THE DIET OF MIDDLE-CLASS Malians has changed in response to colonization and globalization, but although Malians have adopted many new foods, they have kept a culturally Malian food system. This hybrid cuisine integrates them into international food systems but continues to use local ingredients and cooking techniques as well as local social and economic networks for production and distribution. These processes have created a modernized food system with distinctively Malian attributes, not a copy of the Western diet. Yet, given an international discourse that stresses Mali's poverty, this class and what it eats is invisible.

This chapter, on Mali's growing cosmopolitan upper-middle class and its characteristic patterns of food consumption, discusses what is known and what is not known about this food system. An introductory section looks at the changes in Mali's domestic political economy in recent years that have facilitated the growth of an urban middle class and presents the methodology used here. The second section uses the tools of subsector analysis to outline the structure of the food system, looking sequentially at consumers, retailers, processors, wholesalers and transporters, and producers. The final section analyzes the lack of visibility of this system and explores the consequences for our understanding of food globalization and development planning. See the map of Mali in figure 4.1 for an overview of the country.

The Growth of the Malian Middle Class

At independence in 1960, Mali was a socialist democracy that emphasized central planning and government ownership of enterprises. A relatively small bureaucracy attempted to create conditions for economic growth for the country and its mostly rural population (Jones 1976); these civil servants became the core of a small middle class. From the late 1960s through the 1990s, Mali faced many of the

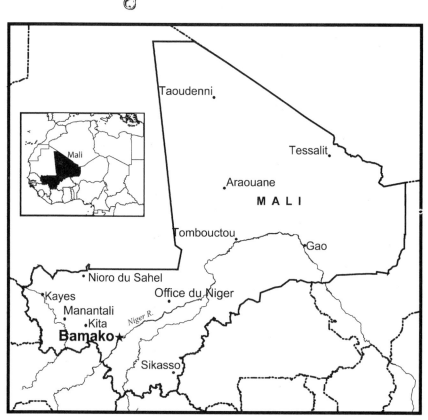

Figure 4.1.   Map of Mali.

challenges common to African countries: failure of its socialist government, coups d'état, drought, structural adjustment, and democratization. These challenges and the responses to them led to economic expansion that increased the size of the middle class. Despite structural adjustment, foreign assistance to Mali increased, creating jobs for qualified Malians as development agencies and donors began to hire local professionals instead of expatriate experts (Koenig, Diarra, and Sow 1998). Humanitarian initiatives and nongovernmental organizations also hired Malian staff and provided temporary contract work to more; for example, my anthropology colleagues at the national social science and humanities research center have seen their opportunities for funded research increase substantially since the 1980s. At the same time, structural adjustment and privatization increased the opportunities for some private entrepreneurs and enterprises. Over the last two decades, the number of banks, computer firms, telecommunications enterprises, and construction companies has increased, offering employment to many. To be sure, structural adjustment in Mali increased poverty for some at the same time as it gave others new sources of income. Those with larger incomes, however, did increase consumer spending. Malians used some of their increased buying power to demand new foods, stimulating other links along commodity chains.

Mali's middle class is primarily composed of educated professionals, not at the top of the power structure, but with professional or entrepreneurial positions that allow them to pursue a Malian middle-class lifestyle, which includes such things as owning a modern home and private transport (usually a car), increasingly sending their children to private primary schools, and, of interest here, changing food consumption habits.[1] This middle class is primarily urban and its size is reflected in the growth of Mali's cities; for example, Bamako, Mali's capital, grew from approximately 130,000 inhabitants in 1961 to an estimated 1.3 million in 2000 (BNETD 2001; UNEP 2001). The growth of the middle class is also seen in the extraordinary growth of neighborhoods laid out in accord with building codes and with access to city water and electricity. In the mid-1970s, the twelve kilometers from the southern bank of the Niger River to the then-new airport had few residents; it is now densely populated with multi-story houses and businesses. Because middle-class neighborhoods were essentially built from scratch, they stimulated a wide variety of work from professional architecture to artisan building trades to construction labor. The desire of middle-class residents to improve possibilities for their children led them to turn from overcrowded public schools to new and expanded private schools, particularly at the primary level; these provided work for administrators and teachers as well as for the many women who sold lunch and snacks to children.

Mali's growing multi-ethnic middle class has developed an urban cuisine that draws upon its many ethnic traditions. This class is also quite cosmopolitan, because few Malians could earn advanced degrees at home until recently, and many educated Malians have spent some time in other countries. During these sojourns, they got to know new foods. Nevertheless, by international standards, this middle class is relatively poor; the monthly salary of the average civil servant remains well under US$1000. People still eat mostly home-cooked meals and as of summer 2004, there were still no major international fast-food chains in Bamako.

Despite the growth of Mali's middle class, there is remarkably little written about it; Mali's international image remains that of a landlocked country of the West African Sahel, one of the world's poorest and least developed countries. Therefore, my knowledge about the middle-class diet comes mostly from participant observation. The emphasis here is on participation; in the twenty-five-plus years that I've carried out anthropological research in Mali, I've eaten many foods with Malian friends and colleagues, in their homes and in small local restaurants. Since the 1970s, I have seen the diversity and quality of food increase markedly. One

Malian colleague remarked that even ten years ago, research teams often needed to bring food with them, but now virtually every town has at least a few small restaurants with adequate meals.

Subsector analysis has generally focused on a single crop to describe empirically its movement from production to the market. It looks at the commodity chain through input distribution, farm-level production, processing, storage, assembly, transportation, wholesaling, retailing, financing, and consumption; its primary goal is to uncover obstacles to productivity and efficiency (Staatz 1997). Subsector analysis can be considered the first descriptive step on the way to commodity-chain analysis, which looks more directly at how power relationships at different points in the system constrain choices. Many studies have used global commodity-chain analysis to understand how products grown in developing countries enter international export markets (Raikes, Jensen, and Ponte 2000), but this type of analysis is also useful for understanding African domestic or regional trade (Chalfin 2001; Ribot 1998). Because of the limited data, this chapter concentrates on description. It stretches the subsector beyond a single crop to look at the multifaceted food system of middle-class Malians.

Middle-Class Malian Consumers

The Malian middle-class diet is based on many different foods. Some are of Malian origin and others come from outside the country, but it is misleading to envision a simple dichotomy of local versus imported foods. Increased demand for some local foods, like rice, cannot be met domestically, so local production is complemented by imports. Other imported foods have come to be Africanized, in the sense that they are now grown or processed locally. This process has been occurring for hundreds of years, as Europeans brought from the Americas many foods now a basic part of African diets, including cassava, maize, peanuts, and tomatoes. French colonialism from the late nineteenth through mid-twentieth centuries also brought new foods, and the international experiences of many Malians opened their eyes to yet others. This section concentrates on those foods that have become part of the typical diet.

The core of urban lunch and dinner, a starch with a sauce, is based on Malian tradition; a grain, which can be processed in a variety of ways, is served in a large bowl, with sauce poured over it. People eat communally from this bowl, each person partaking of the section closest to him or her. In rural areas, men and women usually eat from separate bowls, but in urban middle class households, they may all eat together. Some urban Malians will use spoons or forks, but many continue to use the right hand as their major utensil.

In rural areas, people often eat the same grain every day for lunch and dinner because they draw primarily upon their own food stores; they usually grow only a limited variety of grains. Sauces also vary little; they draw on local production, gathered foods, and a limited number of purchased ingredients. The amount of meat or fish in the sauce is minimal except on feast days and special occasions, and variation in ingredients is mainly a function of seasonal availability. Grain and sauce is often the entire meal, and the only drink offered will be water. The urban diet shows more diversity and quality in the ingredients and has added complementary foods.

Since middle-class consumers buy most of their food, they are not bound by seasonal constraints to the same extent. Although urban households continue to consume millet and sorghum, they increasingly eat rice, which needs less processing and preparation and meets their need to save time. In West Africa, rice has also come to be seen as a more refined and cosmopolitan food, the grain of the urban elite. While millet and sorghum are grown locally in many parts of Mali, rice is grown in only limited areas, since it needs to be irrigated. Although there is an indigenous West African rice (*Oryza glaberrima*), production of white rice (*Oryza sativa*) has become more common; the region also regularly imports rice, mostly from Asia.[2] Urban Malians also buy tubers to replace the staple grain. These include plantains and cassava (especially in a processed form called *attieke*), foods that have been borrowed from higher rainfall neighbors; while some are probably imported from neighboring countries, they may also be cultivated locally on irrigated farms. People also eat potatoes, often as french fries; these may have been introduced by the French during the colonial period, but they are now grown in southeast Mali. Imported pasta is also eaten.

Sauce ingredients are more varied in urban areas as well; they are also more abundant and include more vegetables and more protein, either meat or fish. As noted, many urban households have begun to eat dishes not native to their ethnic group; for example, peanut sauce, considered to be a food of the Malinke, the first large-scale peanut growers, has become a national staple. Vegetable ingredients of sauces include tomatoes, onions, garlic, and okra as well as leaves, eggplant, squash, and other vegetables.

Urban consumption has undoubtedly stimulated increased production of both sauce vegetables and meat, including chicken, beef, and lamb. Economically high-value fruits and vegetables are grown intensively, even in Bamako itself on the banks and islands of the Niger River (cf. Dettwyler 1986). Meat appears to be primarily locally produced; it usually arrives in markets alive and is butchered in place. It has been harder to increase production of fish, still mostly caught in rivers and lakes; ocean fish, sometimes frozen, is imported from neighboring coastal countries such as Senegal and Côte d'Ivoire. While most condiments are grown locally, some seasonings are imported. This includes salt and various brands of seasoning cubes, which substitute for diverse local ingredients.

Urban consumers have also added foods. Bread shows the influence of the French and is available on almost every street corner in Bamako, in virtually every small town, and in some villages. It relies on imported wheat, but the technology of bread making has spread widely, and there are bread ovens even in quite small villages. Bread may substitute for cakes and porridge based on local grains for breakfast, and it serves as a portable food for travelers; it has not replaced local grains as the basic starch for lunch and dinner, however. Salad has also become popular and is served at dinner, especially when there are guests. It includes not only lettuce, but onions, beets, carrots, and tomatoes. The ingredients are mostly locally grown, although they may include some imports; for example, some salads include canned ears of baby corn, brought in via Southeast Asian cuisine because of colonial links.

Finally, middle-class urban Malians have added snacks, desserts, and drinks. Desserts are typically fresh fruit, and depending on the season, include bananas, mangoes, pineapples, oranges, grapefruit, guavas, and dates, mostly of local origin. Snack foods include peanuts and locally produced and processed popcorn, and, increasingly, cookies and sweet cakes. Most cookies are imported, but there is increasing local production of sweets, including cakes, doughnuts, and popsicles. Malians consume industrial soft drinks as well as local juices, based on ingredients such as hibiscus flowers, ginger, mint, and tamarind. Soft drinks as well as beer are processed in a local bottling plant with multinational links; while alcohol is widely available, consumption is lower in this primarily Muslim country than among its non-Muslim neighbors.

The varied middle-class diet has become modernized by drawing on exotic sources and including processed and imported foods, but Malians have Africanized or Malianized many of these new foods, inserting them into a food system still oriented around a communal bowl of starch and sauce. Much production and processing occurs locally, further entrenching these foods in the local economy. This urban middle-class hybrid food system has created a demand for products that retailers have met in various ways.

Bamako Retailers

Urban middle-class Malians buy most of their food in a highly segmented and specialized retail market system, which includes central downtown areas and small neighborhood marketplaces, small stores, and open-air street sellers. Many middle-class consumers try to buy nonperishable products such as grains in bulk, but they continue to buy perishable foods on a daily basis, in part because of Bamako's uncertain electricity supply.[3] Since middle-class households often host family members from rural areas or other towns on a short- and long-term basis, daily purchases of higher-valued foods help regulate food expenditures. This section provides a brief overview of retail options.

Basic staple grains like rice or sorghum are often bought from specialized grain traders located in central market areas, in bulk in fifty- or one hundred–kilogram sacks. Others buy grains from colleagues who have entered the grain trade as a subsidiary occupation; they can often pick up their cereals at work or in their neighborhoods. More perishable starches like potatoes or plantains are bought as needed. Most perishable produce is purchased in open-air markets. Butchers have specific areas, as do fish sellers; markets are found downtown, on major commuter routes (to facilitate purchases on the way home from work), and in neighborhoods. Sauce ingredients, vegetables, and fruits are sold in multiple markets as well. Some markets sell a wide variety of foods, while others are more specialized. For example, Dibida, a subsidiary market in downtown Bamako, specializes in high-quality produce, meat, and fresh fish as well as hardware. The left bank of the Niger River, along a busy commuter route, has citrus sellers in one area and fish in another, with the busiest time the evening rush hour. In addition, small vendors are sprinkled throughout middle-class neighborhoods. For example, local bus stops often have multiple salad, vegetable, and fruit vendors, who catch customers on their way home from work.

Even as fresh foods continue to be sold in open-air markets or by specialized bulk sellers, the number of small and medium-sized groceries has grown substantially. Groceries concentrate on the imported and processed foods that have become staples of Malian life: coffee, tea, powdered milk, sugar, mustard, oil, vinegar, and snacks. They also sell cleaning products, insecticides, cosmetics, and hygiene and other household items. Those with refrigerators often sell cold drinks, yogurt, and other snacks. Small groceries are complemented by tiny neighborhood vendors, who sell coffee, tea, sugar, powdered milk, soap, and other essentials in small quantities.

To the best of my knowledge, there are no comprehensive studies of food retailing in Bamako, although it appears that these markets have some characteristics similar to those in Kumasi, Ghana (Clark 1994). Vending is highly gendered. Large-scale grain traders, butchers, and meat vendors tend to be men. Fish, fruits, and vegetables are more commonly sold by women. Small stores are often staffed by men, but it is impossible to know who owns medium-sized groceries; more men tended to work in these stores, but it was not clear whether they were employees or owner-operators. Much of the open-air food retailing would be characterized as informal sector, in the sense that vendors did not always keep detailed accounts for tax purposes. It is not clear that produce itself is taxed or that open-air small merchants collect or pay value-added tax. However, marketplaces are well organized and vendors usually pay a fee to rent space.

While consumers in some parts of Africa have come to depend more on multipurpose large-scale groceries, this has not happened in Mali or in many other parts of West Africa. The presence of multiple small sellers in middle-class neighborhoods offers consumers a high degree of convenience and jobs to many small vendors. Mali has marketing traditions of considerable time depth, but whether contemporary systems, affected by urban growth and changing government policies, still work in the ways described in the classic works on West African market systems (e.g., Bohannon and Dalton 1965; Meillassoux 1971) is not clear. The classic literature, moreover, does not include new institutions such as small groceries. How much capital, for example, is needed to open a store; what are the sources of retail stock; what issues does management face; do these stores turn a profit and on what goods? Do certain kinds of retailing earn substantially more than others; what kinds of stratification exist among retailers?

Food Processing

Processed foods can facilitate consumption, by saving labor, and create or increase income for processors by adding value. Some processed foods consumed in Mali are created by industrial processing, usually by multinational corporations; others are created locally, at a small scale by individuals or small companies. Imported processed foods can erode local artisanal or industrial processing by replacing local products or by introducing new products that create new tastes. Thus, demand for processed foods may grow from below as consumers need to save time or develop new tastes or it may be imposed from above, as processors try to create new markets.

As in many developing countries, processors have offered new products that may increase external dependence. As elsewhere, powdered milk supplied by multinational corporations is common; large Nestle tins are ubiquitous in Malian markets. Here, powdered milk has augmented an indigenous food. Mali has a long herding tradition and Malian farmers also buy and keep cattle as an investment; both herders and farmers drink the milk from their cows and sell some surplus. Local production is not sufficient to meet the urban demand for local milk products, especially since national policies have concentrated on encouraging herders to furnish the market with meat.[4] In this case, the ready availability of cheap powdered milk may have discouraged investment in local milk production, but it does not appear to have destroyed a local industry, nor has it created a completely new demand.

Seasoning cubes show how a processed product can replace existing traditional products, here local condiments. Instead of buying a variety of ingredients and mixing them to individual taste, cooks can now buy seasoning cubes; these have become so popular that they are found even in remote villages. They are promoted aggressively on Malian television, in commercials that show African families around local foods; in Mali, the dialogue is often in Bambara, the lingua franca. Both the Maggi company, a part of the Nestle corporate family, and its main competitor,

Jumbo Cubes, have tailored their advertising to the African market. Nestle has clearly made a commitment to enter the West African market, investing in regional production facilities as well. For example, according to packages, the Nestle instant coffee that dominates Malian markets has mostly been processed under license in Côte d'Ivoire, Mali's neighbor and a coffee producer. However, few other multinational companies seem to have made similar efforts. In international terms, Mali's middle-class market remains a relatively small percentage of a small population. Moreover, its landlocked location increases the prices of imported goods because of high transport costs. Major western corporations do not always find it in their financial interest to make major sales efforts; at the same time, importers find other sources of processed foods. The growing use of dry cereals provides an example; corn flakes in particular have recently flooded the market. While Bamako has a few upscale supermarkets that sell packaged cereals from major multinational producers at very high prices (about US$6–8 per box), corn flakes are sold in small groceries throughout the city and by street vendors at major intersections for about US$2 per box. The latter appear to be imported from Asian countries, carrying brand names unknown to me; box information is often printed in Arabic, suggesting that the primary market is meant to be North Africa or the Middle East. This example suggests at least a partial decentering of economic globalization, as processors from newly industrializing countries move into developing country markets.[5]

Despite the presence of imported processed foods, Malian processors on a variety of scales also supply the market. They appear to respond to new demands rather than actively creating them. At a large scale, an industrial dairy produces yogurt and individual containers of milk. Medium-scale processors have begun to supply some of the new labor-intensive foods appreciated by urban consumers; for example, local markets now carry *attieke* and pre-cooked *fonio* (a local grain) in meal-size amounts that save substantial labor. Processors have also met the demand for snacks; markets carry locally made snack foods such as roasted peanuts, popcorn, chips, and flavor concentrates for local drinks. Small firms also make and sell peanut butter, a major sauce ingredient. Individuals produce artisanally processed foods; for example, popsicles from local drinks and various sweet cakes, often made at home, are sold throughout the city. Tiny restaurants can be found around major employment sites and schools to provide lunch for workers and students. It is likely that some market vendors process the foods that they sell to increase value, in ways similar to those found in Kumasi, Ghana (Clark 1994). Pilcher (this volume) notes the meager earnings of handmade tortilla vendors in Mexico City; the profit levels of Bamako micro-processors are not known.

Nevertheless, the amount of processed foods consumed by middle-class Malians remains relatively low. On the one hand, the still low disposable income of Mali's middle class means that consumers consider food prices carefully and are not always willing to pay the extra for processing. On the other hand, Malian middle-class women do not face strong pressures to save their own labor, because they usually have domestic help, provided by the many rural young women who come to cities looking for work. Furthermore, there is little enforcement of sanitary standards for artisanally processed foods. Malian media often carry stories, sometimes unsubstantiated, about adulterated food, which discourages people from buying what they have not seen cooked or from vendors they do not know. Therefore, many foods continue to be sold without processing; poultry, for example, is still mostly sold live and butchered only just before it is prepared.

Insofar as academic literature on food processing in developing countries exists, it has concentrated on processing that has increased the dependency of developing countries on major multinational corporations, such as the well-known case of Nestle or that of bread in Nigeria (Andrae and Beckman 1985). Examples of new exports from non-Western countries (e.g., Asia, South Africa) have been much less discussed, as has local processing. Presumably, entrepreneurs who create food processing industries undertake studies to evaluate the potential return to their investments, but much more could be learned about food processing.

Wholesalers and Transporters

Intermediaries move products from production sites to retail outlets close to consumers, with distinctive pathways for locally produced and imported goods (Clark 1994). Throughout Africa, there has been interest in understanding how these pathways work, fueled in part by the belief that high consumer prices were evidence that intermediaries enriched themselves to the detriment of consumers. In fact, evidence suggests that high consumer prices reflect high transaction costs met by intermediaries, who carry out risky work in areas plagued by poor road and transport infrastructure (Clark 1994). Recently researchers have tried to understand how macro-political changes have affected transport and wholesale activities; Lynch (2002), for example, used commodity-chain analysis to understand how economic reform and population growth affected specialization in wholesale markets in Dar es Salaam.

The literature on Mali reflects the fact that studies of wholesale networks have tended to concentrate on basic food grains (cf. Guyer 1987). Since independence in 1960, food self-sufficiency has been a priority of the Malian government and the Sahel droughts of the 1970s and 1980s only increased this preoccupation. Through the 1960s and 1970s, the Malian government regulated transport prices as well as grain prices for consumers and producers. The regulations on grain pricing were not effective, since only an estimated 20 to 40 percent of cereals moved through government channels (Koenig, Diarra, and Sow 1998). However, transport regulations evidently depressed trade by discouraging private transporters, who often could not earn much, if anything, at official prices (Steedman et al. 1976). Structural adjustment in the 1980s brought market liberalization, which in turn encouraged research on cereals markets. Some studies focused on large-scale grain traders and the constraints that affected consumer pricing (Dioné and Dembélé 1986; Dembélé and Staatz 2000). Others looked at the ways in which producers added value, for example the growing participation of farmers in rice marketing and decentralized threshing at the *Office du Niger* (Diarra, Staatz, and Dembélé 2000). Observation suggests that the quantity and quality of transport has increased substantially since deregulation, but I am not aware of studies on the impact of deregulated transport.

Information about intermediaries, wholesalers, and transporters for other foods in the urban middle-class Malian diet is more limited. Observation suggests a chain of market centers, much like that described by Clark (1994) for Kumasi; the range of transport options is also quite diverse. Outstanding questions include the degree of concentration and specialization in wholesale and transport as well as questions about conservation; for example, what do intermediaries do to get fresh fruits and vegetables to the market in salable condition?

Producers

The foods eaten by urban middle-class Malians come from a wide range of sources. Imported foods follow global commodity chains that link distant producers and industrial processors to Malian consumers, but Malians produce many foods. As elsewhere (cf. Guyer 1997), producers have responded to the commercial opportunities provided by growing urban populations. Areas throughout the country have become known for specific crops. Sikasso, in the far southeast, is a center of potato production; Baguineda, irrigated and close to Bamako, is known for fruits and vegetables; Kita is considered Mali's peanut capital. Meat comes mostly from the semi-arid areas of significant livestock production. Given the diverse diet, this chapter can look at only a few products and producers. This section looks at farmers from Kita's hinterland and their choices to produce and sell particular crops; it draws upon earlier research I carried out in 1999 on a sixty-household sample in two village clusters in this zone.

Like many Malian farmers, Kita households try first to assure their own food supply. Men usually grow food grains, primarily sorghum, on household fields where all male household members work. Women have individual fields on which they grow sauce ingredients. At the same time, both men and women often grow other crops, which they may sell to meet personal or household expenses. Since 1995, household heads and other adult males have been encouraged by the Compagnie

Malienne de Développement des Textiles (CMDT) to grow cotton to earn cash; many have done so, but they have been discouraged by low prices, due primarily to falling world market prices. Many farmers looked for alternative incomes by producing for domestic markets. In Kita, they grew four major types of foods: peanuts, orchard crops, watermelon and tobacco, and vegetables and condiments.

Kita became known as Mali's peanut capital in the late 1960s, when a rural development and extension organization began to encourage farmers to produce peanuts for export. By the mid-1970s, this organization faced significant challenges: falling international prices in light of competition from other tropical oils (Steedman et al. 1976); competition within Mali from cottonseed oil (FAO/World Bank 1986); and infestation from aflatoxin, a mold linked to cancer. Structural adjustment required that the organization become economically self-sustaining, but it could not; having stagnated over intervening years, it was abolished by the Malian government in 1996 after the CMDT had begun cotton extension. Nevertheless, Kita's farmers continued to cultivate and sell peanuts to private merchants, who served as intermediaries to the growing urban market. Peanuts have become a major domestic commodity.

Paradoxically, the CMDT itself facilitated private-sector peanut marketing when it improved the transport infrastructure to expedite the movement of cotton. Throughout the late 1980s and 1990s, farmers in peanut-production zones complained about poor prices, but by 1999, they reported substantial price increases, which they attributed to the presence of the CMDT. Some believed that this was due to the dynamics of supply and demand; new cotton fields meant fewer peanut fields and a smaller harvest, the more limited supply increasing the price. Others simply noted that with the arrival of the CMDT, everything farmed could be sold. Kita town and its market grew substantially following the growth in route infrastructure that began with construction of a dam at Manantali, 120 kilometers west of Kita, in the 1980s.

Both men and women grew peanuts in large quantities. Peanuts became the currency of everyday life in Kita's hinterland; easily bought and sold, they were involved in economic transactions of many types. Spouses gave peanuts to each other as gifts or loans; women gave them as gifts at ceremonies. People also used peanut earnings to finance investments in livestock or trade; some women's associations cultivated collective peanut fields to finance other activities.

The number of peanut buyers and sellers was large, and farmers could sell peanuts in many places: in their own village, at weekly markets, in towns like Kita or Nioro du Sahel, or in cities like Bamako or Kayes. Farmers understood clearly that prices varied seasonally, with supply and demand, although they could and did sell throughout the year. Women often sold peanuts regularly in small quantities at weekly markets to buy condiments. Farmers who needed money might sell many of their peanuts at the harvest, but wealthier households often held peanut stocks until prices rose at the beginning of the following rainy season, when they could sell substantial quantities for large lump sums. Many farmers also added value and earned more by shelling. Almost anyone could enter the peanut trade, at least on a small scale, and a number of men and some women in the sample were or had been peanut traders, buying from their neighbors and reselling in other markets. Because of its focus on producers, the 1999 study did not follow the commodity chain and I have little information about intermediaries. While some peanuts may have gone to Bamako's middle class, peanuts from Kita also went west to Kayes and north to Nioro du Sahel.

Kita farmers also moved into new crops for which they believed there was demand. Tree crops were attractive because they earned relatively well and required relatively little upkeep once well established. Anecdotal evidence suggests that Bamako markets were for a long time supplied from orchards near the city, but urban expansion destroyed many of them and wholesalers have been forced to look further. New producers have responded, and, as the route infrastructure has improved, fruits now come from greater distances.

The sixty-household Kita sample had ten mango orchards and one banana orchard; a few grew other fruits, such as oranges, guavas, and sweetsop. These crops were grown primarily to sell, although orchard owners and their families ate the produce as well. There is no evidence that any grower had done a systematic market analysis; young men believed that they could make money because they saw that others had done so. Most learned to grow mangoes by watching other growers and imitating them, although one young man had specifically sought to learn more about orchards by seeking out peri-urban gardeners for seasonal wage labor. On his return home, he received further training in grafting from the CMDT. At initial stages, tree crops required significant labor in regular watering and protection from animals, but more important was long-term access to a single plot of land. Indigenous land tenure favored local men. Women and immigrants rarely had tree crops because they were not given long-term ownership rights over land.

Most growers sold their fruit in local periodic markets; rarely if ever did anyone have a crop large enough to encourage intermediaries to come to the farm, as was the case with peanuts. Many fruits appear to have gone first to Kita, where they were bulked; from there they presumably went to other urban centers, including Kayes, Nioro du Sahel, and Bamako. Kita farmers had only begun to adopt strategies to increase the value of their crop. For example, many were moving out of traditional mangoes to grow more valuable grafted ones, but they did not seem to use more sophisticated technical strategies, such as those to force earlier growth or extend the growing season. It is clear that some suppliers of the Bamako market do so, because mango season begins earlier and ends later than might otherwise be expected.

Farmers also grew dry-season annuals, crops produced at the end of the rainy season in fields which benefited from residual humidity and some hand irrigation. For a long time, Kita farmers had grown tobacco this way; the Kita sample included twenty-one small, sole-cropped, tobacco fields. There were many tobacco consumers in the study villages, mostly older men and women who used snuff. It seems that much of the tobacco was sold to local consumers, although some may have been sold outside the region as well.

Farmers were also turning to a new crop that grew in similar conditions: watermelons. Watermelons were considered relatively easy to grow, particularly in the higher rainfall area south of Kita. One blacksmith would ask clients who could not pay their bills to work in his watermelon field. Another farmer, with half a hectare in watermelons, arranged for a truck to come from Kita to pick them up. In the year before the study, he had sold about six hundred watermelons for a net income of 40,000 FCFA (US$62).[6] Again, there is little information on the remainder of the commodity chain.

Finally, men and women grew and sometimes sold vegetables and condiments, usually in small fields irrigated with dug wells, as second season crops. These included beans and cassava, sweet potatoes, okra, squash, eggplants, onions, tomatoes, peppers, and lettuce. Most were consumed in the household, although the presence of lettuce suggests new middle-class eating habits. Women usually raised garden crops partly for consumption and partly for sale in local markets where they bought consumer goods and sauce ingredients they did not or could not grow. In one of the villages, a women's garden association sold tomatoes and lettuce in their village and in the nearby weekly market. While some men believed that gardening was women's work, other men had begun to grow garden crops to supply what they perceived as a growing market. One young man had just cleared a new half-hectare plot to increase his production of onions, cabbage, lettuce, and tomatoes. Another had cultivated four raised beds of onions, from which he earned 45,000 FCFA (US$69) through sales in local markets.

Clearly, producers from Kita's hinterland were using diverse strategies to meet the demand created by the growing number of urban food consumers. Evidence from producers about where, when, and in what quantities they sold suggests multiple commodity chains, even for a single crop. While some farmers transported peanuts in relatively small quantities to nearby periodic markets, others, with large quantities, brought them to Kita to sell or waited for intermediaries to come directly to their villages. Farmers made selling decisions by calculating transaction costs in relationship to expected prices. However, since the 1999 study concentrated upon family production decisions, I have relatively little information about other links on the commodity chain, including intermediaries, their degree of specialization, overheads and margins, or decisions about choice of sources or sales points. Even though Bamako residents ate the kinds of foods produced by Kita farmers, this food did not necessarily come from them as there were multiple suppliers. At the same time, Kita farmers were sending their produce to several urban areas.

Conclusion

The analysis here must remain incomplete because of lack of data. Although urban middle-class Malians have a diverse and rich diet, little has been written about the foods they eat or the commodity chains that supply them. Because of insufficient data, this chapter has treated an entire group of foods as a single subsector, even though each commodity should be analyzed individually. This conclusion offers some suggestions for why so little is known and suggests theoretical and practical reasons to better understand urban food supplies.

As noted, there is substantial work on agricultural production and markets in Mali, but it is limited; theoretical frameworks have led researchers to focus on some issues, while rendering others invisible. The vision of Africa as a reservoir of crisis has led to an extensive literature on basic food grains, which dates to the Sahel drought and the serious problems it raised about food security. In Mali, this stimulated excellent research about grain production and distribution discussed previously, but it has meant that research on urban food supply has rarely gone beyond this.

At the same time, other crops have been targeted by development specialists, who have stressed the role of global trade in increasing standards of living for poor people in developing countries. The World Bank and the U.S. Agency for International Development (USAID) both accentuate the role of export earnings in providing funds for growth and development and to fight poverty. For example, the unpublished terms of reference for a recent World Bank study noted, "As the cotton sector drives investment and growth for much of agriculture, measures to improve the competitiveness of the cotton sector are critical to the success of the CSLP" (Cadre Stratégique de la Lutte contre la Pauvrété, i.e., the fight against poverty). As one of the world's least developed countries, Mali receives significant foreign assistance to fight poverty and increase the well-being of its citizens, but the emphasis of donors on export crops has meant that studies done within this framework have focused on crops for export.

In the case of Mali, this has meant a concentration on cotton, which provided 22 percent of its export earnings in 2002 (IMF 2004:48). The research on cotton includes but is not limited to issues surrounding production and international trade. Studies have looked at regional, local, and gender impacts, environmental issues, and the development of cotton farmer unions (Bassett 2001; Bingen 1998; Gardner and Lewis 1996; Tefft 2000). Cotton now has a strong place on the contemporary international stage because of recent concern about the negative effects of cotton subsidies in developed countries on earnings of African farmers (e.g., Prestowitz 2003).[7]

In contrast, other crops are targeted only when they are cultivated for export or internationally traded. For example, although there was some literature on peanuts in Mali in the 1970s and 1980s when it was an export crop, very little has been written recently. On the other hand, mangoes came to be of interest to USAID when they were exported, but not when they were grown for a domestic market (USAID 2005:6). Sometimes, crops do serve noneconomic purposes, as when the Helen Keller Foundation encouraged carrot cultivation to prevent night blindness, under the implicit assumption that people would eat the crops they grew. This model of production, based on the old dichotomy of cash crops (primarily for export) and food crops (primarily for self-subsistence), has stimulated research at the two extremes but encouraged ignorance about the many and diverse foods produced locally and for domestic markets.

As this chapter makes clear, this tunnel vision has produced great gaps in knowledge about domestic production, distribution, and consumption. There is little information about how resources are distributed in the system among consumers, vendors, intermediaries, and producers, how recent macro-economic changes have affected the system, and how the system might be improved to provide better earnings and more employment. As the urban middle class grows, initiatives to strengthen the commodity chains that supply its food offer the potential for development and poverty alleviation strategies that complement the existing focus on exports. A greater understanding of Mali's hybrid food subsector may offer alternative pathways to providing foods for the poor as well as additional employment opportunities. The Kita data suggest that farmers are interested in finding new, more profitable products, simple processing, and technologies to increase production. There would seem to be possibilities for facilitating employment and generating income among processors and intermediaries as well. Although the development of domestic market systems may offer a complementary approach to improving the lives of both urban and rural Malians, it is difficult to suggest concrete strategies when there is so little information. We need more information to suggest feasible alternative approaches.

At the same time, a better understanding of the domestic food economy may suggest more complex models of globalization. Although Mali's urban food system depends strongly on locally produced foods, it is not insulated from the world economy, and middle-class Malians regularly consume imported foods. Previous literature has stressed how Western-dominated multinational corporations have introduced processed foods in ways that increase the dependence of developing countries; in Mali, this process can indeed be seen in the penetration of Nestle products. However, as noted, Mali's imported foods do not come only from traditional developed country centers. Insofar as the consumption of imported foods is demand driven by the new tastes of cosmopolitan Malians, nontraditional importers, especially less well-known processors in newly industrializing countries, may meet some of the demand. For example, links between Mali and Asian countries as well as larger African centers (e.g., Nigeria, South Africa) need to be better understood.

Moreover, we need to know more about the consequences of the indigenization of links of commodity chains. Andrae and Beckman (1985) argued that decentralized bakeries actually increased the dependence of Nigeria on new imported bakery technologies by making bread more widely available; whether similar processes are occurring in Mali is an open question. It appears that although Mali does depend on imported wheat, other links in the commodity chain use more local technology and inputs than was the case in Nigeria. As Wilk notes in this volume, food is often prepared in ways that mix ingredients of different origins, with significant action in the interstices between the global and the local. We do need to know more about how indigenization of commodity-chain links affects the distribution of power. This kind of knowledge will improve our ability to furnish what Mintz calls food at moderate speed, good and healthy food for everybody.

Notes

Acknowledgments. This chapter is based on research funded by Fulbright Hays PO19A80001, National Science Foundation SBR-9870628, and USAID LAG-A-00-96-90016-00 (BASIS CRSP). Many Malian and U.S. agencies in Bamako facilitated this research; most important was the collaboration of Malian colleagues from the Institut des Sciences Humaines, especially Tiéman Diarra, Mama Kamaté, and Seydou Camara. I would also like to thank Tiwanna DeMoss for research assistance and Richard Wilk and other reviewers. I bear sole responsibility for the views presented here.

1. Some Malians have also accumulated wealth through more "traditional" occupations such as long-distance and local trade. Their lifestyles may be different from those of the professional middle class discussed here.

2. The Office du Niger, a large irrigated perimeter, has allowed Mali to meet a substantial part of its rice demand, but other countries in West Africa import rice. This has stimulated substantial efforts to increase production and decrease imports.

3. The construction of a power plant at Manantali in western Mali was meant to bring more reliable electricity to a capital city until then plagued by erratic power. When Manantali came on line in 2001, the amount of electricity available to Bamako did increase, but problems in the old distribution network were common and power was still problematic.

4. Despite propositions that African herders act out of traditional noncapitalist logics, they supply Mali's meat markets as well as those of neighboring countries; in 2002, livestock

products were Mali's third major export and contributed 5.6 percent of export earnings (IMF 2004:48).

5. Andrae and Beckman (1985) suggest that imported wheat formed a significant part of import value in 1980s Nigeria, increasing its dependence upon Western industrial economies. Food appears to be a smaller proportion of Mali's imports, while the source of imports seems quite diverse. According to 2002 figures, food formed 13 percent of the value of Mali's imports; about one-third of this was cereal grains. The largest imports were machines and vehicles (24 percent), chemical products (20 percent), and petroleum products (17 percent) (IMF 2004:49). By value, 29.5 percent of imports came from industrial countries, 54.7 percent from other African countries, and 5.9 percent from Asia (IMF 2004:50). However, it appears that these figures do not necessarily indicate the original source of the product; for example, petroleum imports may be attributed to the neighboring country that delivered them rather than to the original producer. Nevertheless, a certain portion of consumer goods and food clearly comes from newly industrializing countries. For example, consumers in Malian markets find Chinese and Indians goods targeted to developing country needs, quality, and price. These include appliances such as cookers and kerosene lamps as well as inexpensive textiles and clothing.

6. At the time of the study, 650 FCFA (the CFA franc) = US$1.00. Average household income from the sale of agricultural produce during the study period ranged from 11,027 FCFA (US$17) to 698,304 FCFA (US$1,075) among groups defined by social stratum and occupation (Koenig 2005). Since household earnings were the aggregate earnings of multiple residents in different activities, 40,000 FCFA from a single crop by one farmer was significant.

7. The use of cotton to draw Malian farmers into the international economy is old, the French having encouraged Malian farmers to grow it since the colonial period (Koenig, Diarra, and Sow 1998). After independence, the cultivation of cotton for export by small farmers became a singular success story, increasing incomes for both farmers and the government (Jones 1976).

References

Andrae, Gunilla, and Björn Beckman. 1985. The Wheat Trap. London: Zed Books.

Bassett, Thomas. 2001. The Peasant Cotton Revolution in West Africa: Côte d'Ivoire, 1880–1995. Cambridge: Cambridge University Press.

Bingen, R. James. 1998. Cotton, Democracy and Development in Mali. Journal of Modern African Studies 36(2):265–85.

BNETD (Bureau National d'Etudes Techniques et de Développement). 2001. Bamako, Mali: City Development Strategy Report. Côte d'Ivoire: BNETD. Electronic document, http://www.unhabitat.org/programmes/ump/documents/Bamako%20detailed%20 summary.pdf, accessed May 27, 2005.

Bohannon, Paul, and George Dalton. 1965. Markets in Africa: Eight Subsistence Economies in Transition. Garden City, NY: Anchor Natural History Library.

Chalfin, Brenda. 2001. Border Zone Trade and the Economic Boundaries of the State in North-East Ghana. Africa 71(2):202–224.

Clark, Gracia. 1994. Onions Are My Husband: Survival and Accumulation by West African Market Women. Chicago: University of Chicago Press.

Dembélé, Niama Nango, and John Staatz. 2000. The Response of Cereals Traders to Agricultural Market Reform in Mali. In Democracy and Development in Mali. R. J. Bingen, D. Robinson, and J. Staatz, eds. Pp. 145–65. East Lansing: Michigan State University Press.

Dettwyler, Steven. 1986. Senoufo Migrants in Bamako: Changing Agricultural Production Strategies and Household Organization in an Urban Environment. PhD dissertation, Department of Anthropology, Indiana University.

Diarra, Salifou Bakary, John Staatz, and Niama Nango Dembélé. 2000. The Reform of Rice Milling and Marketing in the Office du Niger: Catalysts for an Agricultural Success Story in Mali. In Democracy and Development in Mali. R. J. Bingen, D. Robinson, and J. Staatz, eds. Pp. 167–88. East Lansing: Michigan State University Press.

Dioné, Josué, and Niama Nango Dembélé. 1986. Description des Circuits Céréaliers au Mali et Analyse des Données Secondaires de Prix des Céréales mil—maïs—sorgho. Working paper 86.02, Projet Sécurité Alimentaire MSU/CESA. Bamako: Institut d'Economie Rurale.

FAO/World Bank. 1986. Projet ODIPAC: Potentiel de Développement Agricole. Working paper. Rome: FAO/World Bank.

Gardner, Katy, and David Lewis. 1996. Anthropology, Development and the Post-modern Challenge. London: Pluto Press.

Guyer, Jane I. 1987. Introduction and Feeding Yaoundé, Capital of Cameroon. In Feeding African Cities. J. Guyer, ed. Pp. 1–54 and 112–54. Bloomington: Indiana University Press.

———. 1997. An African Niche Economy: Farming to Feed Ibadan 1968–88. Edinburgh: Edinburgh University Press for the International African Institute, London.

IMF (International Monetary Fund). 2004. Mali: Selected Issues and Statistical Annex. Country Report No. 04/10. Washington, DC: IMF.

Jones, William I. 1976. Planning and Economic Policy: Socialist Mali and Her Neighbors. Washington, DC: Three Continents Press.

Koenig, Dolores. 2005. Social Stratification and Access to Wealth in the Rural Hinterland of Kita, Mali. In Wari Matters: Ethnographic Explorations of Money in the Mande World. S. Wooten, ed. Münster: Lit Verlag.

Koenig, Dolores, Tiéman Diarra, and Moussa Sow. 1998. Innovation and Individuality in African Development: Changing Production Strategies in Rural Mali. Ann Arbor: University of Michigan Press.

Lynch, Kenneth. 2002. Urban Fruit and Vegetable Supply in Dar Es Salaam. Geographical Journal 160(3):307–318.

Meillassoux, Claude, ed. 1971. The Development of Indigenous Trade and Markets in West Africa. London: Oxford University Press for the International African Institute.

Prestowitz, Clyde. 2003. As Accusations Fly, Poor Nations Suffer. Washington Post, June 8:B2.

Raikes, Philip, Michael Friis Jensen, and Stefano Ponte. 2000. Global Commodity Chain Analysis and the French Filière Approach: Comparison and Critique. CDR Working Paper 00.3. Copenhagen: Centre for Development Research.

Ribot, Jesse. 1998. Theorizing Access: Forest Profits along Senegal's Charcoal Commodity Chain. Development and Change 29:307–341.

Staatz, John. 1997. Notes on the Use of Subsector Analysis as a Diagnostic Tool for Linking Industry and Agriculture. Staff Paper 97–4. East Lansing: Department of Agricultural Economics, Michigan State University.

Steedman, Charles, Thomas Daves, Marlin Johnson, and John Sutter. 1976. Mali: Agricultural Sector Assessment. Ann Arbor: University of Michigan Center for Research on Economic Development.

Tefft, James. 2000. Cotton in Mali: The White Revolution and Development. In Democracy and Development in Mali. R. J. Bingen, D. Robinson, and J. Staatz, eds. Pp. 213–41. East Lansing: Michigan State University Press.

UNEP (United Nations Environment Programme). 2001. Mali-Bamako: Summary Project Site. Electronic document, http://www.unep.org/DEWA/water/groundwater/africa/English/reports/CountrySummaries/Mali/Eng_Summary_Mali.pdf, accessed May 27, 2005.

USAID (U.S. Agency for International Development). 2005. Group of 8: Reducing Poverty through Trade. Frontlines, April:6.

Taco Bell, Maseca, and Slow Food: A Postmodern **5** Apocalypse for Mexico's Peasant Cuisine?

JEFFREY M. PILCHER

MEXICO HAS A DISTINGUISHED revolutionary tradition, but is the land of Emiliano Zapata ready for the "delicious revolution" of Slow Food? The question may sound a bit facetious at first, but given the movement's origins in the Italian Communist Party, a disquisition on class consciousness in a postmodern era seems appropriate. Of course, class has been virtually banished from postmodern academic discourse, perhaps from the sheer embarrassment of an intellectual vanguard discovering itself to be a petit bourgeoisie on the brink of proletarianization by the forces of global capital. In the script of contemporary revolution, only the villain—global capital—retains its traditional role. Slow Food speaks the lines of the reformist Social Democratic Party (SDP) to José Bové's militant Bolshevism, the international proletariat is now politically suspect for its consumerist tendencies, and the peasantry has become the progressive motor of history. Although Slow Food offers an admirable program for personal life, it will never represent a genuine revolution until it confronts the dilemmas of class that have been complicated but not obviated by increasing globalization. Indeed, the Mexican case reveals the impossibility of drawing a clear dichotomy between slow and fast food in markets where global and local capital compete for the trade of middle-class tourists and equally cosmopolitan "peasants."

The Slow Food snail mascot would no doubt bask contentedly in the shade of Emiliano Zapata's sombrero, for the Mexican agrarian revolution of 1910 likewise sought to preserve traditional agrarian livelihoods. Emerging from the crisis of Italian leftist politics in the late 1980s, Slow Food exalted leisure and pleasure as an antidote to the blind pursuit of efficiency within the United States (Parasecoli 2003). The movement sought to revive artisanal production and to preserve vanishing biodiversity against the homogenizing influence of multinational agribusiness. Nevertheless, tensions remained between the elitism of the official manifesto— "preserve us from the contagion of the multitude" (Parasecoli 2003:xxiii)—and the democratizing ideal of affordable but tasty *osterie* (regional restaurants).

Recent work on the history of Italian cuisine demonstrates that the traditions Slow Food seeks to preserve are largely invented, a point acknowledged by the movement's leaders (Hobsbawm 1983; Petrini 2003). Well into the twentieth century, peasants subsisted on monotonous porridges of maize, chestnuts, broad beans, or rice, depending on the region and the season (Camporesi 1993; Diner 2001; Helstosky 2004). Italy's regional cuisines are not only modern inventions, they may even have been created in the Americas through the industrial production and canning of olive oil, tomato paste, and cheeses to satisfy migrant workers who could afford foods unavailable to peasants at home (Teti 1992; Gabaccia 2004). More research is needed on the nineteenth-century bourgeois diet, but it seems that contemporary Italian cuisine emerged largely from festival foods such as *maccheroni*, which became items of everyday consumption in the United States. The traditional *osteria* that Slow Food seeks to encourage likewise grew out of the *cucina casalinga*, meals served in urban homes to unattached male workers; they only became restaurants with the postwar growth of tourism. The Italian experience in turn provides a useful model for the emergence of Mexico's regional cuisines.

There can be few foods slower than Mexican peasant cooking. For thousands of years, the preparation of the staple maize tortillas required hours of hard, physical labor each day. Women rose before dawn to grind corn (*masa*) on a basalt stone (*metate*), then patted out tortillas by hand and cooked them on an earthenware griddle (*comal*)—all this before men went out to the fields (Redfield 1929; Lewis 1951). Festivals multiplied the workload of women; in addition to preparing special tortillas and masa dumplings (*tamales*), they labored over the metate grinding chile sauces (*moles*) and cacao while men sat around drinking (Stephen 1991). The metate was so intrinsic to Mexican patriarchy that when mechanical mills capable of adequately grinding masa finally reached the countryside in the first half of the twentieth century, one villager described it as a "revolution of the women against the authority of the men" (Lewis 1951:108). As women transferred their labor from domestic reproduction to market production, tamales and moles were gentrified by restaurants catering to national and international tourists (Pilcher 2004).

Mexico has had two competing visions for the modernization of its cuisine. Attempts by local investors and engineers to industrialize tortilla production have culminated in the rise of Grupo Maseca, a multinational producer of *masa harina* (dehydrated tortilla flour), which can be reconstituted with water to save the trouble of making fresh masa, thus making them popular among migrant workers. Although connoisseurs can distinguish fresh from industrial corn tortillas, both are quite different from the wheat flour tortillas most common in the United States. Meanwhile, Taco Bell has led the way in applying North American fast food technology to Mexican cooking. Neither approach proved satisfactory to aficionados, leaving a space for Slow Food to catch on among middle-class Mexicans and foreign tourists.

Yet attempts to save traditional Mexican cuisine have been plagued by the same contradictions of elitism, gender bias, and even a measure of imperial arrogance—treating Native Americans like southern Italians—that typified the movement at home.

Maseca

Although the industrialization of Mexico was generally characterized by imported technology and capital, the modernization of the tortilla was a uniquely national enterprise. The complex skills involved in making tortillas were mechanized in three distinct stages at roughly fifty-year intervals around the beginning, middle, and end of the twentieth century. The arduous task of hand grinding maize at the metate was first replaced by forged steel mills. Next came the technology for automatically pressing out and cooking tortillas, which facilitated the spread of small-scale tortilla factories throughout the country. Finally, the industrial production of masa harina allowed the vertical integration of food processing under Grupo Maseca. Tortilla futurists envisioned these technologies as a complete package, but the three distinct processes could in fact be combined or separated according to circumstances, and each was tied into complex culinary, social, and political relationships. Ultimately, the fate of the tortilla resulted more from questions of political economy than of consumer choice.

Corn mills arrived in Mexican cities by the late nineteenth century but took decades to spread through the countryside, in part because of concern among women about their position within the family. The ability to make tortillas was long considered essential to a rural woman seeking marriage, and any who neglected the metate risked unfavorable gossip. Even the few centavos charged by the mills posed a significant cost in subsistence communities, but poor women often had the greatest incentive to grind corn mechanically because the time saved could be used to engage in artisanal crafts or petty trade. Wealthy families, by contrast, were among the last to give up the metate on a daily basis; this form of slow food offered a status symbol, in part because the rich could pay others to do the actual work. As the benefits of milling gained acceptance, women often organized cooperatives to purchase the machines. By midcentury, corn mills had arrived in virtually every community in Mexico, transforming social relationships and helping to incorporate rural dwellers into the monetary economy (Lewis 1951; Bauer 1990).

The mechanization of the tortilla and the development of masa harina posed more technological than social problems. Conveyer belt cookers were first introduced around 1900, but only at midcentury could they produce a tortilla that satisfied Mexican consumers. Once these machines were created, a cottage industry of tortilla factories quickly spread to all but the most remote rural communities. Although these shops generally sold tortillas by the kilo made from commercially purchased maize, they also ground corn for customers who wished to prepare their own tortillas at home. Both small-scale tortilla factories and their eventual corporate challenger developed under the aegis of a welfare program intended to subsidize food for poor urban consumers. The first masa harina factories were established in 1949 by Molinas Azteca, S.A. (Maseca) and a parastatal corporation, Maíz Industrializado, S.A. (Minsa). The two firms collaborated on research and development for more than a decade before arriving at a suitable formulation that could be transformed into tortilla masa with just the addition of water. By the 1970s, tortilla flour accounted for 5 percent of the maize consumed in Mexico. Sales grew steadily over the next two decades until Maseca alone held 27 percent of the national corn market. Nevertheless, the subsidy on maize supplied to small-scale tortilla factories slowed the firm's expansion.

The dismantling of the state food agency in the 1990s assured Maseca's triumph. President Carlos Salinas de Gortari (1988–1994) first curtailed the corn subsidy while also selling Minsa to a consortium rivaling Maseca. For the fifty-one thousand small-scale tortilla factories, subsidized corn had been essential for their commercial viability. Led by a trade organization, the Association of Proprietors of Tortilla Factories, and Nixtamal Mills, they launched a vocal political campaign to retain the subsidy, citing scientific studies concluding that traditional tortillas were more nutritive than those made with Maseca, which they dubbed "MAsaSECA" ("dry masa"). They also accused Maseca of manipulating corn markets and attempting to monopolize supplies, thereby tapping popular memories of hunger that remain vivid in many sectors of Mexican society. But the proprietors found themselves on the wrong side of a neoliberal political avalanche, and the subsidy was eliminated in January 1999. The sudden change left tortilla factories unable to establish competitive sources of supply, and they were reduced to mere vendors for the multinational company, as masa harina quickly cornered an estimated 80 percent of the national tortilla market. Maseca, in turn, claimed nearly three quarters of these sales (Pilcher 1998; Ochoa 2000; Cebreros, n.d.).

The results of this change have been mixed. Proponents of modernization considered tortillas to be essentially tasteless, anyway, and found no difference in the new product. Journalist Alma Guillermoprieto (1999:46) took a different view, claiming that "when the privatization program of Mexico's notorious former President Carlos Salinas delivered the future of the tortilla into their hands . . . [the tortilla magnates] served up to the Mexican people the rounds of grilled cardboard that at present constitute the nation's basic foodstuff." Campesinos are quite sensitive to tortilla quality, and many have resisted Maseca (see, for example, González 2001:173). Nevertheless, the exigencies of subsistence often require small farmers to sell their best produce to urban markets. Meanwhile, Mexican food faced a still more uncertain fate abroad.

Taco Bell

Even as the tortilla market evolved under government protection at home, tacos slipped across the border into greater Los Angeles, where they fell into the hands of scientists and industrialists. While migrants labored in corporate agribusiness, their foods underwent a process of Taylorization to become more standardized and efficient. Neatly packaged under the trademark of Taco Bell, these brave new tacos subsequently traveled around the world, ultimately colonizing their native land. But despite their best efforts, the food formulators and advertising executives could not determine the global reception of the cyborgs they had created.

Sociologist George Ritzer (1993) has examined most comprehensively the threat of corporate fast food to local traditions, extending Max Weber's theory of rationalization, the process whereby modern technology has made society more efficient, predictable, and controlled. One would, indeed, be hard pressed to find a better example of those values than the Big Mac. The result of this process has been, first, the standardization of food, replacing the endless variety of local cuisines with the artificial choice of numbered selections from a "value menu." The creation of so-called McJobs has further alienated labor by requiring only minimally skilled workers who respond to the commands of machinery. By stifling the social interactions customarily associated with dining, fast food has supposedly dehumanized the process of eating.

The McDonaldized taco, like the hamburger, had its origins in southern California in the mid-1950s. Glen Bell, a telephone repairman from San Bernardino, was impressed by the original McDonald's restaurant, but rather than compete head-on for the hamburger trade, he applied the new industrial techniques to a separate market segment, the Mexican American taco stand. As he described it: "If you wanted a dozen, you were in for a wait. They stuffed them first, quickly fried them and stuck them together with a toothpick. I thought they were delicious, but something had to be done about the method of preparation" (Taco Bell 2001). That something was to pre-fry the tortillas, anathema to any Mexican, but a blessing to Anglos who preferred to drive off with their food rather than eat at the stand while the other tacos were freshly cooked.

Corporate mythology attributing the North American taco to Glen Bell is questionable, but whatever the origins of the pre-fried taco, precursor to the industrial taco shell, it made possible the globalization of Mexican food by freeing it from its ethnic roots. No longer would restaurateurs or home cooks need a local supply of fresh corn tortillas to make tacos; the shells could henceforth be mass-produced and shipped around the world, albeit with some breakage. The extent to which the taco has been alienated from the Mexican community can be seen in the job description given by a Taco Bell employee in *The New Yorker* (2000): "My job is I, like, basically make the tacos! The meat comes in boxes that have bags inside, and those bags you boil to heat up the meat. That's how you make tacos."

By the mid-1990s, as the Tex-Mex fad spread worldwide, restaurants in Europe and East Asia abandoned even the pretense of serving Mexican food. Nevertheless, critics have questioned the homogenizing effects of the McDonaldization thesis by emphasizing the diverse ways in which people around the world experience restaurants. Although travelers may find the bland uniformity of the Golden Arches disturbing, locals embrace the new choices made possible by the arrival of fast food. The protests of burger-Luddite José Bové notwithstanding, French cuisine has little to fear from the spread of McDonalds, as sociologist Rick Fantasia (1995) has pointed out, because the fast food chains and upscale restaurants cater to quite different markets. The contributors to James Watson's (1997) volume, *Golden Arches East*, found the experience of U.S. culture, rather than actual food, to be the chain's biggest selling point in Asia. Customers were enthralled by the democratizing influence of waiting in line, the freedom from the social demands of competitive banqueting, and the novelty of clean public bathrooms.

The opening of Taco Bell's first Mexican outlet in 1992 illustrates the divergent expectations of corporate executives and local consumers. The Tricon conglomerate already operated a number of fast food restaurants in the country, and it tested the market by offering a selection of tacos at a Kentucky Fried Chicken location in an upscale mall in the suburbs of Mexico City. Skeptics murmured about "coals to Newcastle," but company spokesmen blithely applied the usual justification for fast food in the United States that "the one thing Mexico lacks is somewhere to get a clean, cheap, fast taco" (quoted in Guillermoprieto 1994:248). In fact, countless *taquerías* offered precisely that, although Guillermoprieto conceded that "no Mexican taco stand looks like a NASA food-preparation station." Even the company acknowledged its doubts by obtaining a supply of fresh tortillas and offering the standard taquería fare of the 1990s, pork *carnitas* and shredded beef. But middle-class customers responded with disappointment, for they could get Mexican tacos anywhere. One woman complained: "This doesn't taste like the real thing, does it? What I wanted was those big taco shells stuffed with salad and Kraft cheese and all *kinds* of stuff, like what you get in Texas" (quoted in Guillermoprieto 1994).

Mexico thus replicates the global experience of fast food as a middle-class privilege, with its own versions of authenticity. The initial opening of Taco Bell in Mexico in 1992 failed due to the economic crisis of that year, but by the end of the decade the company had opened a number of successful outlets. Even in the United States, fast food need not entail the complete obliteration of local culture; witness the spread of "fresh Mex" restaurants such as Chipotle, a subsidiary of the

McDonald's corporation. Moreover, by introducing customers to an artificial version of Mexican food, chains may well have expanded opportunities for marketing the genuine article.

Slow Food
In its mission to preserve and advertise distinctive regional foods, Slow Food created an "Ark of Taste" along with awards for biodiversity to promote awareness of and support for ecologically beneficial practices around the world. Despite their relatively small size, organizations from developed nations wield disproportionate power in a country such as Mexico, and as a result, they slant local activist movements toward middle-class agendas with little relevance for the needs of common people. Moreover, the fascination with Mexico's folkloric and Native American heritage diverts attention from the *mestizo* (mixed-race) majority, who do not speak an indigenous language but still suffer economic and political marginalization.

Mexico has done very well through the Slow Food movement, although it is unclear how much of this attention is due to its rich culinary heritage and how much to the Zapatista rebellion in Chiapas. The indigenous uprising gained international acclaim almost from the first shots fired on January 1, 1994, the day the North American Free Trade Agreement (NAFTA) went into effect. While brandishing an AK-47, the charismatic Subcomandante Marcos shunned terrorist bombings and instead waged his campaign with anti-globalization *pronunciamientos* fired across the World Wide Web. Stylish, balaclava-clad guerrillas held particular fascination for the Italian left.

Regardless of the inspiration, Mexicans have topped the list of Slow Food's Award for the Defense of Biodiversity. The jury consists of about five hundred food writers and other culinary authorities from around the world, although the United States and Italy provide the largest number. In the first four years, Mexicans received five out of fifty nominations, worth €3,500 each, and three out of twenty jury prizes, providing an additional €7,500. The United States, by comparison, received four nominations but no jury prize winners. The first Mexican jury prize, in 2000, went to Raúl Manuel Antonio, from Rancho Grande, Oaxaca, for establishing an indigenous vanilla-growing cooperative to supplement the incomes of small coffee producers. The following year, Doña Sebastiana Juárez Broca, known in her Tabasco community as Tía Tana, won a prize for reviving traditional cacao production techniques as an alternative to an official marketing organization that had impoverished farmers. Finally, in 2003, the jury honored historian José Iturriaga de la Fuente for organizing a fifty-four-volume series documenting Mexico's regional and indigenous cuisines (Slow Food n.d.).

Just as Slow Food began in Italy with a 1986 protest against the opening of a McDonald's restaurant below the historic Spanish Steps in Rome, Mexico has had its own showdown with McDonald's on the main square in Oaxaca City, the mecca of indigenous gastronomy. The company had already had one restaurant in a middle-class shopping mall on the outskirts of the city, like hundreds of others from Cancún to Tijuana, but when the local franchise holder sought permission for an outlet on the Zócalo in the summer of 2002, the intelligentsia mobilized its opposition. The campaign, led by renowned Oaxacan artist Francisco Toledo, asserted that burgers and fries were simply too different from the indigenous version of fast food, *chapulines*, fried grasshoppers sold from baskets and eaten with tortillas and guacamole. Bowing to the complaints of such high-profile figures, the government withdrew the permit, but the controversy had little importance, either culturally or economically, for ordinary Oaxacans who could not afford a Big Mac (Weiner 2002).

A similar protest had already played out in Mexico City against Maseca. As masa harina became ubiquitous in tortilla factories throughout the capital, the local branch of Greenpeace began issuing warnings about the use of GM-maize. In September 2001, self-styled ecological guerrillas changed the slogan on a giant billboard depicting flute-shaped crispy tacos from "Flautas with Maseca are tastier," to "Flautas with Maseca are genetically modified." Héctor Magallón explained the action by pointing out that in a recent survey, 88 percent of Mexicans indicated that they wanted GM-food to be labeled as such, and as a significant importer of maize from the United States, Maseca made an obvious target (Greenpeace 2001). While the desire for accurate labeling is certainly understandable, the protest movement has traveled a long way from the struggles of family-owned tortilla shops against a multinational giant.

For most poor Mexicans, surviving the shock of neoliberal reforms meant increased labor migration. Oaxacans were relative latecomers to the United States, but by the 1970s, Zapotecs and Mixtecs had become an important source of seasonal labor for California agriculture, and many lived year-round in Los Angeles. Despite difficult working conditions and vulnerability due to their undocumented status, migrants generally succeeded in improving their economic position and their remittances were vital for the survival of their families in Mexico. Over time, patterns of migration changed, from predominantly single males to include women and children as well, creating complicated transnational family networks. Higher incomes and tastes for consumer goods have caused significant cultural changes among migrants, especially those who settle permanently in the United States, but ties to home communities often remain strong nevertheless (Kearney 1996; Cohen 1999).

Migrant remittances form only one part of broader family survival strategies based on precarious subsistence agriculture in rural Oaxaca, as elsewhere. Farming has always been difficult in this region, but population growth and revenue from migrant labor has fostered urbanization, placing even greater pressure on cultivable land (Cohen 1999). Even successful artisans catering to the tourist trade spend much of their time in agriculture and depend on local food production (Chibnik 2003). Although often unlettered, these peasant farmers possess an extraordinary empirical understanding of their land and crops (González 2001). Nevertheless, such local knowledge may count for little if the economic necessities of competing with agribusiness cause a downward spiral of ecologically devastating practices, a sort of Gresham's Law of farming (Raikes 1988:62).

In seeking to encourage sustainable agriculture, Slow Food recognized a crucial problem for poor commodity-producing nations, the failure of branding. Mexico exports high-quality pork and vegetables but gains relatively little value from them because of the lack of global cachet associated with, for example, prosciutto ham or Tuscan olive oil. The case of cacao is symptomatic; once the drink of Maya lords, it is now a commodity subject to cutthroat international competition. Small farmers in Mexico suffered further exploitation, having just two options for marketing their harvest, a corrupt monopoly union or multinational buyers, both of which paid desperately low prices. With the assistance of two Mexican biologists and the Dutch organic certifying organization NOVIB, Sebastiana Juárez Broca parlayed her indigenous origins into a valuable brand name, Tia Tana Chocolate. But the adoption of capitalist advertising techniques conferred de facto property rights to a single individual rather than a village cooperative. As the Slow Food citation reads, Tia Tana "produces chocolate using traditional methods employing village women and encouraging the expansion of biological and economically compatible cultivation" (Slow Food n.d.). Yet the picturesque image of local production for tourists can conceal exploitative class relations within indigenous communities. Néstor García Canclini (1993) has observed that profits from craft sales to foreigners generally end up in the hands of local merchants and intermediaries.

Corporate control of international marketing further complicates the prospects for such ecological initiatives. Warren Belasco (1993) has shown the skill with which the food industry has co-opted counterculture movements and created its own forms of ersatz authenticity. Cookbook publishers likewise shared in the bonanza, offering up picturesque images of peasant cuisine to affluent readers (Pilcher 2004). The complicated recipes for traditional festival dishes may even be prepared occasionally by the leisured elite, but slow food offers little to single parents working overtime to support a family in the collapsing ruins of the U.S. welfare state.

Apocalypse Now?

The United States' campaign to spread GM food represents only the latest version of the "white man's burden" to uplift backward peoples through modern agricultural technology, although in practice the so-called Green Revolution has succeeded in promoting capitalist farming, rural unemployment, and urban shantytowns. Yet the Slow Food program likewise bears more than a passing resemblance to the *mission civilisatrice* of nineteenth-century imperialism. While more benign than military intervention, the missionary approach still conceals uneven power relationships that limit the opportunities available to the Mexican people. Moreover, the movement's goal of reducing agricultural overproduction resonates clearly with the dilemmas of the European Union's Common Agricultural Policy, with its mountains of surplus foods. International commodity markets can have complex implications for developing countries (see Raikes 1988), but the agricultural trade wars between Europe and the United States have caused tremendous harm to poor farmers around the world. One of the latest victims of this imperial struggle has been famine-ridden Zambia, the subject of widespread criticism for rejecting U.S. food aid out of fear that GM grain would contaminate domestic crops and forfeit European sales (Annear 2004). Viewed at this level, Sebastiana Juárez Broca appears as simply a colorful indigenous brand to sell Mexican chocolate to upscale consumers.

From the global struggles of industrial food retailers, Grupo Maseca has emerged as an unlikely champion of authentic Mexican cuisine. Mechanization has been essential to the survival of tortillas as the daily bread of Mexican wage laborers, who cannot afford the luxury of slow food on an everyday basis. In foreign markets, the company has launched ambitious expansion plans, and United States and Europe make up nearly 50 percent of total sales (Vega 2003). Occupying foreign territory has meant using local knowledge of fresh corn tortillas to challenge taco shell stereotypes. Although condemned at home as the antithesis of traditional cooking, bags of masa harina have become essential care packages for migrants and aficionados in exile from Aztlán.

With multinational corporations increasingly determining the availability and even the authenticity of food, class-based issues of market power become ever more crucial. While in many European countries restaurant service is an honorable trade paying a living wage, in Mexico it is often the last resort of the most impoverished people. Self-exploitation ultimately makes possible the Slow Food ideal of "good regional cuisine at moderate prices" (Petrini 2003:15). Moreover, Michael Kearney (1996:107) has offered a cautionary note about the conservative embrace of ecological projects generally: "one need not be cynical to see in official support of sustainable development and appropriate technology a de facto recognition that rural poverty in the Third World is not going to be developed out of existence. All peoples will not be brought up to the comfort level of the affluent classes and must therefore adapt to conditions of persistent poverty in ways that are not ecologically, economically, or politically disruptive." He concludes that "the de facto project of such right romantics is to sustain existing relations of inequality." Historically minded observers will note also that much of the program and even the slogan of "alimentary sovereignty" adopted by José Bové was promoted earlier by the fascist regime of Benito Mussolini (Parasecoli 2003:37; Helstosky n.d.). Slow Food has likewise replaced the developmental ideal of Prometheus with the more defensive symbol of Noah. As Petrini (2003:86) explains: "Faced with the excesses of modernization, we are not trying to change the world anymore, just to save it." Yet Oaxacan migrant workers, who must cross a militarized frontier in order to save their own communities, may ask themselves: will they find a place on the Ark?

This is not to deny that Slow Food offers hope for the survival of peasant cuisines. Indeed, the contemporary situation in Mexico parallels that of Italy a century ago. Just as half of all Italian labor migrants ultimately returned home, with new attitudes and more money but still part of their old communities, so do Mexican sojourners continue to follow their circular routes, notwithstanding hysterical media accounts of "a border out of control." Of course, it would be absurd to think that NAFTA will ever lead to income redistribution programs comparable to those of the European Union. Nevertheless, attempts to improve conditions in Oaxaca, like those in the Mezzogiorno, must adopt a continental vision. The indigenous political revival, with roots in both southern California and southern Mexico, offers a model for revalorizing ethnic communities (Kearney 1996). Those who sympathize can help most by allowing transnational families to flourish in their own neighborhoods rather than by indulging in exotic tourism to distant lands. The true foundation of sustainable agriculture in Mexico is outside labor paying decent wages—as it is for any American family farm.

Note

Acknowledgments. This essay was inspired by Martín González de la Vara and greatly improved by the suggestions of Richard Wilk, Donna Gabaccia, William Beezley, Sterling Evans, Glen Kuecker, and the anthropologists of SEA, who graciously welcomed an imposter in their midst.

References

Annear, Christopher M. 2004. "GM or Death": Food and Choice in Zambia. Gastronomica 4(2):16–23.

Bauer, Arnold J. 1990. Millers and Grinders: Technology and Household Economy in Meso-America. Agricultural History 64(1):1–17.

Belasco, Warren. 1993. Appetite for Change: How the Counterculture Took on the Food Industry. Ithaca: Cornell University Press.

Camporesi, Piero. 1993. [1989] The Magic Harvest: Food, Folklore, and Society. Joan Krakover Hall, trans. Cambridge, U.K.: Polity Press.

Cebreros, Alfonso. n.d. Grupo MASECA: Un Caso Exitoso de Transnacionalización Agroalimentaria. Electronic document. http://ciat-library.ciat.cgiar.org/Alacea/v_congreso_ memorias/V_grupo_maseca.htm, accessed September 6, 2003.

Chibnik, Michael. 2003. Crafting Tradition: The Making and Marketing of Oaxacan Wood Carvings. Austin: University of Texas Press.

Cohen, Jeffrey A. 1999. Cooperation and Community: Economy and Society in Oaxaca. Austin: University of Texas Press.

Diner, Hasia. 2001. Hungering for America: Italian, Irish, and Jewish Foodways in the Age of Migration. Cambridge, MA: Harvard University Press.

Fantasia, Rick. 1995. Fast Food in France. Theory and Society 24:201-43.

Gabaccia, Donna. 2004. The Atlantic Origins of Italian Food. Conference on American Popular Culture. Toronto, Ontario.

García Canclini, Néstor. 1993. Transforming Modernity: Popular Culture in Mexico. Lidia Lozano, trans. Austin: University of Texas Press.

González, Roberto J. 2001. Zapotec Science: Farming and Food in the Northern Sierra of Oaxaca. Austin: University of Texas Press.

Greenpeace. 2001. Greenpeace etiqueta anuncio espectacular de Maseca. Boletín 173, September. Electronic document. http://www.greenpeace.org.mx/php/gp.php?target= %2Fphp%2Fboletines.php%3Fc%3Dtrans%26n%3D173, accessed April 22, 2004.

Guillermoprieto, Alma. 1994. The Heart That Bleeds. New York: Vintage.

———. 1999. In Search of the Tortilla. The New Yorker, November 26:46.

Helstosky, Carol. 2004. Garlic and Oil: The Politics of Italian Food. London: Berg.

———. n.d. In press. Mussolini's Alimentary Sovereignty.

Hobsbawm, Eric. 1983. Introduction: Inventing Traditions. In The Invention of Tradition. Eric Hobsbawm and Terence Ranger, eds. Pp. 1–14. Cambridge: Cambridge University Press.

Kearney, Michael. 1996. Reconceptualizing the Peasantry: Anthropology in Global Perspective. Boulder, CO: Westview Press.

Lewis, Oscar. 1951. Life in a Mexican Village: Tepoztlán Revisited. Urbana: University of Illinois Press.

The New Yorker. 2000. Day Job: Taco Bell Employee. April 24–May 1:185.

Ochoa, Enrique C. 2000. Feeding Mexico: The Politics of Food Since 1910. Wilmington, DE: Scholarly Resources.

Parasecoli, Fabio. 2003. Postrevolutionary Chowhounds: Food, Globalization, and the Italian Left. Gastronomica 3(3):29–39.

Petrini, Carlo. 2003. Slow Food: The Case for Taste. William McCuaig, trans. New York: Columbia University Press.

Pilcher, Jeffrey M. 1998. ¡Que vivan los tamales! Food and the Making of Mexican Identity. Albuquerque: University of New Mexico Press.

———. 2004 From "Montezuma's Revenge" to "Mexican Truffles": Culinary Tourism across the Rio Grande. In Culinary Tourism. Lucy M. Long, ed. Pp. 76–96. Lexington: University Press of Kentucky.

Raikes, Philip. 1988. Modernising Hunger: Famine, Food Surplus and Farm Policy in the EEC and Africa. London: James Currey.

Redfield, Margaret Park. 1929. Notes on the Cookery of Tepoztlan, Morelos. American Journal of Folklore 42(164):167–96.

Ritzer, George. 1993. The McDonaldization of Society. Thousand Oaks, CA: Pine Forge Press.

Slow Food. n.d. Premio Slow Food. Electronic document. http://www.slowfood.com/eng/sf_premio/sf_premio.lasso, accessed April 22, 2004.

Stephen, Lynn. 1991. Zapotec Women. Austin: University of Texas Press.

Taco Bell. 2001. History. Electronic document. http://www.tacobell.com, accessed March 17, 2004.

Teti, Vito. 1992. La cucina calabrese: è un'invenzione americana? I viaggi di Erodoto 6(14):58–73.

Vega, Marielena. 2003. Grupo Industrial Maseca. El Economista, September 3.

Watson, James L., ed. 1997. Golden Arches East: McDonald's in East Asia. Palo Alto: Stanford University Press.

Weiner, Tim. 2002. Mexicans Resisting McDonald's Fast Food Invasion. New York Times, August 24.

From Hunger Foods to Heritage Foods: Challenges to Food Localization in Lao PDR

6

PENNY VAN ESTERIK

"**A** COMMODITY CHAIN is a series of interlinked exchanges through which a commodity and its constituents pass from extraction or harvesting through production to end use" (Ribot 1998:307). The end of the commodity chain for a small basket of crisps made of Lao river algae purchased for 40,000 kip (around $4.00 U.S.) at a local market in Vientiane, Lao People's Democratic Republic (Lao PDR), is my kitchen. But before I simply consume the algae chips, and their sweet counterparts, cassava chips, I want to place them in a broader interpretive framework than commodity chains and use them to interrogate the ethics of exotic foods. I do this first by placing these two food items in the context of Lao national food security, and then in the context of Southeast Asian culinary traditions. But the story of these chips is neither linear nor unambiguous. Nor are these food products centrally important to anyone's diet. They are marginal in the Lao diet where the chain begins and in the North American diet where it ends—marginal in multiple ways and in multiple contexts. It is their marginality I want to reflect upon in this chapter.

Under conditions of food insecurity and seasonal scarcity, Lao cooks—usually women—rely heavily on collecting wild foods from the forest. They make ingenious use of wild foods considered exotic by outsiders, such as crickets, green tree ant eggs, river algae, wild cassava, and wild yams. These regionally specific seasonal foods are not always part of the regular diet of the lowland Lao; we might refer to them as *hunger foods*—foods that act as insurance against hunger in times of seasonal or catastrophic food shortages.

This chapter argues that the rarer and harder these foods are for the Lao to obtain, the more valued they have become to North American and European chefs. How have seasonal hunger foods become heritage foods in the gourmet boutiques of Europe and North America? In the quest for new ingredients and new tastes for chefs and consumers, some importers have discovered elements of the Lao cuisine that can be sold as specialties in niche markets. These include products that are produced in the northern region of Luang Prabang, Lao PDR, like *khai pen* (river algae sheets), and products created out of cassava such as *khao kiep* (cassava crisps). These items have been redesigned to meet Western tastes. In California, where food boutiques and food banks stand side by side, these two Lao food items have begun to appear in specialty food shops and online shopping services, provisioners of yuppie chow.

Being Food Insecure

Lao People's Democratic Republic (Lao PDR), a landlocked country in Southeast Asia, is classified as a low-income, food deficit country. After decades of war, including fighting for independence from French colonial control and surviving the bombing inflicted by the American secret war in Laos, the country remains food insecure.

With a per capita income of around $400, Lao PDR is one of the poorest and least developed countries in Asia. This poverty is reflected in the nutritional status of its population. Forty percent of children under five are underweight, 41 percent stunted, and 15 percent wasted (Health Status of the People in Lao PDR, 2001). The prevalence of wasting among children increased to 15 percent in 2000, and the presence of chronic energy deficiency among adults was "alarmingly high (19 percent), even higher than reported during a previous survey in 1995 (14 percent)" (FAO country profile). According to the Food and Agriculture Organization (FAO) country profile on Lao PDR, "the daily dietary energy supply per capita increased from 2030 kcal in 1968 to 2400 kcal in 1995." Almost 30 percent of the population is below the minimal level of dietary energy consumption. Household food insecurity is defined by the government as the inability to provide 2,100 calories per person per day. To reduce the number of poverty households, the government reduced the minimal dietary energy requirements to 1,983 calories per day (Millennium Development Goals 2004:6). Clearly there is a poor fit between the measurement of calories nationally and the hunger and malnutrition experienced by individuals in households.

Local and national food shortages are not relieved by trade in food items. Food imports and exports are minimal, government controlled, and directed toward urban markets. Lao PDR is a closed, protected trading system—but one where informal and nonformal trade with China, Vietnam, and Thailand thrives. Stocks of stored rice are available neither nationally nor locally, as most households do not produce enough rice to meet their needs and have to purchase it. About half the provinces regularly fail to reach rice self-sufficiency because of drought, flooding, or underproduction related to irrigation problems. Since rice provides over 80 percent of total calorie intake (UNDP 2003), many households are food insecure and have to stretch rice with other foods. In Lao PDR, as in Vietnam, gruels made from broken rice grains, rice flour, and tubers such as cassava or yam "saved a lot of people from famine" (Nguyen 2001:94). In short, for some households in some communities in some seasons, food itself is a scarce commodity.

In response, the Lao government has developed policies to improve the nutritional status of Lao families by enhancing Lao food self-sufficiency and encouraging the production and export of cash crops. Lao government planning gives highest priority to reducing poverty especially in rural areas, by improving the food security and nutrition situation through diversification of the Lao diet. Integration into global markets is part of this plan: "The Lao government believes in the globalization process since it considers that it will create a propitious environment for achieving the over-arching goal of alleviating poverty and creating a more prosperous and peaceful society" (Lao PDR 2000:29).

But has Lao PDR always been food insecure? Recently (2001) the Asian Development Bank concluded that poverty in Lao PDR is "new poverty," produced by the process of development. The policy imperative driving market integration has made things worse for most Lao, and better for a few. Efforts to increase market integration are increasing this policy-induced new poverty, so that the more remote communities are actually more food secure than communities close to roads (EU 1997:20). Yet, government policies operate on the assumption that remoteness and lack of market integration is a cause of poverty. This chapter provides one example of what happens when the market comes to remote locations where food insecurity is common. Market integration makes possible the movement of some food products out of the Lao food system and into the North American, and the constant devaluation of the Lao currency (*kip*) makes some food products more valuable outside the country than inside.

Culinary Complexes of Southeast Asia

That poverty and food shortages may be recent experiences for the Lao explains why the country retains its self-identity around concepts of hospitality and food sharing. A Lao proverb states: "You can live in a narrow space, but it's hard to live with a narrow heart" (Rakow 1992:54); failure to share food is evidence of a narrow heart. Southeast Asian cuisines, including the Lao, are born of festive meals, communally prepared and eaten (Ho 1995:8).

Food as a focus of interest in Southeast Asia has been a matter of praxis not analysis, unless by analysis we consider the endless evaluations of food, flavors, and eating experiences that dominate discussions in rural and urban communities. Food matters to people at many levels, but it has rarely figured analytically in the work of anthropologists of Southeast Asia. However, the area is favored by food writers such as Alford and Duguid, whose award-winning books on Asian foods (*Hot Sour Salty Sweet: A Culinary Journey through Southeast Asia*, 2002; *Seductions of Rice*, 1998) easily delineate the boundaries and characteristics of Southeast Asia as a culinary area.

In addition to cookbook authors, linguists have also provided clues that suggest food is something worth talking and thinking about throughout Southeast Asia. Different Southeast Asian language families make similar distinctions between cooked and uncooked rice and contain multiple verbs for drying and cutting (Matisoff 1992), hinting about the existence of a regional culinary complex. Culinary terms are critical to aligning otherwise distinct cultures, even before globalization made *pad Thai* (Thai fried noodles) a household word (cf. Van Esterik 1992).

For economic anthropologists, using food systems as a means of defining ethnic and agricultural boundaries within a Southeast Asian culture area suggests an outmoded theoretical concern with classification, diffusion, and typologies. But without a perspective on the structure of typical meals, we are more likely to consider food items such as river weed and wild cassava in isolation, rather than as parts of historically produced complexes. O'Connor's (1995) model of agricultural change in Southeast Asia calls for a regional anthropology that situates agro-cultural complexes within regional history. In our admiration for fieldwork-driven empiricism, he argues, we have avoided regional comparisons, lest we be accused of returning to a theoretically antiquated culture area concept, unsuitable for addressing questions of globalization and transnational migration. Although only the broadest outlines of the regional food system are provided here, Lao food systems emerged out of past systems and bear some relation to comparable systems elsewhere in the region.

Southeast Asian culinary complexes include: rice as the central source of calories and a dominant cultural symbol of feminine nurture, fermented fish products, soups, local fresh vegetables and herbs, spicy dipping sauces to add zest to bland rice, and meat or fish in variable amounts. Most meal formats feature rice in a common bowl with side dishes presented simultaneously. Throughout Southeast Asia, and particularly in Lao PDR, we taste the rural roots of the cuisine.

Lao Food System

The Lao government recognizes sixty-five distinct ethnic groups, although it stresses "unity in diversity" among all ethnic groups. The food system discussed here is characteristic of lowland Lao *Lum* groups, the dominant majority making up 68 percent of the population. Lao PDR is a country of subsistence rice farmers, with some minority groups growing maize and cassava in addition to rice. As elsewhere in the world, rice as the key staple is valued far beyond its nutritional value (Bray 1986; Ohnuki-Tierney 1993; Goody 1982; Hanks 1972). The key marker of the collective identity of lowland Lao is the use of glutinous or sticky rice. Only more recent arrivals to the country such as the Yao and Hmong prefer nonglutinous rice (Schiller et al. 1998:228). Recent rice surveys have found over 3,200 varieties in the country, 85 percent of them glutinous (Rao et al. 2001). Most glutinous rice is consumed less than fifty kilometers from its place of production (Nguyen 2001:112). And no rice tastes better than the rice grown at home. While Lao and Vietnamese who use glutinous rice as their daily staple celebrate the taste of their local rice varieties, a European visitor in 1877 did not like the "stickiness" of glutinous rice, referring to it as that "ghastly rice of Laotians" (Nguyen 2001:64).

Glutinous rice is by far the preferred rice for the lowland Lao. It is an understatement to say that the Lao appreciate the qualities of glutinous rice; like the Vietnamese, they deeply believe that glutinous rice is more nutritious and more aromatic than any other kind of rice. In Vietnam, contests were held to perfect glutinous rice steaming skills for young girls and men (Nguyen 2001:57). Lao are very conscious of the aromatic and cooking qualities of glutinous rice, as well as its keeping quality (Schiller et al. 1998:234). This is equally true of families with adequate rice and families who must buy rice because their own fields have not produced enough, or because they have no access to rice fields.

Accompanying most rice meals is a sauce or paste made from fermented local fish or shellfish. The fish are salted, dried, pounded, and packed with toasted rice and rice husk in jars for a month or more. Fish sauce (*nam pa*) is a crucial ingredient in many dishes. In its thicker form (*padek*), it is served as a dish with rice. The strong-smelling product is not appealing to many westerners who have little tolerance for fermented, fishy foods, but overseas Lao speak longingly of the taste of local versions recalled nostalgically from their homeland.

Fresh greens and herbs are available from household gardens and local markets. Recent development projects on home gardens have dramatically increased the amount of fresh vegetables available to households. In pilot projects, families participating in these projects consumed three times more vegetables than they sold. However, households need land, labor, and seeds to benefit from these initiatives. Vegetables are served in soups; stir fried with onion, garlic, meat, or fish; or served raw with fermented fish products or dipping sauces (*jeaw*).

There is a clear continuity between medicinal and culinary use of herbs and other forest products. Ginger, coriander root, and aromatic woods play important roles in both medicinal and culinary systems. Elders, both male and female, generally know where to locate these products if they still live in the same localities where they were taught to locate and process these items when they were young. However, relocated individuals and households may not know where to obtain wild foods, particularly medicinal herbs, and may not know how to process them to remove toxins. Correct processing and prescribing requires specialized knowledge. For example, wild cassava needs to be carefully processed to remove toxins; elders report that young people may have no idea how to find or process wild cassava, although they recall eating it mixed with rice when rice supplies were low. In other parts of the world knowledge of how to process toxic tubers has already been lost, resulting in deaths from cyanide poisoning (Cardoso et al. 2005).

In Lao PDR, as elsewhere in Southeast Asia, dipping sauces add zest to bland rice, stimulating appetites, and tempting intemperate eaters to consume more calories from starchy staples. With the early adoption of chili peppers, originally from America, Lao developed local sauces (*jeaw*) made from ingredients such as peppers, garlic, lime, sugar, fish sauce, onions, and coriander—each combination unique to a region, community, or household. Some dry *jeaw* consist primarily of salt and chili peppers and are not given to children.

Meat and fish are valued parts of Lao diets. Variable amounts of fish or meats are mixed with herbs and spices in stews and soups; large amounts of meat or fish are grilled mainly for communal festive meals. Meat or fish may also be used in soups served in communal or individual dishes. Soups are particularly valued as they allow cooks to stretch ingredients, make use of bones, and generally expand the meal to serve more people.

Squirrels, snakes, frogs, crickets, and insects also supply protein, along with freshwater fish, although there is clear preference for chicken, pork, duck, or beef, should cash be available to purchase meat. Domestic animals in Lao communities do not fare well without regular vaccinations, although development projects attempt to increase domestic livestock and poultry. Most projects fail unless external aid projects are able to provide extension support.

Fermented rice liquor (*laolao*) plays a key role in all celebrations, as consumption of alcohol creates links between the living and the dead, humans and spirits, and guests and hosts. Among minority groups living north of Luang Prabang, rice alcohol is kept in heirloom jars (Nguyen 2001:73), and in the past was a necessary ingredient for oath taking and other rituals. Producing *laolao* used to be a household enterprise in the past, but more recently, liquor is purchased from local enterprises where glutinous rice is grown specifically for this purpose. Steamed sticky rice is fermented with balls of yeast for about a week, when it is distilled and consumed (Schiller et al. 2001:236).

Food in Motion

Describing the structure of the Lao food system as I have done above overstresses the continuity of traditional food items and meal formats. But the structure of systems of food production and consumption in Lao PDR may provide valuable opportunities for examining diversity and continuities, including historical transformations brought about through processes of colonization, development, and globalization.

Colonialism affected the Lao food system in many ways: French bread, pâté, and salads clearly came from the French colonial experience. Many urban and overseas Lao substitute baguettes for glutinous rice for breakfast. What is known as Luang Prabang salad exemplifies the fusion of French salad traditions and the Lao practice of providing plates of raw or steamed vegetables and herbs to go with dipping sauces. Foo (2002:18, 88) describes Lao long lunches as a colonial remnant, and notes that the popularity of French baguettes endured longer than the bricks of colonial buildings. However, apart from freshly baked baguettes, the French had less impact on the Lao food system than on the Vietnamese (cf. Norindr 1996).

Other changes can be linked to development processes within Lao PDR. Because of government policies to reduce slash-and-burn upland agriculture and to increase production of cash crops, Lao farmers with access to irrigated fields have been encouraged to produce nonglutinous rice for sale. The few new varieties of glutinous and nonglutinous rice grown in irrigated fields in the central region of Lao PDR since 1993 require fertilizers, mechanical threshers, and hand tractors in order to make a profit (Schiller et al. 1998:226). The small amount of glutinous rice exported for use by overseas Lao comes from northeastern Thailand, and overseas Lao find Thai rice less flavorful than the rice they remember from home villages.

While Lao make distinctions between people who eat glutinous rice and those who eat nonglutinous rice, in fact, the distinction is somewhat arbitrary and is breaking down rapidly. Ordinary or nonglutinous rice can become glutinous, and glutinous rice can become ordinary rice, as the glutinous character of the rice endosperm is reversible (Nguyen 2001:26). Lao have selected for glutinous characteristics that increase with domestication (Nguyen 2001:20). Just as the product itself can change over time, so too is the way rice is served. Several Hmong and lowland Lao households I visited in 2005 had both glutinous and nonglutinous rice in their kitchens, and rural restaurants served both kinds of rice in the same meal. Glutinous rice can no longer be considered unambiguously as the primary marker of Lao ethnic identity.

Conversion of forests to agricultural land and the expansion of commercial logging have reduced forests in many parts of Lao PDR. Villagers complain that it is now more difficult to collect wild greens from these shrinking forest reserves. In addition, the valuable nontimber forest products (NTFP) that have provided both emergency food for poor households and income for many more households can now be sold more conveniently by locals or, more often, by middlemen who are able to access NTFP and new markets more directly, thanks to new roads.

Wild Meat and Fish

Forest animals are harder to find now than in the past. To obtain meat, Lao villagers now need to go deeper into the forest and become even more skilled hunters. Where a dozen years ago, villagers in Champassak province in southern Laos reported an abundance of animals and fish close to their villages, now many species have disappeared; a two-day trek might yield nothing and an hour fishing might yield half a kilogram of fish (UNDP 2003:82).

Villagers speak with nostalgia of the days when the giant Mekong catfish (*Pangasianodon gigas*), now close to extinction, could still be caught (Heldke 2003:74; Davidson 1975; Levy 1986). Like river algae, the rarity of the giant catfish makes it doubly appealing to Western food adventurers. After eating Lao catfish soup, food writer Levy comments: "Certainly, a local fisherman did catch one of the huge creatures some time that week. It's a horrible thought, but it could have been the last one. And, readers, we ate it" (1986:190).

There is a well-developed trade in endangered species across the borders to Thailand and Vietnam. Eating exotic animals, including eating uncustomary parts of customary animals, and eating animals rarely consumed in North America such as bears, dogs, and cats, as well as wild animals that are dangerous to catch or process, is thrilling for a food adventurer (Heldke 2003:71).

The wild animals are not always eaten but rather may be traded for the body parts with medicinal value (horn, antler, teeth, bone, gallbladder, shell, blood, excrement, urine [Baird 1995]) as part of systems of contagious magic. Lao healers report that an animal part used for medicine can "last a lifetime" (Baird 1995:22), and some claim that the overharvesting of endangered species is driven by the demand for these products in Vietnam, China, and Thailand.

Exports for Gourmets

Globalization has brought in new stakeholders who are looking at Lao food resources from very different perspectives. In spite of national food insecurity—or perhaps because of it—Lao PDR has become a site for agricultural, pharmaceutical, and gastronomic bioprospecting. Agribusinesses want to patent the incredibly diverse rice varieties found in different regions of Lao PDR. "The development of 'boutique rices' that combine the glutinous endosperm and aromatic character of many traditional Lao rices is regarded as having the greatest potential for the export market," concludes a report from the Lao-IRRI project and the National Agricultural Research Institute (Schiller et al. 2001:240). Pharmaceutical companies want access to the herbs and other plant resources (most are wild NTFP), along with the specialized knowledge of traditional healers, in order to discover, develop, and patent new drugs to combat malaria, cancer, and HIV/AIDS. Lao communities have used these products for centuries as medicinal cures and ingested them in soups and tonic drinks in the absence of adequate primary health care. These products are now being exported to make medicinal tonics in China, Vietnam, and Thailand, endangering the herbal resources available for future generations of Lao.

Khai Pen *and* Khao Kiep

Culinary bioprospecting in Lao PDR has attracted new entrepreneurs—both Lao and non-Lao—who want rare ingredients and new tastes for chefs and Western consumers. This brings me back to the seasonal hunger foods mentioned at the beginning of the chapter. Few Westerners have the opportunity to visit exotic Luang Prabang, the former royal capital. But they can consume rare foods that come from there—foods like *khai pen* (river algae sheets) and *khao kiep* (cassava crisps) that have been romanticized by association with the former royal palace. The recipe book of the former royal chef includes a dish made from river algae mixed with ground pork (Sing 1981:235).

A few well-traveled individuals discovered these foods and publicized their features, while others developed the products, arranged their export, and introduced them into new markets. The sale of these rare, exotic food items is neither a large nor a particularly profitable business, but it requires a great deal of culinary capital on the part of the distributors and their customers.

Khai pen is made from a river weed (*khai*), as it is known in the north of the country, a variety of green algae (*chlorophyceae*) collected from the fast-flowing rivers of northern Laos and Thailand. It is harvested in winter, from November to January; the algae identified as *thao* was also collected from stagnant water in the rainy season (Sing 1981:25). Although it was used in royal households, it was more common in poor households: "Households that routinely suffer from food insecurity in the form of insufficient rice often depend on wild aquatic resources to compensate for this deficiency" (Meusch et al. 2003:22). River algae was consumed two to four times a week by more than half the households surveyed in a study of the value of aquatic resources in southern Attapeu province (Meusch et al. 2003:31). It was probably consumed in simple water-based soups rather than used to make *khai pen*.

Families, including children, collect the bright green algae that looks like fine seaweed from rocks on the sides of rivers. To make *khai pen*, the algae is spread in the sun to dry and processed by pressing dried tomatoes, garlic, chilies, sesame seeds, and salt into the dried sheets. The sheets are held together with tamarind paste. They can be cut into strips and used as flavoring in vegetable dishes or fried rice (Alford and Duguid 2000:165) or grilled and served as a snack with drinks. In Lao PDR, it is primarily served to men in town bars. According to *New York Times* food writer Florence Fabricant, *khai pen* has a "pleasantly earthy, slightly spinach-like flavor that is both nutty and peppery" (Fabricant 2002:D3).

Once the algae is removed from the subsistence system, commodified, and reintroduced into Lao markets as *khai pen*, it is expensive to purchase; it costs approximately one dollar for four large sheets in the markets of Luang Prabang and $7.49 (reduced from $9.99) for four very small sheets from a California-based, online food boutique.

One Lao couple in Vientiane has been producing Lao algae chips for three years; they estimate they have sold between three and five hundred kilos in that period. They developed and marketed the product because they are interested in preserving traditional Lao recipes. The algae is collected by networks of women who gather it by hand, helped by their children, from fast-flowing rivers around Vang Vieng and Luang Prabang. They could also collect river algae from the southern provinces, and thus expand their market without endangering the river environment. Locals, they say, are not yet aware of the possibility of collecting and selling the algae.

In order to control the quality, insure the cleanliness of the product, regulate its taste, and insure proper preservation, they process the product themselves in their house in Vientiane. They have increased its shelf life up to six months by drying it in special ovens to remove the moisture and destroy the germs. The algae chips are distributed through a few outlets in the capital frequented by foreigners, where four small sheets are sold in a Lao basket for forty thousand kip (with five thousand kip profit for the company). It is also sold at the airport, where Japanese visitors and visiting Lao expatriates buy it in great quantities—forty to fifty boxes at a time—often for gifts. They complain that few local shops are interested in their products because of the demand for imported food.

In some parts of Southeast Asia, cassava is collected wild as an emergency food; in other areas, it is planted in upland fields as a dry season crop; in Thailand, it is grown for animal fodder. But wherever root crops are grown in Southeast Asia, they are freely given up for the more prestigious rice: "Rice advances across Southeast Asia as if it were addictive" (O'Connor 1995:986). But root crops are never entirely abandoned. In the forests of Lao PDR, wild yams, cassava, and taro are collected by women who know where to find them and how to process them to remove poisons, if necessary, by soaking, cooking, and drying the roots. Once harvested, cassava tubers are very perishable and hard to store. Cassava tubers have a high carbohydrate content and are a good source of potassium, iron, magnesium, vitamin C, and other vitamins. Currently, the same entrepreneurs who are marketing *khai pen* are also marketing sweet and savory cassava cakes for sale in California and online. Their household-based production involves forming the flat cakes in a simple wooden press and sun-drying them. Cassava crisps—semi-savory or sweet—are also available from Lotus foods for $7.49 (reduced from $9.99) per package. These products are too expensive for Lao families to purchase in either country.

The products were promoted by a luncheon presentation in New York on May 30, 2002, where well-known chefs from New York and Chicago prepared them in specialties such as "grilled *kaipen* wrapped seabass with somen noodles and cilantro vinaigrette," "*kaipen* with Asian guacamole," "smoked corn and *kaipen* fritters," and "cassava sesame crisp tacos with grilled shrimp, rice noodles, bean sprouts and tangy dipping sauce."

New roads in Lao PDR made it possible for these products to leave the localities where they were produced; the newly integrated market economy made it possible for them to make their way to food boutiques in San Francisco and Toronto.

Conclusion

Foods and their meanings are increasingly mobile in a globalized food market. But the same foods have very different meanings in different contexts—river algae in soup as a side dish with sticky rice for a Lao subsistence farmer, or as grilled *kaipen*-wrapped sea bass with noodles and cilantro vinaigrette in an upscale Chicago restaurant; wild cassava to stretch sticky rice in a Lao community, or as the base for cassava sesame crisp baskets with lobster, chorizo, and lobster stock emulsion in that same Chicago restaurant.

Lao farmers use these products as part of their seasonal subsistence strategies and as insurance against crop failure. North American chefs use them to experiment with new taste combinations and perhaps to attract new admirers. Further examination of the commodity chain linking Lao river algae chips and cassava cakes to North American specialty food markets requires close attention to the meaning of *scarce, rare,* and *exotic.* The Oxford English Dictionary defines *scarce* as "restricted in quantity, size or amount, accessible in deficient quantity or limited number" (2658); *rare* denotes "seldom appearing, infrequent, uncommon, exceptional, unusual in respect to some good quality, of uncommon excellence" (2417). These foods are scarce to Lao farmers who harvest them, but rare to the North American chefs who cook them. It is their rarity that makes them exotic to the latter group.

Hunger foods and heritage foods represent disconnected discourses. My task here has been to identify these discourses and link them together, acting as the broker of these stories, just as food importers act as business brokers to provide exotic foods to North American consumers. Yet it would be a mistake to overstate the obvious binaries inherent in this story: slow food in Lao PDR becoming fast food snacks in North America; hunger over there, abundance over here; traditional food being given new life in another locale; poverty food necessities used as exotic expensive luxuries; here and there, then and now.

Such binaries force us to make moral judgments about the interconnections between food systems. On the one hand, a few Lao households are making extra income by providing these products to local entrepreneurs. On the other, the export of these products might destroy the scarce resource base both locals and exporters depend on. But the products are of interest in California and Toronto only as long as they remain exotic and rare. These particular items are no longer found in Toronto gourmet shops but must be ordered on the internet. In fact, the long-term demand for river weed and wild cassava would reduce their availability to Lao households as emergency hunger foods.

This chapter also questions the contrast between poverty foods and luxury foods. Lao villagers might well prefer pork loin to boiled pork backs, chicken breast to chicken feet, shrimp to crickets. Chicken feet and crickets are not the poverty foods that become exotic rare treats for foodies, notwithstanding the craze for chocolate-covered insects in the 1960s—foods used by teens to "gross people out." These latter products were food fads of short duration. Similarly, the interest in *khai pen* and *khao kiep* in North America is unlikely to last long.

The slow-fast distinction makes little sense in the Lao case. Lao food is unusually slow in preparation compared to Thai and other Asian cuisines. Rice must be soaked and steamed, fish products fermented, vegetables, fruits, and herbs collected and eaten fresh, or sun dried. But this is not the slow food envisioned by the Italian Slow Food movement.

When hunger foods, whose origins are inextricably linked to a place or tradition, are taken out of such traditions, away from their roots, their *terroir* (flavor unique to a particular region and soil), they no longer function as seasonal insurance and become instead markers of elite consumption in very different food systems. This decoupling of food from people and culture, of production from consumption, raises a question for future research: What are the boundaries between fascination with food—its taste and textures—and food fanaticism, with its prescriptive rules and border patrolling of what is ingested? How do these boundaries shift during globalization and the development of transnational commodity chains when the food deprived and the food obsessed eat the same food? *Bon appetit!*

Note

Acknowledgments. I would like to thank Richard Wilk for encouraging me to attend my first Society for Economic Anthropology meeting and to transform my poster presentation into a paper. His insights into what I wanted to say through my Lao food poster combined with his critical commentary about how to get there shaped this final chapter. I have benefited from participating in a project on community-based natural resource management at the Department of Forestry, National University of Laos, giving me an opportunity to meet others interested in Lao food. In addition, I recorded details about most meals I consumed in the country, and I thank those who fed me and ate with me for their patience with my questions. In the end, this chapter emerged more from trips to the table and the market than from trips to the library.

References

Alford, J., and N. Duguid. 1998. Seductions of Rice. New York: Artisan.
———. 2000. Hot Sour Salty Sweet: A Culinary Journey through Southeast Asia. Toronto: Random House.

Asian Development Bank (ADB). 2001. Participatory Poverty Assessment: Lao People's Democratic Republic. Manila: ADB.

Baird, Ian. 1995. Lao PDR: An Overview of Traditional Medicines Derived from Wild Animals and Plants. A TRAFFIC Southeast Asia Consultancy Report.

Bray, Francesca. 1986. The Rice Economies: Technology and Development in Asian Societies. Berkeley: University of California Press.

Cardoso, P., E. Mirione, M. Ernesto, F. Massaza, J. Cliff, M. Rezaulttaquei, and J. Bradbury. 2005. Processing of Cassava Roots to Remove Cyanogens. Journal of Food Composition and Analysis 18(5):451–60.

Davidson, Alan. 1975. Fish and Fish Dishes of Laos. Rutland, VT: Charles Tuttle and Co.

EU (European Union). 1997. Micro-projects. Unpublished report, Luang Prabang, Vientiane.

Fabricant, Florence. 2002. In Laos, a Regional Specialty Goes Global. New York Times, May 22:D3.

Food and Agriculture Organization (FAO). 2005. Nutrition Country Profiles: Lao Peple's Democratic Republic. Rome: FAO.

Foo Check Teck. 2002. No Cola, Pepsi Only. Bangkok: White Lotus.

Goody, Jack. 1982. Cooking, Cuisine and Class. New York: Cambridge University Press.

Hall, Michael, E. Sharples, R. Mitchell, B. Cambourne, and N. Macionis, eds. 2003. Food Tourism around the World: Development, Management and Markets. Oxford: Butterworth Heinemann.

Hanks, Lucien. 1972. Rice and Man: Agricultural Ecology in Southeast Asia. Chicago: Aldine Atherton.

Harrison, Julia. 2003. Being a Tourist: Finding Meaning in Pleasure Travel. Vancouver: UBC Press.

Heldke, Lisa. 2003. Exotic Appetites: Ruminations of a Food Adventurer. New York: Routledge.

Ho, Alice Yen. 1995. At the Southeast Asian Table. Kuala Lumpur: Oxford University Press.

Lao PDR. 2000. Fighting Poverty through Human Resource Development, Rural Development and People's Participation. Government report, Vientiane.

Levy, Paul. 1986. Out to Lunch. New York: Harper and Row.

Matisoff, James A. 1992. International Encyclopedia of Linguistics. Oxford: Oxford University Press.

Meusch, E., J. Yhoung-Aree, R. Friend, and S. Funge-Smith. 2003. The Role and Nutritional Value of Aquatic Resources in the Livelihoods of Rural People. Bangkok: FAO.

Millenium Development Goals. 2004. Progress Report. Vientiane, Lao PDR.

Ministry of Health. 2001. Health Status of the People in Lao PDR. Vientiane, Lao PDR.

Nguyen Xuan Hien. 2001. Glutinous-Rice-Eating Tradition in Vietnam and Elsewhere. Bangkok: White Lotus.

Norindr, Panivong. 1996. Phantasmatic Indochina. Durham: Duke University Press.

O'Connor, Richard. 1995. Agricultural Change and Ethnic Succession in Southeast Asian States: A Case for Regional Anthropology. Journal of Asian Studies 54(4): 968–96.

Ohnuki-Tierney, Emiko. 1993. Rice as Self: Japanese Identities through Time. Princeton: Princeton University Press.

Oxford English Dictionary. 1971. Oxford: Oxford University Press.

Rakow, Meg. 1992. Women in Lao Morality Tales. Southeast Asia Paper No. 35, Center for Southeast Asian Studies, Schools of Hawaiian, Asian and Pacific Studies, University of Hawaii at Manoa.

Rao, A., C. Bounphanonsay, J. Schiller, and M. Jackson. 2001. Collection of Rice Germplasm in the Lao PDR between 1995 and 2000. National Rice Research Program (NAFRI), Vientiane, Lao PDR.

Ribot, Jesse. 1998. Theorizing Access: Forest Profits along Senegal's Charcoal Commodity Chain. Development and Change 29:307–341.

Schiller, J., A. Rao, and P. Inthapanya. 1998. Glutinous Rice Varieties of Laos: Their Improvement, Cultivation, Processing and Consumption. In Specialty Rices of the World. R. Duffy, ed. Rome: FAO.

Sing, Phia. 1981. Traditional Recipes of Laos. Devon: Prospect Books.

Trankell, Ing-Britt. 1995. Cooking, Care and Domestication: A Culinary Ethnography of the Tai Yong, Northern Thailand. Uppsala Studies in Cultural Anthropology 21, Uppsala, Sweden.

Trubek, Amy. 2003. Food from Here. Expedition 45(2):22–25.

UNDP (United Nations Development Program). 2003. Human Development Report.

Van Esterik, Penny. 1992. From Marco Polo to McDonalds: Thai Cuisine in Transition. Food and Foodways 5(2):177–93.

Tasting the Worlds of Yesterday and Today: Culinary Tourism and Nostalgia Foods in Post-Soviet Russia

MELISSA L. CALDWELL

THROUGHOUT THE TWENTIETH CENTURY, when Russians' abilities to travel abroad were limited by government restrictions and their own personal finances (see Barker 1999), food travel offered a unique means to experience foreign cultures. For Soviet citizens, the Soviet Union's Moscow-based Exhibition of the Achievements of the National Economies (*VDNKH*) exposed domestic tourists to the cultural and technological treasures of each of the fifteen republics. Included in these virtual tours were national dishes of the various republics (Glants and Toomre 1997). More recently, travel themes were again prominently displayed when McDonald's opened its first Soviet restaurant in January 1990, nineteen months before the breakup of the U.S.S.R. In a documentary recording the grand opening festivities in Moscow, provocatively titled *A Taste of the West*, one Russian customer was asked why he had made the trip to the Moscow restaurant on its opening day. The man replied that he wanted to be able to travel abroad without leaving the country.[1] Travel themes are reproduced inside this restaurant, which is decorated with a "see-the-world" motif: miniature replicas of world landmarks like the Eiffel Tower decorate one room; large, red Chinese gates lead into a room with an Asian theme; a third room resembles the inside of a Dixieland steamboat, complete with "windows" that look out onto scenes along the banks of the Mississippi River. A mural painted on the walls of another McDonald's restaurant in Moscow depicts Ronald McDonald and his friends riding a train bound for various destinations in Russia and Ukraine. During the restaurant's early years in Russia, the company also aired on Russian television a children's animated program that followed the adventures of McDonald's characters as they traveled around the world—of course, only to destinations with McDonald's restaurants (Hume 1990:51).

In the current post-Soviet moment, restrictions on Russian citizens' abilities to travel domestically and abroad have eased, and the Russian public's preoccupation with travel has become more apparent. As modes of travel have become more accessible, local ideas about desirable tourist destinations have diversified. In Moscow, pedestrians are constantly forced to navigate around the young women who crowd sidewalks and the exits at metro stations and distribute flyers for organized tours and vacations to exotic destinations. Travel agencies have sprung up in all corners of the city; it is not uncommon for multiple agencies to compete for space and customers in the same building. Magazine kiosks offer a wide variety of newspapers and magazines devoted to travel, and travel-themed programs and advertisements appear ever more frequently on Russian television.

This growth and diversification in Russia's budding tourism industry is paralleled by developments in the food industry. At the same time that Russia's increasingly global connections have created new opportunities for foreign travel beyond Russia's borders, they have also facilitated the spread of foreign foods, restaurants, and eating practices within Russia (Patico and Caldwell 2002). Moscow's dining scene has been transformed by the rapid proliferation of restaurants and food shops offering cuisines from around the world. Restaurants and individual food products promise to transport adventurous diners on culinary journeys to foreign lands. Irina, a schoolteacher in her early thirties, uses blue cheese and red wine to travel to France via her taste buds while she waits for the necessary legal documents that will enable her to leave the country. Food companies sponsor contests that promise to send lucky winners on trips to other countries, while tourists incorporate culinary experiences into their foreign vacations.

In this chapter, I explore these intersections of food and travel in Russia by focusing on the phenomenon of culinary tourism as a mode of experiencing the foreign Other. In particular, I am concerned with the ways in which forms of food travel evoke multisensory experiences of foreignness that are simultaneously imaginary and real. I suggest that the corporeal aspects of culinary tourism create a type of virtual travel that mobilizes a multidimensional reality. Finally, I conclude by examining the consequences of this culinary tourism. Travel has left Muscovites with acute feelings of homesickness that are satisfied by a good serving of nostalgia cuisine. Intriguingly, the type of nostalgia cuisine that has emerged in Moscow in the last few years is not aimed at bringing Russians back to a physical place, but rather to moments in time—notably, in both the distant and recent past. Consequently, nostalgia cuisine becomes the means for Muscovites to engage in a form of time travel.

The ideas and examples discussed in this chapter come from fieldwork that I conducted in Moscow between 1995 and 2004.[2] The majority of data presented here are drawn from the 2001–2002 period, when overlapping discourses of travel and food were most widespread and visible in Moscow. During a short research trip in May 2004, I encountered only two publicly posted advertisements that linked food and travel, and both announced contests to win trips. The discourses and images of culinary travel that I found were confined largely to articles and advertisements in travel magazines and to articles, recipes, and advertisements in magazines devoted to food and cooking.[3] This was in marked contrast to the 2001–2002 period, when advertisements linking food products and travel motifs appeared with much greater frequency.

Rethinking Fast Food and Slow Food through Culinary Tourism

Culinary tourism offers a provocative point of departure for rethinking the nature and consequences of food globalization in two important respects.[4] First, culinary tourism presents a critical variation on the "traveling foods" genre of globalization studies. This genre's conventional focus on foods and food practices as objects that are circulated through global flows and across borders orients analyses around local responses to foreign trends and the relationships that are constituted through these movements (e.g., Bestor 2000; Freidberg 2001; Goldfrank 1994; Jing 2000; Mintz 1985; Sutton 2001; Watson 1997, among others). By contrast, culinary tourism's preoccupation with food as the medium through which consumers traverse global boundaries redirects attention to the forms of global travel and the experiences of actors who engage in this travel.

Second, culinary tourism complicates the configurations of time and space that have been articulated in globalization studies. At one end of the spectrum are models that suggest that the rapidly increasing "intensification of global interconnectedness" of today's world (Inda and Rosaldo 2002:2) results in the collapse of temporal and spatial boundaries (see discussion in Inda and Rosaldo 2002; see also Barber 1995; Harvey 1989). Within the specific realm of "fast food," distinctions between local and foreign and between near and far are diminished (Ritzer 2004). Consequently, there is no "there" there, as Barber illustrates with his cynical observation that "You are nowhere. You are everywhere. Inhabiting an abstraction. Lost in cyberspace" (Barber 1995:99). At the other end of the spectrum are models that attempt to restore and maintain temporal and spatial distances (Giddens 1990). From this perspective, globalization produces opportunities for local communities to emphasize—and in some cases reinvent—cultural particularities of time and place (Watson 1997; Wilk 2002). In this respect, the insistence on the local is itself a response to global forces.

This emphasis on the local features prominently in the ideals of the Slow Food Movement. Initially presented by its founder, Carlo Petrini, as an antidote to the pathologies of fast living, as exemplified by the culture of "fast food," the Slow Food Movement encourages new arrangements of time and place in everyday life (Petrini 2001; see also Leitch 2003; Parkins 2004). These new ideals of time involve the cultivation of a slower pace of life in which consumers' sensibilities are oriented to leisure, pleasure, and contemplation. New formations of place entail, among other elements, appreciation and preservation of local cultures (Petrini 2001). Accordingly, as both Penny Van Esterik and Jeffrey Pilcher illustrate in their chapters in this volume, the Slow Food perspective privileges foods that symbolize regionally specific cultural traditions (see also Leitch 2003). Within this rubric, the form of "gastronomic tourism" that Petrini proposes is not one of frivolous entertainment, but rather a practice that is "meant to be aware and well-informed about the places visited: respectful, slow, reflective, and as distant as possible from the culture of 'use and discard'" (Petrini 2001:57).

Nevertheless, Petrini's preference for local cultures is insufficient for understanding the forms of culinary tourism currently in play in Russia. Specifically, in contrast to the Slow Food Movement's efforts to distance the local from the foreign and the global, the significance of Russian culinary tourism is that it mediates distinctions between past and present, distance and nearness, local and foreign, a quality also observed by Turgeon and Pastinelli for ethnic restaurants in Quebec City (2002). Turgeon and Pastinelli's observation that ethnic restaurants "represent microspaces allowing for intercultural contact, deterritorialized places where diners can see and touch, even consume the culture of the other on home ground" (2002:257) offers instructive parallels for understanding the role of culinary tourism in Russia today.

What makes Russian culinary tourism such a compelling means to access and interact with foreign cultures is food's capacity to evoke bodily responses in different sensory registers: sight, taste, smell, touch, and sound. This overlapping of multiple sensory experiences, a phenomenon that David Sutton (2001) terms "synesthesia" in his work on sensory food memories in Greece, transforms food into a mnemonic device that not only transports diners to other cultures (see also De Silva 1996; Linger 2001; Mankekar 2002; Turgeon and Pastinelli 2002) but also facilitates the transmission of different cultural realities across space and time (Seremetakis 1993). Consequently, consideration of the corporeal experience of culinary travel (see also Clifford 1997; De Certeau 1984) pushes the discussion of food and globalization in Russia beyond the more customary examinations of rigid Self/Other, local/foreign, and real/virtual boundaries that are pursued in analyses of global encounters.[5] Moreover, the physicality of culinary travel redirects discussions of speed, tempo, and place away from analyses of external processes and structures and back to the very social actors who are caught up in these forces.

Geogastronomia: Food as Place-Making

The crossover appeal of food and travel is evident in the types of advertisements that appear regularly in both food and travel magazines. For instance, the tour company

Rusal-Tur placed the following advertisement in the Russian culinary magazine *Restaurant Bulletin* (*Restorannye Vedemosti*). To promote its tour packages to Europe, Asia, and the Middle East, Rusal-Tur used the slogan "Travel with taste!" (*Puteshestviute so vkusom*). The word *vkus* is associated both with taste as a sense of style and taste as a sensory experience. By using this word, Rusal-Tur explicitly played up the notion of travel as an experience that evoked physical responses.[6] A more explicit play on taste is evident in the following advertisement placed in *Gurman*, the Russian version of the magazine *Gourmet*, by the tour company Kredo-Servis Tur. The caption to the advertisement offers "An exotic menu for gourmands—and travelers." The rest of the advertisement lists various countries tourists can visit and the increasingly exotic foods and beverages that might be encountered in those destinations: "The Czech Republic and Germany—wine; . . . Portugal—port; Switzerland—fondue; Galapagos islands—turtle soup; . . . Thailand—durian; Spain—paella; . . . Korea—monkey brains; . . . Kenya—crocodile meat and elephant meat."[7]

Themes of food travel also appear explicitly in feature articles in these magazines, such as one article titled "Around the World—by Mushrooms" (Ogorodnikov 1998). Periodic issues of *Restaurant Bulletin* include a special section called "Culinary Geography." Articles focus on the culinary history and culture of different parts of the world—such as the Netherlands (Litvencheva 1998)—accompanied by colorful pictures of foods and recipes for readers to prepare the dishes at home. Similarly, the magazine *Kulinar* includes a section titled "Culinary Journeys" that explores parts of the world ranging around the Caribbean, South America, Southeast Asia, Europe, and North America. An article on Indonesia in the September 1998 issue (Borisova 1998) is representative of these food journeys. The article includes a map of the region, and the author provides descriptions of Indonesia's climate, fauna, agriculture, history, religious practices, and economy, among other topics. These detailed summaries, complete with rich color photographs, segue into a series of beautiful, full-page photographs of local foods and five pages of recipes (Borisova 1998). Similar pairings of food and travel appear in *Gurman*. For instance, the February–March 1998 issue contains a section called simply "Exotica" that is devoted to the world and cuisine of Eskimos (Milovskii 1998). In the December 1997–January 1998 issue, the "Exotica" section first explores the culinary history of Provence, France (Kuznetsov 1997–1998), before moving to a special feature, "Calendar for Traveler-Gourmands" (*Gurman* 1997–98:68–69). Focusing specifically on Denmark, this brief article describes notable Christmas culinary traditions in Denmark and then provides readers with travel information on hotels and restaurants specializing in Christmas foods.

To a great extent, magazines such as *Restaurant Bulletin*, *Gurman*, and *Kulinar* cater primarily to members of Russia's business and financial elite. The restaurants, food shops, and other services advertised in these magazines tend to be expensive and thus out of the reach of most Moscow consumers. Nevertheless, themes of food travel are just as prevalent in the magazines and advertisements marketed to ordinary, middle-class Russians. For instance, the women's magazine *Good Appetite* focuses primarily on recipes, practical cooking utensils, and widely available and affordable ingredients that ordinary working women can use to prepare healthy and satisfying meals for their families. Most recipes are variations on traditional Russian dishes, often accompanied by suggestions for how to preserve Russian holiday traditions. Each issue of this magazine also includes a food travel section that presents the history and culture of another country, with easy-to-prepare recipes that have been adapted to Russian tastes and ingredients. In one issue, an article devoted to the food culture of Catalonia includes a recipe for a salad of peas, onions, and oil. A small box at the bottom of the recipe advises: "If you prefer a more satisfying dish, serve the peas with sour cream"—a nod to the customary use of sour cream in Russian dishes and the preference expressed by a number of my informants for heartier dishes over light salads (*Priyatnogo Appetita!* July 1998:41).

Underscoring further the significance of these linkages between food and travel is the term *geogastronomic,* coined by the anonymous author of a food travel article in *Restaurant Bulletin* (Anonymous 1998:8). Although the author used this term to call attention to the number of foreign restaurants located in one specific region of Moscow, this term is useful for capturing the broader idea that topographies themselves can be arranged and made meaningful through food. For instance, McDonald's, among other restaurants in Moscow, has successfully plotted the physical landscape of the city with the prominent display of billboard maps inside metro stations and underground walkways that use the restaurant's logo as a landmark for navigating city streets. It is important to note that Muscovites also use McDonald's as a landmark when giving directions. One acquaintance drew a map directing me to a local market and used McDonald's as the reference point (she then commented on the irony of using McDonald's as a landmark).

The phenomenon of geogastronomia flourished in summer 2002, when soccer's World Cup tournament focused people's imaginations even more closely on international border crossing. An American-style coffee shop in downtown Moscow invited its patrons to travel the world by drinking "Mexican coffee" and "Irish coffee," among other varieties. Pepsi-Cola capitalized on the World Soccer Cup by offering a contest in which lucky winners could win trips to a soccer country, an opportunity that was continued in May 2004, when the company used soccer players to promote a contest to win a trip to Portugal. Also in 2002, Coca-Cola aired a series of commercials in Russia for a contest in which winners received cellular telephones. Using the slogan, "A summer without borders," the commercials depicted people representing a range of ethnicities and attire from all over the world phoning each other freely. A similar strategy of mapping the world through food-related products was presented in a series of advertisements for tobacco in Moscow in 2002. The cigarette company advertised its products through a travel-oriented contest. In a series of posters hanging in Moscow metro cars, the company invited customers to participate in "A unique opportunity to go where tobacco for [the company] grows: Indonesia, Tanzania, Brazil, and Turkey!" The physical de-marcation of the world into tobacco-growing and non-tobacco-growing regions was further emphasized by the inclusion of a map that highlighted all of the company's tobacco-growing regions.

These examples of geogastronomia illustrate clearly the symbolic and actual power of cuisines and tastes to constitute meaningful geographies just as convinc-ingly as political borders, language groups, or historical events. In this respect, geogastronomia is not an act of consuming geography (cf. Turgeon and Pastinelli 2002:251), but rather an active process of place-making that is viscerally created and experienced. As such, the phenomenon of Russian culinary tourism is more than simply "experiencing" the world's geography vicariously, as a simulacrum" (Harvey 1989:299, 300, cited in Roseberry 1996:771; cf. Fjellman 1992). Rather, the synesthetic qualities of sight, smell, taste, and touch that are evoked by foods transform physical spaces into meaningful geographies that Russian travelers access and inhabit with and through their bodies.

The holistic sensory experience of food and drink has been employed by theme restaurants in Moscow that present totalizing foreign dining experiences. Visitors to one Georgian restaurant in Moscow walk into a building that has been designed to resemble a traditional Georgian house and courtyard. The interior is decorated with artwork, cooking implements, and other items that one might find in a Georgian home, and staff members are dressed in Georgian costumes. Similar design strategies have been used in Irish, Thai, Tibetan, Japanese, and other foreign restaurants in Moscow. The overlapping combination of tastes with smells, sounds, and visual cues in these restaurants offers both images and sensations of dining in another culinary culture. Other restaurants promise diners even more explicit forms of travel. In an advertisement that appeared in a Moscow-based English-language newspaper read by both foreigners and English-speaking Russians, the Gandhara restaurant described itself as a combination "restaurant and museum" that offered diners "an exquisite culinary and cultural journey" to "experience the ambience of 1st century B.C. while you feast on traditional Pakistani and nouveau continental cuisine."[8]

At the same time that food evokes a powerfully subjective experience of travel, it can also be the conduit for actual travel. Television commercials for one brand of Russian beer appealed to potential customers with the succinct phrase, "Do you want to go to the sea?" (*khochetsia k mor'iu?*). The phrase turned out to be part of the company's promotional campaign to give away trips to Sochi, a popular beach destination for Russian vacationers. In a similar move, another Russian brewing company marketed its brand of beer, "*Ruski*," with a series of television commercials that suggested that people in different countries drank their beer differently. The commercials depicted people drinking beer in a variety of national "styles" that each invoked stereotyped costumes, behaviors, and settings. For instance, characters who drank "in the Finnish style" were portrayed in recognizably Finnish costumes and sitting in a wooden house. Characters who drank "in the Japanese style" were dressed as sumo wrestlers and sat at a table on the floor. At the end of the commercials, the Russian hero is described as someone who prefers "beer in the Russian style" (*pivo po-russki*) and then is shown dancing with women dressed in traditional Russian folk costumes, in the midst of a Russian folk festival in the Russian countryside.

Collectively, this diverse set of examples—beer commercials, restaurants, and print advertisements—underscores food's capacity to compress temporal and spatial distances as well as its potential to transport consumers across space and time. As these examples also illustrate, these time-space relationships take shape in different ways in different contexts. At some times, time and space are stretched out; at others, collapsed. And Russian consumers are left to navigate these multiple, competing realities.

Time Travel and Homesickness in a Displaced World: The Emergence of Nostalgia Cuisine

One of the consequences of multiple and competing mobilities in today's Russia is the sense of temporal and spatial rootlessness experienced by consumers as they are overtaken by events and forces beyond their control. Svetlana Boym describes this alienation as a condition in which sufferers feel "inside and outside the crowd, alienated while engaged, but not too much" (Boym 1994:227), and she suggests that this sense of disorientation and displacement has prompted the emergence of a collective homesickness for familiar places and times, where life is imagined to be more stable, manageable, and familiar (Boym 2001).[9] One of the arenas in which cures for this homesickness have emerged most vividly is nostalgia cuisine. Food companies increasingly rely on comforting images of home and family to advertise their products, such as one Russian dairy company that promotes its products with stylized representations of grandmothers and summer cottages.

In her article on culinary nostalgia among Indian immigrants in Silicon Valley, Purnima Mankekar observes that it is the sensory cues of Indian grocery stores that endow these spaces with a sense of familiarity and comfort for its customers (Mankekar 2002). The particular combination of scents, sights, tastes, and sounds contained within these stores creates an imagined community for Indians who are otherwise separated from home and family.[10] Mankekar's findings resemble Daniel Linger's account of Brazilian expatriates working in Japan who seek out the Brazilian restaurant 51 "not just to eat, as they might in Brazil, but to eat Brazil" (Linger 2001:75).[11] What distinguishes Russian nostalgia cuisine from the cases described by Mankekar and Linger, however, is that the Russian nostalgia cuisine industry is not designed for émigrés who are permanently displaced geographically from their homelands. Instead, Russian nostalgia cuisine is domestically produced and designed for Russian travelers who are temporarily displaced from home, such as individuals who have traveled abroad for work or vacation and will return to the comforts and safeties of home within a short period of time.

This emphasis on home as a safe and comfortable space appears clearly in the August 1998 issue of the culinary magazine *Restaurant Bulletin*. In this issue the magazine expanded its culinary travel section to include a special feature for Russians who travel abroad. The specific geographic focus of the article is food in the United Arab Emirates, and the author undertakes to find restaurants, foods, and settings that are acceptable to the unique sensitivities of Russian stomachs (Nazarov 1998). The author then translates local foods into terms and descriptions that are familiar to Russian consumers. Ultimately, the author is concerned with the health of the Russian nation as it is manifested by the bodies of its citizens abroad. By seeking out foods that are familiar and comfortable to his Russian readers, the author reveals his concerns with protecting the body of the nation as it is represented by the physical bodies and food habits of its citizens. These aspects are presented vividly in his introduction to this article:

> Russians are found not just in Russia. Millions of "dear Russians" have dispersed around the world and, thank God, they no longer take with them electric tea kettles so that they can boil instant soup at night in their hotel bathrooms. Even more importantly, after having gone crazy from the unexpectedly cheap prices of foreign squashes in comparison with Russian squashes, our people begin to hammer away at them, one after another, with the expected consequences of upset stomachs. Hence *Restaurant Bulletin* should constantly fulfill [its] function as a restaurant compass not just toward Russian restaurants [i.e., restaurants in Russia] but also on a global scale. We are obligated to fight with every means for healthy national stomachs! (Nazarov 1998:43)

The issue of national preservation that appears in Nazarov's article resonates with the emphasis on nostalgia that characterizes Slow Food movements (Petrini 2001; see also Leitch 2003, Pilcher this volume). As Penny Van Esterik and Jeffrey Pilcher both describe in this volume, the rootedness of foods in particular places and historical moments makes them effective symbols of cultural heritage and tradition. Consequently, heritage foods become the commodities through which national and regional traditions are identified and preserved. Even as Carlo Petrini has argued that Slow Food activists are not "museum curators" (Petrini 2001:52), he nonetheless acknowledges that one of the goals of the Slow Food Movement is "preserving our agricultural and alimentary heritage" (Petrini 2001:8).[12]

Russian nostalgia cuisine differs from the variety promoted by the Slow Food Movement in several respects, however. Russian nostalgia cuisine focuses not on the preservation of foods, but on the preservation of consumers who feel increasingly alienated from the world around them. At the same time, although geographic origins are prominent in Russian nostalgia cuisine, temporal origins have emerged more conspicuously as Russian nostalgia cuisine takes the specific shape of time travel to events and periods in Russia's past. Finally, the concerns with recreating authenticity in terms of time and place that are so important in Slow Food trends are present only peripherally—if at all—in Russian nostalgia cuisine. Rather, Russian nostalgia cuisine resembles processes of "structural nostalgia" (Herzfeld 1991), in which time scales and events are collapsed into generic, imagined, and stylized accounts of "the good old days."

The temporal compressions found in Russian nostalgia cuisine are evident in the absence of a consensus on precisely which past is being invoked. In some cases, the past is presented as the pre-Soviet days of Imperial Russia, as with restaurants that claim to use ancient recipes and historically authentic Russian ingredients. Advertisements for the restaurant located in the State Historical Museum in Red Square enticed diners in 1999 with "a selection from the Coronation Menus of Russian Emperors." In other cases, Russian history is presented as an idyllic peasant past. The Russian restaurant chain Yelki-Palki invites diners to imagine that they have been transported back to the simplicity of an old peasant village. The interiors of Yelki-Palki restaurants in Moscow are decorated to resemble a traditional peasant house and farm courtyard. Servers are dressed in peasant attire, and Russian cookware adorns the walls. A spring 2004 company magazine announcing the opening of the first Yelki-Palki restaurant in Nizhnii Novgorod declared that the placement of the restaurant in the historical center of the city was designed to be a setting where "tourists from all corners of the country would gather to be imbued [proniknyt'sia] with the atmosphere of the old days, with which the walls were impregnated" (Yelki-Palki 2004:2). The announcement continued with a description of the historical significance of the interior architecture and decorations.[13]

More recent pasts can be accessed via socialist-inspired restaurants, like the Moscow restaurant Spetsbufet #7 (a shortening of the name Special Buffet #7). This deliberately Soviet-themed restaurant is strategically located in a building along the embankment of the Moscow River that was at the center of Stalin's purges.[14] The extensive menu of the Spetsbufet #7 consists of typical Russian fare: blini with sour cream and caviar, Russian soups, pelmeni, broiled chicken and potatoes, vodkas, and teas, among many others.[15] Some dishes have been given Soviet-themed names such as "bourgeoisie" or "komsomol." Although the

Russian-language menu simply lists the names of the dishes and their prices, the English-language menu includes definitions and descriptions of the dishes' historical significance. Descriptions include details such as which particular dish was prepared for the tsar. The interior space is decorated primarily with political posters and photographs from the Soviet period, including a large framed picture of Lenin, and other period memorabilia such as an antique record player and books that were in vogue during the Soviet era.[16]

Each of these examples illustrates deliberate, albeit ironic, manipulations of food to evoke imagined homelands located in imagined pasts. In a global world characterized by dizzying feelings and images of displacement, the powerful lure of culinary tourism is precisely that it grounds people while also giving them possibilities for mobility. Consumers can enjoy the performative aspects of movement and experiencing the Other without straying too far from home. Just as significant, however, are the ways in which nostalgia cuisine redirects the emotional attachments that Russian consumers have to specific places and times. At the same time that this culinary time travel presents the distant past in romantic hues, it also renders the horrors of the Soviet past into ironic forms of entertainment.

Conclusion: The New Exoticism of Foreign Travel

In this analysis I argue that the overlapping of food and travel that appears so comfortably and prominently in Moscow's commercial sphere offers Muscovites new forms and modes of tourism. As a mnemonic device that engages all the senses, culinary travel is a form of virtual reality that provides a totalizing experience of both foreign and domestic Others. Yet the past several years have been marked by two diverging trends. On the one hand, the enchanting nature of culinary tourism seems to be receding in importance for some Moscow consumers. By late spring 2004, advertisements and magazines promoting geographic and historical food travel were conspicuously absent. This shift has coincided with a notable increase in the frequency with which Muscovite acquaintances are discussing actual travel—both planned and completed—to such destinations as Egypt, Turkey, France, and England. Even one elderly friend, a retiree who barely scrapes by on her monthly pension, mentioned possibilities for visiting friends in the United States of America. Collectively, these changes suggest that for Muscovites who are coming closer to realizing their dreams of traveling abroad, the virtual experience offered by culinary tourism becomes less important.

On the other hand, foreign restaurants have become even more prominent in Moscow. Most notable are the Japanese restaurants—especially sushi bars—that have suddenly popped up on what seems like every corner of town. Although conclusive statements about the long-term significance of these trends are beyond the scope of this current analysis, it seems plausible that the popularity of Japanese food reflects the changing borders of Russians' navigable world. As the geographic locales associated with Irish, French, and Middle Eastern cuisines come within grasp of Muscovite travelers, they lose their appeal as different and exotic. As the borders of Russians' navigable worlds recede so that Asia is at the edge, Japan now represents the boundary between the familiar and the exotic. And Japanese restaurants, with their kimono-clad servers and pseudo–sumo wrestling entertainment, offer the easiest and safest way for diners to pretend that they are in Japan.

Ultimately, for analyses of global processes, culinary tourism is significant because it prompts critical reconsideration of polarizing categories such as self and other, national and foreign, homogenous and heterogeneous, and "Fast" and "Slow." As the case of Russian culinary tourism illustrates, these distinctions are not absolute but instead represent different aspects or stages of the same processes. More important, however, the mediating capacity of culinary tourism provides new ways of thinking about relationships between the local and the global. Rather than presenting the local and the global as two ends of the same spectrum, culinary tourism offers possibilities for seeing how these two processes simultaneously coexist within each other and also maintain their respective distinctiveness. Russian culinary tourists who inhabit both the global and the local, the "Fast" and the "Slow," resemble the cosmopolitans described by Ulf Hannerz (1990). Unlike a "local," Hannerz's cosmopolitan is someone whose orientation or perspective entails "a stance toward diversity itself, toward the coexistence of cultures in the individual experience" (1990:239), and for whom participation in—not just observation of—this foreign Other is significant (1990:241). The key to Hannerz's definition of the cosmopolitan, however, is this: "The cosmopolitan may embrace the alien culture, but he does not become committed to it. All the time he knows where the exit is" (1990:240). By knowing where this "exit" is located, cosmopolitans are able to inhabit multiple worlds simultaneously. It is this aspect of Hannerz's idea of the cosmopolitan that is most instructive for understanding how the bodily experience of travel opens possibilities for thinking through how Russian consumers can ground themselves in one culture while traveling to another—or to put it another way, how Russian consumers can simultaneously be both here and there, and both now and then.

Notes

Acknowledgments. This chapter is based on materials gathered in Moscow, Russia, between 1997 and 2004. Funding for this research was generously provided by the Davis Center for Russian and Eurasian Studies, Department of Anthropology, and Committee on Degrees in Social Studies at Harvard University, the Mellon Foundation, and a Foreign Language

Area Studies Fellowship. I am grateful to Richard Wilk for the opportunity to present my research at the 2004 Society for Economic Anthropology meeting and his thoughtful recommendations for improving this chapter, and to my colleagues at this meeting for their comments and suggestions. I would also like to thank Catherine Dolan and Stanislav Shectman for reading and commenting on earlier versions of this article.

1. This documentary was produced by McDonald's of Canada, which founded the joint venture in the former Soviet Union. Because of the politics of the Cold War, it was McDonald's of Canada, and not McDonald's USA, that opened in Russia. For more information on McDonald's in Russia, see Caldwell 2004.

2. These fieldwork periods include: summer 1995, November 1997–October 1998, May–July 1999, summer 2000, summer 2001, summer 2002, and May 2004.

3. Curiously, one of the contests was for a brand of ravioli; lucky winners could win a trip to Turkey. Although most advertisements make the connection between a particular type of food and a destination clear, there was nothing presented in this promotional that indicated why Turkey should be paired with ravioli.

4. For general overviews of anthropological research on tourism, see Adler 1989, Benthall 1988, and Werner 2003.

5. See also Clifford 1988. In her work on heritage tourism, Susan Terrio (1999) observes that it is the performed aspects of craft chocolates that appeal to tourists in France.

6. This advertisement appeared in *Restorannye Vedemosti*, August 1998:45.

7. This advertisement appeared in *Gurman*, June–July 1998:39.

8. This advertisement appeared in *The Moscow Times*, May 25, 2004, 2926:3.

9. Compare Boym's ideas about homesickness and nostalgia with Michael Herzfeld's ideas about structural nostalgia (1991).

10. For additional discussions of connections between nostalgia and food, see Leitch 2003 and Sutton 2001.

11. As Linger documents, by offering Brazilian food, beverages, clothing, reading materials, videos from Brazilian television, and other items, this restaurant sells the idea of being transported to Brazil, not just to its Brazilian customers but also to its Japanese regulars who dream of traveling to Brazil (2001:79–81).

12. For an excellent discussion of the Slow Food Movement's program of culinary nostalgia, see Leitch 2003.

13. This description appears in the May 2004, 3(124) issue of the advertising magazine for *Yelki-Palki*.

14. According to accounts by Moscow acquaintances, residents of the building listened at night for footsteps in the hallways and waited in fear for the knocks on their doors that signaled the KGB had come to take them away.

15. When I visited the Spetsbufet #7 in May 2004, I was amused to see that the Soviet-era decorations were accompanied by a large-screen flat television turned to the Eurosport channel. Also, despite mediocre reviews in a popular English-language guidebook that criticized the quality of the food and service and a review in a local Moscow newspaper

noting that the low-quality service was in keeping with the Soviet ambience, my waitress was very friendly and efficient and the food ranked among the best I have eaten in Russia.

16. These simultaneously ironic and affectionate commentaries on the socialist past seem to be growing in the postsocialist world. Elsewhere in downtown Moscow, sports enthusiasts can watch their favorite athletic events on Eurosport and other cable television channels at a sports bar named *Das Kapital*. Among the nostalgia restaurants identified by Stanislav Shectman (personal communication) is a St. Petersburg restaurant that venerates Stalin in one dining room and then mocks him in another. For the case of urban China, James Watson has documented "Mao Restaurants" as sites where "veteran Red Guards of the Cultural Revolution era (1966–76) meet to reminisce over corn fritters, ant soup, and roast locust—key dietary items from their revolutionary experiences in the Chinese countryside." Watson and Caldwell also note that these gentlemen are frequently interrupted from their stories "by cellphone calls from their secretaries or business partners" (Watson and Caldwell 2005:8, n. 6).

References

Adler, Judith. 1989. Travel as Performed Art. The American Journal of Sociology 94(6):1366–91.

Anonymous. 1998. *Moskva na ostrie shampura* (Moscow on a sharp skewer). Restorannye Vedemosti February 1:4–10.

Barber, Benjamin R. 1995. Jihad vs. McWorld: How Globalism and Tribalism Are Reshaping the World. New York: Ballantine Books.

Barker, Adele Marie. 1999. The Culture Factory: Theorizing the Popular in the Old and New Russia. *In* Consuming Russia: Popular Culture, Sex, and Society since Gorbachev. Adele Marie Barker, ed. Pp. 12–45. Durham, NC: Duke University Press.

Benthall, Jonathan. 1988. The Anthropology of Tourism. Anthropology Today 4(3):20–22.

Bestor, Theodore C. 2000. How Sushi Went Global. Foreign Policy 54–63.

Borisova, Natalya. 1998. *Indoneziya: Kak zhivut i chto edyat v strane vechnogo leta* (Indonesia: How they live and what they eat in the land of eternal summer). Kulinar 9:4–19.

Boym, Svetlana. 1994. Common Places: Mythologies of Everyday Life in Russia. Cambridge, MA: Harvard University Press.

———. 2001. The Future of Nostalgia. New York: Basic Books.

Caldwell, Melissa L. 2004. Domesticating the French Fry: McDonald's and Consumerism in Moscow. Journal of Consumer Culture 4(1):5–26.

Clifford, James. 1988. The Predicament of Culture: Twentieth-Century Ethnography, Literature, and Art. Cambridge, MA: Harvard University Press.

———. 1997. Spatial Practices: Fieldwork, Travel, and the Disciplining of Anthropology. *In* Anthropological Locations: Boundaries and Grounds of a Field Science. Akhil Gupta and James Ferguson, eds. Pp. 185–222. Berkeley: University of California Press.

De Certeau, Michel. 1984. The Practice of Everyday Life. Steven Rendall, trans. Berkeley: University of California Press.

De Silva, Cara, ed. 1996. In Memory's Kitchen: A Legacy from the Women of Terezín. Bianca Steiner Brown, trans. Northvale, NJ: Jason Aronson Inc.

Fjellman, Stephen M. 1992. Vinyl Leaves: Walt Disney World and America. Boulder, CO: Westview Press.

Freidberg, Susanne. 2001. French Beans for the Masses: A Modern Historical Geography of Food in Burkina Faso. Journal of Historical Geography 29(3):445–63.

Giddens, Anthony. 1990. The Consequences of Modernity. Palo Alto: Stanford University Press.

Glants, Musya, and Joyce Toomre. 1997. Introduction. In Food in Russian History and Culture. Musya Glants and Joyce Toomre, eds. Pp. xi–xxvii. Bloomington: Indiana University Press.

Goldfrank, Walter L. 1994. Fresh Demand: The Consumption of Chilean Produce in the United States. In Commodity Chains and Global Capitalism. Gary Gereffi and Miguel Korzeniewicz, eds. Pp. 267–79. Westport, CT: Praeger.

Gurman magazine. 1997–1998. Kalendar': Puteshestvennika-Gurmana (Calendar of a Traveler-Gourmet). December 1997–January 1998:68–69.

———. 1998. June-July.

Hannerz, Ulf. 1990. Cosmopolitans and Locals in World Culture. Theory, Culture & Society 7:237–51.

Harvey, David. 1989. The Condition of Postmodernity. Oxford: Blackwell Publishers.

Herzfeld, Michael. 1991. A Place in History: Social and Monumental Time in a Cretan Town. Princeton: Princeton University Press.

Hume, Scott. 1990. How Big Mac Made It to Moscow. Advertising Age 61(4):16, 51.

Inda, Jonathan Xavier, and Renato Rosaldo. 2002. Introduction: A World in Motion. In The Anthropology of Globalization: A Reader. Jonathan Xavier Inda and Renato Rosaldo, eds. Pp. 1–34. Malden, MA: Blackwell Publishers.

Jing, Jun, ed. 2000. Feeding China's Little Emperors: Food, Children, and Social Change. Palo Alto: Stanford University Press.

Kuznetsov, Sergei. 1997–1998. Shalandy, polnye Kefali (Barges full of mullet). Gurman December 1997–January 1998:62–67.

Leitch, Alison. 2003. Slow Food and the Politics of Pork Fat: Italian Food and European Identity. Ethnos 68(4):437–62.

Linger, Daniel Touro. 2001. No One Home: Brazilian Selves Remade in Japan. Palo Alto: Stanford University Press.

Litvencheva, Aleksandra. 1998. Kulinarnye progulki po Niderlandam (Culinary Strolls around the Netherlands). Restorannye Vedemosti February 1:58–61.

Mankekar, Purnima. 2002. "India Shopping": Indian Grocery Stores and Transnational Configurations of Belonging. Ethnos 67(1):75–98.

Milovskii, Aleks. 1998. Zhir kitovii: Lyubimoe lakomstvo Eskimosov (Whale Blubber: The Favorite Delicacy of Eskimos). Gurman February–March: 50–54.

Mintz, Sidney. 1985. Sweetness and Power: The Place of Sugar in Modern History. New York: Penguin Books.

The Moscow Times. 2004. Advertisement. May 25 (2926):3.

Nazarov, Oleg. 1998. *Za stolom s sheikhami* (At the table with Sheikhs). Restorannye Vedemosti (13):42–45.

Ogorodnikov, T. 1998. *Po miry—po griby* (Around the world by mushrooms). Restorannye Vedemosti August, 7(13):4–11.

Parkins, Wendy. 2004. Out of Time: Fast Subjects and Slow Living. Time & Society 13(2/3):363–82.

Patico, Jennifer, and Melissa L. Caldwell. 2002. Consumers Exiting Socialism: Ethnographic Perspectives on Daily Life in Post-Communist Europe. Ethnos 67(3):285–94.

Petrini, Carlo. 2001. Slow Food: The Case for Taste. William McCuaig, trans. New York: Columbia University Press.

Priyatnogo Appetita! 1998. February.

Restorannye Vedemosti. 1998. 7(13), August.

Ritzer, George. 2004. The Globalization of Nothing. Thousand Oaks, CA: Pine Forge Press.

Roseberry, William. 1996. The Rise of Yuppie Coffees and the Recognition of Class in the United States. American Anthropologist 98(4):762–75.

Seremetakis, C. Nadia. 1993. The Memory of the Senses: Historical Perception, Commensal Exchange and Modernity. Visual Anthropology Review 9(2):2–18.

Sutton, David E. 2001. Remembrance of Repasts: An Anthropology of Food and Memory. Oxford: Berg Publishers.

Terrio, Susan J. 1999. Performing Craft for Heritage Tourists in Southwest France. City & Society XI(1–2):125–44.

Turgeon, Laurier, and Madeleine Pastinelli. 2002. "Eat the World": Postcolonial Encounters in Quebec City's Ethnic Restaurants. Journal of American Folklore 115(456):247–68.

Watson, James L. 1997. Introduction: Transnationalism, Localization, and Fast Foods in East Asia. *In* Golden Arches East: McDonald's in East Asia. James L. Watson, ed. Pp. 1–38. Palo Alto: Stanford University Press.

Watson, James L., ed. 1997. Golden Arches East: McDonald's in East Asia. Palo Alto: Stanford University Press.

Watson, James L., and Melissa L. Caldwell. 2005. Introduction. *In* The Cultural Politics of Food and Eating. James L. Watson and Melissa L. Caldwell, eds. Pp. 1–10. Malden, MA: Blackwell Publishers.

Werner, Cynthia. 2003. The New Silk Road: Mediators and Tourism Development in Central Asia. Ethnology 42(2):141–59.

Wilk, Richard. 2002. Food and Nationalism: The Origins of "Belizean Food." *In* Food Nations: Selling Taste in Consumer Societies. Warren Belasco and Philip Scranton, eds. Pp. 67–80. New York: Routledge.

Yelki-Palki. 2004. Advertising Magazine 3(124).

THE CONTRADICTIONS OF INDUSTRIAL FOOD   III

Kaiten-zushi and Konbini: Japanese Food Culture in the Age of Mechanical Reproduction

8

THEODORE C. BESTOR

T HIS CHAPTER EXAMINES two different kinds of commercial establishments engaged in the mass distribution of foodstuffs in Japan, both of which have become *sine qua non* of the contemporary urban commercial landscape. The first of my two types of examples are known as *kaiten-zushi*, sometimes translated as "conveyer belt sushi" or "rotary sushi," restaurants. The second are chain stores known as *konbini*, "convenience stores" (from a Japanese contraction of the English term *convenience*), which are discussed in much greater detail in Gavin Whitelaw's chapter that follows. At first glance, these two examples perhaps appear to have little in common with one another. One is a kind of restaurant; the other is a kind of retailer. One sells fresh or at least perishable prepared dishes, usually consumed on the spot; the other is a purveyor of packaged, processed foodstuffs, usually to be taken away even if not taken home.

But *kaiten-zushi* and *konbini* are closely linked phenomena in the production, distribution, and consumption of food in contemporary Japan. The connections, parallels, and contrasts that can be drawn between these two genre of businesses provide broader perspectives on food distribution and consumption as an activity deeply embedded in complex domestic as well as global dynamics of Japanese cuisine, consumption, diet, domesticity, labor, leisure, social structure, and the commercial applications of information technology and standardization.

Both types of retailing have become particularly prominent during and after the economic boom (the so-called "Bubble economy") of the 1980s, a period of high inflation, conspicuous consumption, and speculative investment that has been followed (since about 1990) by a prolonged domestic recession during which the Japanese retail environment has adjusted dramatically with increased consolidation of large retail chains (and bankruptcies of small enterprises), steady increases in technological sophistication in production and distribution, greater dependence on foreign imports, and waning consumer spending.

My interest in the relatively new popularity of these retail outlets for indus-trialized fast food started from the perspective of distribution, based on research at Tokyo's massive Tsukiji wholesale fish market and the supply channels lead-ing to, through, and from it. Tsukiji is the world's largest marketplace for fresh seafood, a hub in both global and national distribution systems, where changing trends of food supply and Japanese consumption directly affect the business of food and the construction of food culture (T. Bestor 1999, 2000, 2001, 2004, in preparation; V. Bestor 1998). The growth of *kaiten-zushi* and *konbini* is not just an incremental perturbation in an already complex system of distribution for seafood and related products; rather, these two commercial forms reflect and have helped effect a complex rewiring of the circuitry of food distribution, both domestically and globally.

Fast Food

In Japan, as is true in many other parts of the world, "fast food" is not a necessarily modern notion. Although sushi has acquired the patina of "high culture"—as something that is simultaneously hip and demanding of connoisseurship both in Japan and in the West—it originated as street food, as pre-industrial fast food, as did many other kinds of Japanese cuisine, such as the *onigiri* (rice balls) that Gavin Whitelaw discusses in chapter 9. These and many other dishes, including *bentō* (box lunches), *yakitori* (grilled chicken skewers), *oden* (vegetable stew), and noodle dishes (*udon* and *ramen*), have been sold by street vendors for generations, in some cases centuries, and are now also the stock-in-trade for the explicitly "Japanese" segments of the Japanese fast food industry (see also Noguchi 1994).

But the identification of dishes as part of a distinctive "traditional" Japanese cuisine also does not necessarily imply historical stasis. Like all other aspects of "tradition," food culture constantly evolves. Many dishes and delicacies now widely regarded as hallmarks of Japanese cuisine are actually of relatively recent introduction or invention. For example, even the basic form of *nigiri-zushi*, a thin slice of fish atop a compact oblong block of vinegared rice—the style characteristic of Tokyo's cuisine and now the world's de facto sushi standard—was an innovation of the mid-nineteenth century, and many of its contemporary features, including exquisitely fresh fish (rather than various kinds of pickled or salted seafood), only became possible in the twentieth century with the advent of mechanical refrigeration and ice manufacturing.

The particular style of Edo-Tokyo sushi, called *nigiri-zushi* ("squeezed" or "hand-molded" sushi) or *Edomae-zushi* (sushi from "in front of Edo"), became the rage of Edo in the 1820s or 1830s (Nishiyama et al. 1984:259–62). One common story of *nigiri-zushi's* origins puts it in the hands of a famed chef, Hanaya

Yohei (1799–1858), who invented or perfected the technique in 1824 at his shop in Ryōgoku (then one of Edo's major entertainment districts), a shop that survived until the 1930s. A nineteenth-century verse celebrated his popular innovation:

> Crowded together, weary with waiting
> Customers wring their hands
> As Yohei squeezes sushi[1]

Sushi is just one example, but the point is that the dishes served up by *kaiten-zushi* and *konbini* have *not* brought Japanese consumers a new concept of "fast food."[2] What they have brought is fast food even faster and in enormous but precisely controlled volumes!

Industrial Food

In this volume Sidney Mintz writes about the creation of a new global food system (see also Mintz 1997), and Japanese contemporary fast food is certainly deeply embedded in this global system. Part of this system is what Jack Goody refers to as "the industrialization of cuisine" (Goody 1982), a macroscopic and multifaceted set of transformations in which the entire character of a society's sustenance—selections of food resources; methods of production and processing; techniques of distribution, sales, and advertising; daily rhythms of eating; the nutritional content of the daily diet; the re-engineering of familiar foods for mass distribution; and the creation of entirely new foodstuffs as well—is adapted to and shaped by industrial, capital-intensive production.

Typically, industrialization of food changes the repertory of goods available to consumers, increasingly substituting highly standardized, processed, and manufactured foodstuffs for widely varied, locally produced, raw and semi-processed ones. The industrialization of food affects consumers, of course, but the transformations are fundamentally propelled by changes in the economic, political, and social institutions that produce, process, and distribute foodstuffs.

Clearly, twentieth- and twenty-first-century technologies of the food industry—including aquaculture, food additives, freeze-drying, high-speed transportation (on a global scale), and mechanical devices to replace hand-processing—have expanded dramatically the ability to invent and produce "new food." At the same time, new techniques of food processing develop together with new channels of distribution, new kinds of retailers, and new forms of marketing. Proprietary brand names become attached both to newly developed products and to products that previously had been simply generic items from the culinary public domain, and consumers, especially in Japan, come to expect "branded" merchandise, even in culinary domains.

If one looks at the industrialization of cuisine from the perspective of the growth of a "food culture industry," then it is essential to look across an entire food system as an integrated social and cultural phenomenon, including production, content, and reception. Within the scope of this chapter, I cannot touch on all elements of the Japanese food culture industry, ranging across both symbolic and material substance, including: the material realities of harvesting, shipping, and processing, and the social contexts of production, distribution, and consumption; the semi-stable social worlds of producers and the shifting social relations of consumption; the role of the mass media; the symbolism of cuisine and identity; changes in diet and domestic living arrangements; gendered divisions of labor; formal and informal labor markets; issues of food security and insecurity; and the impact of global trade on Japan's retail and service sectors.

What I focus on are the elements of mass production—even assembly line production—that are at the core of the *kaiten-zushi* and *konbini* phenomena, which I conceive of as examples of "Fordist food culture."

The elements of Fordism are well-known characteristics of industrial societies, and include: the simultaneous development of both mass production and mass consumption; the substitution of industrial for craft production; the development of process engineering and standardization of both production and products; patterns of vertical integration among economic sectors, in order to control information flows and to manage financial risks; and the invention of the de-skilled assembly line.

Second-stage Fordism—the Japanese version perfected during the high-growth years from the 1960s through the 1980s—made some critical refinements to these basic principles. These include: the creation of flexible systems of industrial pro-duction, including "just-in-time production" and "just-in-time distribution" partly based on extensive networks of very-well-coordinated subcontractors (dependent not on direct vertical integration but on "relational contracting" among well-established partnerships); philosophies of "total quality management" based on careful collection and statistical analysis of production and distribution informa-tion; extremely rapid product cycles; and the micro-segmentation of market niches and product differentiation.[3]

This second-stage Fordism, the "Model-J" rather than the "Model-T," enabled the industrial transformation not only of production, but also of the retail and service sectors. Nowhere has that transformation been pushed as relentlessly as in Japan, especially in the 1990s. Time and space have not been annihilated, but have been process-engineered and micro-managed to create ever-finer increments of advantage in distribution, retailing, and the provision of services. *Kaiten-zushi* and *konbini* are exemplars of that acceleration.

Kaiten-zushi

Kaiten-zushi ("conveyor-belt sushi" or "rotary sushi") gained wide popularity among consumers during the late 1990s as an inexpensive but increasingly trendy (and increasingly sophisticated) form of consumption. Restaurants that specialize in *kaiten-zushi* are now ubiquitously part of the urban landscape; some are stand-alone restaurants, others are parts of chains (currently about a dozen national chains exist);[4] their décor ranges from nonexistent to high tech; their common characteristic is an emphasis on low-priced sushi.

Kaiten-zushi arrives on a conveyor belt; kitchen workers make small batches of different kinds of sushi and place them on a moving track, and customers take one plate of this or that. Each serving is priced according to the color or shape of the plate itself, and at the end of a meal, an employee simply sorts and then counts the different kinds of plates the customer has stacked up to calculate the total. *Kaiten-zushi* shops make a point of their low prices: 100, 150, or 200 yen per serving for basic offerings (roughly $1.00, $1.50, or $2.00 respectively) with higher prices for servings that go around on fancier plates (see figure 8.1).

Figure 8.1.   A kaiten-zushi *shop's display, with colored plates indicating prices in Tokyo, 2003. Photograph by T. C. Bestor © 2003.*

Kaiten-zushi was invented in the 1950s and gained a reputation (deservedly so, in many cases) as quick, cheap, and often tasteless. At wholesale markets like Tsukiji, proprietors of *kaiten-zushi* shops were regarded as bargain hunters, bottom feeders, who bought the cheapest products at the end of the day, items that were overstocked or at the margins of salability. As restaurants, they appealed to a primarily male and often solitary clientele. Such restaurants were places to catch a bite before catching a train; ambience did not come around the belt.

During the 1970s and 1980s, however, a number of factors began to change the character (if not immediately the image) of *kaiten-zushi* shops. One key development, which affected Japanese seafood markets generally, was the decline of the Japanese fishing industry, both in terms of local off-shore production (because of environmental degradation) and the withdrawal of major Japanese fisheries companies from distant water fisheries (because of the shifting geo-politics of fisheries, the expansion of two-hundred-mile fishing zones by many coastal nations, and international criticism of the environmental effects of Japanese fishing fleets). As a result, an increasing proportion of seafood consumed in Japan was imported, often in frozen form and, as food processing technology advanced, often in pre-sliced, portion-controlled packaging. The major Japanese fisheries companies began to shift their focus from direct production to coordination of joint ventures and seafood processing in foreign locations (where labor costs were cheaper than in Japan). Equipment that can skin, de-bone, and custom slice several hundred fish per hour revolutionized the processing of seafood, and super flash freezing (for tuna, to minus 60 degrees Celsius) transformed distribution; in both instances, there was extensive crossfertilization between European and Japanese manufacturers of processing technologies.

In many ways, therefore, seafood from around the globe became widely available, bypassing established wholesale markets, and sushi shops and other retailers are now able to obtain seafood products in portions and styles that exactly match their needs. At least one major (former) fisheries company has a division that is exclusively focused on the processing and distribution of sushi toppings (*sushidane*). *Kaiten-zushi* restaurants are no longer bargain hunters at Tsukiji; they are more likely now to get their fish from channels that run outside the market than from those within it, and this reflects the growing power of large trading companies active in the food import-export business.

Other technological innovations, on the domestic front, included the development of what are known as "sushi robots," an array of mechanical devices that can automatically cook rice, squeeze it into blocks, and plop precut pieces of fish on top, all in the back room where the conveyor belt slips out of sight. Still others depend on pre-made sushi, often frozen, sometimes prepared overseas and shipped to

Japan. Aesthetics aside, these enabled high-speed production of highly standardized sushi that could rely on relatively unskilled (and cheaper) labor.

Another unanticipated boost for *kaiten-zushi* came from abroad. In the 1970s *kaiten-zushi* shops began to appear in a few North American cities like San Francisco, Los Angeles, and New York (and later, in the 1980s, in European and Southeast Asian cities (Cwiertka 1999, in preparation; Ng 2001). Non-Japanese clientele were attracted to these restaurants, according to people in the industry, in part by the growing popularity of things Japanese and by the fact that one could see exactly what one was getting without having much if any prior knowledge about sushi; the novelty of Japanese gadgetry—an important aspect of the Western imagery of postwar Japan—was an additional draw. And, as such restaurants acquired a following in foreign cities frequented by Japanese tourists, the idea of *kaiten-zushi* as an aspect of cosmopolitan popular culture was imported back to Japan (Tamamura 2000), a reflection of "Japan's Gross National Cool," a concept now widely embraced *within* Japan (McGray 2002).

In the Japanese recession of the 1990s, *kaiten-zushi* became widely popular at home and its image (and quality) dramatically improved (Akamoto 2002; Anonymous. 2001; Watanabe 2002; Yagyū 2003). Its newfound popularity (and the idea—oxymoronic to some—of gourmet *kaiten-zushi*) reflects the impact of the recession on consumer spending habits and the wider availability of inexpensive imported seafood (mentioned previously). In addition, the technology of the fast-food industry more generally has been applied to sushi: careful portion control, scanners that can read barcodes or microchips embedded in each plate, and low-paid staff who simply assemble sushi rather than master it.

A major aspect of its appeal is in the demystification of production and consumption. "Traditional" sushi shops—at least during the past generation or two—implicitly valorized the expertise of the *itamae-san*, the sushi chef, as a skilled and discerning *shokunin* (artisan), whose discernment and connoisseurship rendered the customer a passive agent. Many upscale sushi shops were largely male domains where businessmen on expense accounts entertained themselves and developed personal ties with particular chefs. Knowing and trusting a good chef was a sign of a certain kind of consumer connoisseurship, in which price was no object. Young couples, let alone young women on their own, were rarely part of the scene, and for a casual customer, someone who was not an expense-account regular, waiting for the bill—in a system where prices were rarely posted—could be a tense experience.

Kaiten-zushi demystifies the expertise, the discrimination, of the chef, and makes prices transparent. The popularity of *kaiten-zushi* therefore reflects a desire on the part of consumers to know what the meal will cost. The sushi on the conveyor belt provides direct information about what is available (just as, for generations, many

Japanese restaurants have displayed extremely accurate plastic models [*mihon*] of their menus in shop windows so that customers can see exactly what their order will look like). Contemporary *kaiten-zushi* shops also have opened consumption up to a much wider spectrum of ages (and genders) and have enabled a feeling of relaxation (or anonymity) that results from uncoupling a meal from one's interactions or relationships with the chef. The chef is no longer an auteur nor an artisan, but simply a service worker in a convivial setting, and a person with whom you do not really need to interact, unless you want to. The automat has been reborn.

Konbini

Konbini are franchised chains of "convenience stores" such as 7-Eleven, Lawson, Family Mart, Sunkus, and AM-PM, whose stock-in-trade are ready-to-eat meals, box lunches, and highly processed snack foods. In many Japanese urban areas, *konbini* have all but replaced traditional small-scale food sellers, especially since the late 1980s.

The first Japanese chain of convenience stores began operation in 1969. Many of the currently dominant chains had their start as joint ventures between American franchise chains and large Japanese trading companies and retail stores; initially, the Japanese side's interest was in acquiring the management expertise for developing highly standardized franchising chains and in training franchisees and workers in highly standardized work routines.[5] Between 1975 and 1995, the number of *konbini* outlets in Japan rose 1600 percent, from about 2,500 to approximately 40,000, a number that has now increased by several fold. As of 1996, one survey estimated that there was one convenience store for every 3,100 residents of Japan; in some urban areas, the density of *konbini* was one per 1,500 residents (Yamashita 1998). In 2005, I personally stood on a street corner in central Tokyo where I could swivel my neck and see six *konbini* (three of them outlets from a single chain).

Konbini are medium-sized, brightly lighted, streamlined shops, usually open twenty-four hours a day and generally located in high-traffic sites. The stores sell ready-to-eat and simple packaged foods, beverages, magazines, toiletries, and basic household goods. Initially, *konbini* were popular primarily with young adults and commuters, but their appeal has spread and their repertoire has expanded enormously. They have become general stores, touted as "lifestyle centers," for young, mobile, free-spending Japanese consumers. They are popular (for many consumers, but not all) because of their hours, the careful branding both of chains and the goods they carry, and the almost total anonymity of the shopping experience; one does not chat or gossip with a *konbini* employee as they scan your purchases.

Current *konbini* services include: selling computer software; providing copying and fax services; offering downloads of music CDs; selling postage stamps and telephone cards; selling tokens for toll expressways; and acting as rail and airline reservation agents. *Konbini* serve as a customer's point for picking up and paying for products ordered over the internet directly from other companies. The advantages for consumers are that they do not have to use a credit card over the internet and that they can arrange for delivery at a time and place convenient for their daily commute (for example, ordering online from their office for a product to be picked up at a branch near their apartment that evening). *Konbini* are also closely linked to the ubiquitous "home delivery services" (*takkyūbin*) that can send a purchase (or deliver something to a *konbini* pick-up point) almost any place in Japan within twenty-four hours.

Food remains the mainstay of *konbini*, however. *Konbini* benefit from long-established patterns in Japanese shopping behavior—frequent shopping trips for small quantities—which reflect a combination of consumer preference for daily shopping with practical limitations on domestic storage space in densely populated Japanese cities. Small-scale, family-owned shops have been a major feature of the urban retail, wholesale, and service sectors for generations, and, traditionally, urban neighborhoods were dotted with small-scale shops strung along shopping streets or arcades (known as *shōtengai*) that enabled residents to shop quickly, often, and close to home. *Konbini* are heir to this shopping and retailing pattern, but without any of the social relationships that typically existed between shop owner and customer.

During the enduring Japanese economic slump since the late 1980s, *konbini* chains have increased their market share vis-à-vis other categories of large-scale retailers such as supermarket chains and department stores. In 2000, the *konbini* retail sector had an estimated sales volume of six trillion yen, roughly 70 percent of the total sales of department stores and 40 percent of supermarket sales (according to unpublished figures from the Ministry of External Trade and Industry). For many young and single consumers (and some who are neither), a convenience store *is* the local food store.[6]

Large trading firms actively developed *konbini* as a strategy to work around restrictions on the size and scale of retail stores (under Japan's Large Retail Store Law) which effectively prevented the expansion of supermarkets and department stores into many commercial districts and most residential neighborhoods: the compact size of *konbini* sets them outside the scope of restrictive law. Building on franchising know-how initially acquired from American retailers, major Japanese trading and retailing corporations engineered ultrasophisticated distribution and inventory systems appropriate to dense networks of small-scale outlets and adapted to the geographic, social, and consumer contexts of contemporary Japan. Food processors have devoted enormous attention to creating products specifically suited to *konbini* product cycles.[7] And, as with *kaiten-zushi* shops, supply channels flow through large trading companies and their domestic and overseas subcontractors; seafood, for example, is obtained by direct imports, processed in central commissaries, and delivered as box lunches, sushi rolls, or stuffed rice balls direct to shops, in several deliveries a day. *Konbini* and supermarkets, along with chain restaurants of all genres, have effectively excluded wholesale markets from their supply chains.

7-Eleven, in particular, is noted for pioneering a retail "just-in-time" distribution and inventory system, which relies on deliveries daily or more often. Their system incorporates sophisticated real-time point-of-sale data collection for inventory control and ordering, as well as consumer analysis and market forecasting. The aggressive use of information technology by *konbini* has also enabled the big chains to become major providers of a wide (and increasingly wider) range of electronic services for customers, and they have moved aggressively into e-commerce (examples of which are mentioned previously), through links made with major Japanese manufacturers and merchandisers.

The extensive technological know-how and infrastructure provided by large *konbini* chains has been a critical factor in their successful marketing of franchises to local business people, many of whom have converted old-line specialized retail shops—corner grocers, rice shops, or liquor stores—into *konbini*. Many family-owned businesses occupy valuable commercial locations, but in the past generation this small-scale sector of the economy has faced enormous labor difficulties, between the aging of the population engaged in family enterprises and the reluctance of children to follow in parental footsteps and take over the businesses. *Konbini* therefore offer many small-scale family businesses a good opportunity to capitalize on real estate assets and to retain ownership of a local business, much of the management of which is embedded in the technical know-how and efficiently engineered distribution systems of the large franchise chains. These systems may rely on hands-on management by local proprietors, but that management is framed by chain policies, and the stores themselves can be operated largely with relatively low-cost, low-skilled retail labor. Many stores rely to a great extent on part-time labor (for example, college students and housewives, as well as on the new working class of "freeters" or "free-timers," semipermanent part-time workers).

Fordist Fast Food and Its Discontents

My description and discussion of *kaiten-zushi* shops and *konbini* stores has necessarily been brief and schematic. But some of the commonalities of these two relatively new forms of retailing seem quite clear. In the first instance, they both represent substantial breaks from or transformation of the traditional small-scale sectors of the urban Japanese retail and service economy. Many of their common features reflect aspects of what I call Model-J Fordism, but perhaps an even later model that includes an enormously expanded reliance on global flows of capital, managerial know-how, technological innovation (both in production and information management), and supply networks of foodstuffs, both raw and processed. Both *konbini* and *kaiten-zushi* shops have resulted directly (in the case of *konbini*) and indirectly from huge investments by large corporations, especially Japanese general trading companies, both in Japan and overseas, and from structural realignments within the Japanese fishing and food industries. Both have benefited from sophisticated process-engineering, which in turn relies on intensive use of information technology, including extremely sophisticated POS (point of sales) data collection for inventory control, scheduling of micro-customized deliveries, control of labor costs, and micro-analysis of consumer behavior (known as "data mining"). And both kinds of establishments make use of new managerial models of franchising, which rely on de-skilled labor performing repetitive tasks according to pre-established scripts.

And both kinds of shops are wildly popular. They obviously cater to consumer demand with extreme efficiency, not only in the range of products they provide but also in the social contexts of consumption they establish (or overthrow).

The success of Model-J Fordism as it has been applied to the Japanese retail and service sectors, however, has also spawned controversy, feeding into various of the "moral panics" that regularly sweep through Japan's mass media and the statements of conservative politicians.

Critics of *konbini* and *kaiten-zushi* see them as garishly intrusive shops that purvey a highly impersonal popular culture of consumption that especially targets alienated teenagers and young adults, and indeed encourages that social alienation. The homogenization of foodways and the disappearance of local foodstuffs and specialty dishes is a cause for concern among some, as is the realization that younger Japanese neither know very much about eating Japanese cuisine nor how to prepare it themselves. Equally, these fast-food outlets, of whatever stripe, are seen to destroy local retail competitors and push aside local production and distribution networks in favor of highly centralized major corporations. This economic trend has the side effect of hollowing out the social infrastructure of regional and community life.

Of course, another one of the raps against chain stores is the quality of the food they provide. There is a standard indictment of a nutritional wasteland: preservatives, additives, high sodium, high sugar, high starch, high calories. And in my own informal surveys of the shelves of *konbini*, I have noted that they rarely stock many foodstuffs that would qualify as "ingredients": things out of which one could construct another dish. There is milk, cheese, butter, eggs, *tofu*, *miso* paste, maybe a potato, an onion, a carrot, an orange or a banana (each individually wrapped in plastic), salt, pepper, and sugar, but rarely any other vegetables, fruits, let alone fresh fish, meat, or poultry. *Konbini* food is off the rack. (No doubt some future marketing campaign will tout this as "prêt-a-porter" cuisine.)

Konbini shoppers are themselves pathologized. The pejorative term *konbini house-wife* floats around as a scornful comment directed toward young (and some not-so-young) homemakers who rely almost entirely on the pre-packaged and ready-to-eat foodstuffs in which *konbini* specialize; these homemakers hence are assumed to be unable or unwilling to perform the normative role of "good wife and wise mother." A Japanese physiologist recently announced the results of his research on adolescents who hang out at *konbini*, and made a claim that the excessive lighting in such stores (about 2,000 lux compared to 900 lux in typical residential space) creates mood disorders. Concerns about crime and public safety often attach themselves to *konbini*.[8] Another nutritionist has calculated the amount of chewing required to eat meals from *konbini* compared with "traditional" meals and claims that today's "soft" cuisine is reshaping the musculature of the jaw and hence the facial shapes of young Japanese (Yamashita 1998). And the anonymity of *kaiten-zushi* and other fast-food restaurants are thought by some to reflect or encourage a form of extreme withdrawal from everyday social contacts that is currently seen as a major problem among young people.

Linguistically, *konbini* and the new service sector have brought criticism as well. Many older Japanese react negatively to the "service voices" that chain store workers affect. Part of it is corporate scrip; some *konbini* chains instruct their employees to greet each customer with the jarring expression: "*Konnichi wa, Irrashaimase!*" Simply translated, this and equivalent phrases simply say, "Good day! Welcome!" This may be grating because the traditional mercantile greeting is simply "*Irrashaimase!*" (Welcome!) spoken in a variety of registers, none of them requiring a customer's response. "*Konnichi wa,*" however, is a cue to interaction; sociolinguistically it requires a response. "*Howya doin?*" "*Fine thanks.*" It is a linguistic stealth tactic to get customers to interact with employees, and, according to people in the business, the commercial logic is twofold. First, even minimal interaction is more likely to lead to purchases, but second and more important, interaction dampens the likelihood of shoplifting; pilferage is a major problem in the anonymous world of *konbini*.

Another linguistic annoyance is the affectless, robotic voices that young workers use, seemingly modeled on the speech patterns of video games. For older Japanese, this monotonal, nasal voice is a marker of the "free-timer" phenomenon, the Japanese equivalent of "Generation X," the young part-time workers who are criticized by their elders for a lack of ambition and work ethic, but who—in their defense—are cast into an economy where the only growth sector is in dead-end, de-skilled service jobs.

Conclusion

Taken together, these and other critiques point toward the loss of what Sidney Mintz describes elsewhere in this volume as "the thick texture of daily interaction" that underlies the sociability inherent in local and regional food systems. The circumstances of *kaiten-zushi* and *konbini* reflect the ascendance of what Mintz calls "the freedom from intimacy." Although Japanese pundits, politicians, and business people congratulate themselves on Japan's success in revolutionizing mass consumption, seeing this as an exportable commodity, as part of Japan's new "Gross National Cool" (McGray 2002), this freedom from intimacy engendered by the automation and process-engineering of mass consumption may raise other significant issues.

The dependence of these highly engineered food systems that rely on the mass and rapid distribution of food from distant and unknowable sources, handled by gigantic and impersonal multinational firms, gives rise to what I call "fast food monoculture," highly susceptible, culturally, to almost instantaneous panics over food security and the contaminations of globalization. And, given the well-documented ability of Japanese mass media to seize on issues of food safety and global risk, recently including *e. coli*, BSE, GMOs, avian flu, and SARS, highly publicized outbreaks or fears of food safety may immediately disrupt Japanese distribution channels on hitherto unimaginable scales and send shock waves throughout the global food system.

And, although the new Japanese food system is inherently dependent on the globalization of food supply, technological innovations, and managerial skills and corporate forms, I would argue that the controversies or moral panics about the domestic changes wrought by (or reflected in) *konbini*, *kaiten-zushi*, and many related genres of business, are much less about domestic change than they are indications of profound ambivalence in contemporary Japan about globalization, perceived as an external rather than an internal or interdependent phenomenon.

Notes

Acknowledgments. Many institutions have generously supported aspects of the research upon which this chapter is based, including: the National Science Foundation, the New York Sea Grant Program, the Center for Global Partnership of the Japan Foundation, the East Asia Program of Cornell University, and the Reischauer Institute of Japanese Studies of Harvard University. I cannot mention them by name, but I am also extremely grateful to the dozens of individuals throughout the Japanese fishing and food industries who have been willing to answer my many questions and share with me their own expertise. Richard Wilk's extensive comments have dramatically sharpened the focus and improved the style of this chapter. Of course, I am solely responsible for the facts and interpretations expressed in this chapter. Additional information about my research is posted at www.people.fas.harvard.edu/~bestor.

1. The humor of the original verse is in the word *nigiru*, used in two senses: wringing one's hands in anticipation, and molding or squeezing rice for sushi, which is known also as *nigiri-zushi* ("hand-molded sushi").

2. Throughout this chapter I restrict my discussion of "fast food" to culinary genres that are identified by contemporary Japanese as distinctively "Japanese" dishes, and exclude

discussion of hamburgers, fried chicken, curried rice, donuts, ice cream, pizza, and coffee, all of which are also major segments of the contemporary "fast food" industry in Japan.

3. Many anthropologists have focused recently on the culture of capitalism and on "multiple capitalisms" as distinct cultural and social forms in different societies (see, for example, Blim 2000; Miller 1997). Japanese economic organization itself has been the object of debates about specific cultural and social characteristics of capitalism (T. Bestor 2004, ch. 1). Business and political commentators have at various times either lauded the Japanese economy as a harbinger of future forms of global capitalism based on tight integration and coordination among government, business, and labor (e.g., Johnson 1982), or condemned it as a highly insular, inefficient, and intensely corrupt system that works against consumer interests (van Wolferen 1990).

4. By Japanese restaurant chain standards, the *kaiten-zushi* chains are quite small; the largest consists of only 250 shops, whereas the largest chains serving "Western" food (e.g., McDonalds, KFC, or Starbucks) each have thousands of outlets (Anon. 2001).

5. The 7-Eleven chain of convenience stores is owned in both Japan and the United States by the Japanese retailing giant, Itō Yōkadō. In 1973, Itō Yōkadō opened its first convenience store in Japan under license from the Southland Corporation, the Texas-based originator of the 7-Eleven franchise, and it began to use the 7-Eleven name in Japan in 1978. In 1991, Itō Yōkadō acquired 70 percent of the shares of the Southland Corporation. In 1993, the 5,000th Japanese 7-Eleven store was opened, according to the 7-Eleven website.

6. Occasional surveys on shopping patterns for perishable foodstuffs conducted by the Tokyo Metropolitan Government illustrate larger shifts within which the *konbini* boom has occurred. In 1996, shoppers in their twenties were most likely to patronize small supermarkets and convenience stores (30.4 percent); those in their thirties were most partial to large supermarkets (36.0 percent); and shoppers over the age of sixty favored retail fishmongers (37.1 percent). During the preceding five years, consumers who shopped regularly at retail fishmongers declined by more than 20 percent and those who shopped in supermarkets and convenience stores increased by 16 percent (Tōkyō-to 1992:108; 1995:119; 1996:8–13).

7. I have had several opportunities to visit *konbini* with food chemists from one of Japan's leading food additive manufacturers. My chemist guides are intimately familiar with almost every product on *konbini* shelves and how they have been engineered to specifically meet the needs of *konbini* sales. They tell me that among many other projects, they are actively working on ways to recreate the smell of freshly cooked rice for pre-packaged meals, to duplicate the freshly made "sushi smell" for box lunches, and to mask the subtly different flavor of imported Chinese-raised eels, which are used in the traditional summer delicacy of *kabayaki* (grilled eel).

8. A national government survey of 3,000 adults, conducted in 2005, found that overall 57 percent of respondents (88 percent of respondents in their 20s, 82 percent in their 30s, and 70 percent in their 40s) considered late-night or 24-hour convenience stores to be a "necessity." However, 41 percent of respondents overall regarded convenience stores

as having a negative influence on youth, 28 percent were concerned about noise, and 27 percent worried about crime and safety around such stores (*Japan Times*, July 17, 2005:2).

References

Akamoto, Mariko. 2002. New, Improved *Kaiten* Shops Herald a Revolution in Dining. Asahi Shimbun, September 14–15:36.

Anonymous. 2001. Kaiten-zushi dake! 1200-kan! (Rotary sushi only! 1200 servings!). Tōkyō Isshūkan, December 25.

Apparudai, Arjun. 1990. Disjuncture and Difference in the Global Cultural Economy. Public Culture 2(2):1–24.

Bestor, Theodore C. 1999. Wholesale Sushi: Culture and Commodity in Tokyo's Tsukiji Market. *In* Theorizing the City: The New Urban Anthropology Reader. Setha M. Low, ed. Pp. 201–42. New Brunswick, NJ: Rutgers University Press.

———. 2000. How Sushi Went Global. Foreign Policy, November/December:54–63.

———. 2001. Supply-Side Sushi: Commodity, Market, and the Global City. American Anthropologist 102(1):76–95.

———. 2004. Tsukiji: The Fish Market at the Center of the World. Berkeley: University of California Press.

———. In preparation. Global Sushi. Book manuscript.

Bestor, Victoria Lyon. 1998. Who's Cooking, Whose Kitchen? Paper presented at the New York Asian Studies Conference, New Paltz, NY, October.

Blim, Michael. 2000. Capitalisms in Late Modernity. Annual Review of Anthropology 29:25–38.

Cwiertka, Katarzyna. 1999. Culinary Globalization and Japan. Japan Echo, June.

———. In preparation. From Ethnic to Hip: Circuits of Japanese Cuisine in Europe. *In* Japanese Globalizations. H. Befu, T. Bestor, and M. White, eds. Book manuscript.

Goody, Jack. 1982. Cooking, Cuisine, and Class: A Study in Comparative Sociology. Cambridge: Cambridge University Press.

Japan Times. 2005. 57% "need" convenience stores. Poll, Japan Times, July 17:2.

Johnson, Chalmers. 1982. MITI and the Japanese Miracle. Palo Alto: Stanford University Press.

McGray, Douglas. 2002. Japan's Gross National Cool. Foreign Policy, May/June 2002:44–54.

Miller, Daniel. 1997. Capitalism: An Ethnographic Approach. Oxford: Berg Publishers.

Mintz, Sidney. 1997. Swallowing Modernity. *In* Golden Arches East: McDonald's in East Asia. J. L. Watson, ed. Palo Alto: Stanford University Press.

Ng, Wai-ming. 2001. Popularization and Localization of Sushi in Singapore: An Ethnographic Survey. New Zealand Journal of Asian Studies 3(1):7–19.

Nishiyama, Matsunosuke, et al., eds. 1984. *Edogaku jiten* (Encyclopedia of Edo studies). Tokyo: Kōbundō.

Noguchi, Paul. 1994. Ekiben: The Fast Food of High-Speed Japan. Ethnology 33(4):317–30.

Tamamura, Toyō. 2000. *Kaiten-zushi sekai hitomeguri* (Rotary sushi around the world). Tokyo: Sekaibunkasha.

Tōkyō-to. 1992. *Shijō Memo* (Market memo). Tokyo: Tōkyō-to Chūō Oroshiuri Shijō.

———. 1995. *Shijō Memo* (Market memo). Tokyo: Tōkyō-to Chūō Oroshiuri Shijō.

———. 1996. *Dai jurokkai seisen shokuryōhin oyobi kaki shōhi-kanbai dōkō: Chōsa kekka* (Results of the sixteenth survey of consumption and sales trends for perishable foodstuffs and flowers). Tokyo: Tōkyō-to Chūō Oroshiuri Shijō Tsukiji Shijō.

van Wolferen, Karel. 1990. The Enigma of Japanese Power. New York: Vintage.

Watanabe Yonehide. 2002. *Kaiten-zushi no keizaigaku* (The economics of *kaiten-zushi*). Tokyo: Besuto Shinsho.

Yagyū Kyūbe'e. 2003. *Kaiten-zushi no sa-sushi-se-so* (The ABCs of *kaiten-zushi*). Tokyo: Ekusunoreji.

Yamashita Machiko. 1998. *From Kitchen: Katei no Shokuji*. Osaka: Osaka Gasu Enerugi Bunka Kenkyūjo.

Rice Ball Rivalries: Japanese Convenience Stores and the Appetite of Late Capitalism 9

GAVIN HAMILTON WHITELAW

SIMPLE IN INGREDIENTS and easy to make, the rice ball, or *onigiri*, is one of Japan's oldest "fast foods" and the nation's ultimate convenience meal. Japan's rice ball roots are traceable back to the Heian period. Ancient court poetry and military ballads celebrated the *onigiri*'s portability and the fact that no plate was required for it to be served. While some of the *onigiri*'s ingredients have changed with time, its basic form has not. Consisting of a heaping fistful of rice pressed into a round, cylindrical, or triangular shape, the *onigiri* is a fast food at its slowest—a convenient meal whose shape literally bears the mark of its maker. Its very name comes from the verb *nigiru*, meaning to press or pack together with one's hands. Today, *onigiri* remain a common food for those on the move. They are eaten for lunch by school children and harried workers, carried in hikers' backpacks, handed out at community events, and even dispensed as emergency rations in the wake of disasters.[1] Although still seen as an easy way to quickly feed a large number of people or to conveniently use up leftover rice from the previous night's meal, the *onigiri* image has evolved from that of a traditional family food to one that is purchased outside of the home, in stores and supermarkets.

Perhaps no retail industry relies on the *onigiri* more than Japan's convenience stores. For *konbini* (the Japanese contraction for "convenience store"), the rice ball plays an important role in redefining convenience and establishing chain distinction. Shortly after the American convenience store franchise model was introduced to Japan in the late 1960s, the *onigiri* became a key product in domesticating the foreign retail form for the Japanese palate. Corporations seeking to provide a familiar, convenient, and freshly packaged food that would still be considered a meal by the Japanese consumer embraced the *onigiri*. This attention to the rice ball led to innovations in its production and content. Today, the *onigiri* remains a focus of creativity, profit, and competition. *Onigiri* are available in various shapes and sizes. Their flavorful fillings range from pickled plum and tuna-and-mayo to *kimchi* and Hokkaido salmon. Priced between 85 and 260 yen apiece, the *onigiri* is a multi-billion-yen business for Japan's convenience store franchises. 7-Eleven Japan alone sold 1.4 billion *onigiri* in 2003 (Yoshioka 2005:17), the statistical equivalent of eight rice balls for every Japanese man, woman, and child.[2]

In this chapter, I explore the *onigiri's* commodification by Japan's convenience store industry. I argue that the *onigiri's* "convenience" as a product is linked to the food's rich cultural resonance that companies hope to freely tap. However, the corporate embrace of the culturally value-added *onigiri* and the phenomenon of commodification that the food undergoes is not a simple process with predetermined outcomes. Drawing on particular case studies, my research points to tensions inherent in late "consumer" capitalism and its concomitant tendencies to commercialize private needs and increase industrial efficiency. Rather than eroding the rice ball's store of cultural meanings, the contradictions between the *onigiri's* commodity nature and its emotional, cultural, and historical significance have contributed new meanings to the food itself.

The *Onigiri*: From the Heian Court to Heisei Households

People have made and consumed the rice ball in Japan for millennia. Heian Period (794 A.D.–1192 A.D.) court documents mention ceremonial exchanges of dense, egg-shaped bundles of glutinous rice between aristocratic households and loyal vassals. Ancient military ballads also contain references to the *onigiri*. Rice balls could be produced in bulk, rapidly distributed, carried into battle, and consumed when necessary. Fillers such as bean, millet, and wild vegetables weakened the rice ball's cohesiveness, making it necessary to wrap or bind (*musubu*) the rice ball together with large leaves or rice straw. The term *omusubi* is still used as an alternative word for *onigiri*, although seaweed and plastic wrap have replaced the leaves and straw of yore.

During the Meiji Restoration (1865–1912), agricultural reforms coupled with improvements in transportation and distribution helped make rice a more prominent part of the Japanese diet. The *onigiri* punctuated particular moments of the nation-state's expansion into everyday social life. One milestone was the opening of Japan's first rail line. In 1885, the national railway approved the sale of the first *ekiben* (train station lunchbox), which contained two rice balls lightly seasoned with sesame salt (*gomashio*) as a preservative. The Ministry of Education's first school lunch program, piloted at a rural northern elementary school in 1889, also featured the rice ball. The *onigiri* remains on school lunch menus to this day.

Although the appearance of *onigiri* in school lunches and in train station food stalls are important developments in the rice ball's modern historical trajectory, undoubtedly the *onigiri's* strongest set of associations is with the home, family, and motherhood. For many Japanese, the *onigiri* is seen as a "comfort food," one that reflects the skill, nutritional acumen, and even flavor of the mother and wife. More akin to the matzo ball than the hamburger, the *onigiri* is a culinary composition whose external simplicity often belies its internal complexity. According to popular women's magazines, the *onigiri*'s ingredients must be carefully chosen. Beginning with grades of rice and *nori* (seaweed) and proceeding through a myriad of fillings such as pickled plum, grilled salmon, and marinated sea kelp, every component of the rice ball is a decision unto itself. Attention paid to using a particularly famous regional product (*meibutsu*) or a seasonally appropriate ingredient bespeaks not only the housewife's knowledge but also the degree to which she cares about what her family ingests.

The *onigiri* is as much about form as content. Its size and shape are literally determined by the hands of the creator. Some scientists have gone so far as to study how naturally occurring salts and oils from the woman's palms subtly alter the taste of rice, thus giving the homemade *onigiri* a distinct flavor that is traceable to the mother who created it.[3] The *onigiri*'s ability to connect the child to the home and caregiver has been reinforced, and some might argue exploited, by the state educational system. A majority of Japanese nursery schools and kindergartens do not offer lunch programs, thus making parents, usually mothers, responsible for creating a lunch box (*obentô*) filled with tasty, easy-to-consume foods like *onigiri*. Anthropologist Anne Allison argues that such a lunch box policy serves the dual purpose of reinforcing a gendered state ideology while opening the household to a subtle yet effective form of surveillance. Through the daily production and consumption of lunch boxes, both mother and the child are observed, judged, and disciplined by school officials and, by extension, the national education system (Allison 1996). Teachers and school officials critique the mothers' *obentô*-making skills from nutritional and aesthetic standpoints. A half-eaten *onigiri* will accompany the child back to the home and kitchen along with a note from the teacher on how to improve tomorrow's meal.

The critical role of homemade lunch box design in a child's (and family's) early educational evaluation has spawned a minor media industry focusing on *obentô* menu ideas. As a popular component of the *obentô* repertoire, the *onigiri* is reinvented monthly in magazines and TV cooking programs. The homey rice ball becomes a canvas on which a mother may exercise her expertise and creativity. The strategic placement of strips of seaweed and circles of processed cheese on a ball of rice by loving hands transform an *onigiri* into the face of a cat or a panda. In recent years, the attention given to *obentô* has generated problems of its own. Lunch box creativity wars among overly zealous mothers led some kindergartens to instruct parents to pack only *onigiri* in hopes of toning down the competitive drive toward more elaborate boxed meals (Iwamura 2004).

The *onigiri*'s power as a cultural symbol continues to be reinforced in folktales and films where rice ball production and consumption embody care, loyalty, and magic. In popular children's stories, like *Sarukani Gassen* ("Showdown between the Monkey and the Crab") and *Omusubi Kororin* ("The Tumbling Rice Ball"), the gift of a rice ball, even when by accident, ultimately leads to reciprocity, prosperity, and deeper interpersonal ties. Even contemporary storytelling makes use of the *onigiri*'s magical dimensions. A pivotal moment in the Academy Award–winning animated film *Sen to Chihiro no Kamikakushi* ("Spirited Away") occurs when the young heroine, Chihiro, accepts a rice ball from her dragon-prince friend, Taku. The strength Chihiro gains from her meal enables her to undo an evil spell that turned her parents into swine and Taku into a fantastical beast. When asked why so many Japanese viewers cry as Chihiro eats her *onigiri*, film director Miyazaki Hayao explains that the scene is a powerful reminder of commensality and human interdependence. "As a child or a parent, you understand that the *onigiri* is a food sculpted by the hands of someone you know and whose tireless efforts give you life" (Miyazaki 2002).[4] For Miyazaki, the rice ball is infused with a kind of emotional magic powerful enough to humanize, or rehumanize, his story's animated characters.

Stories about the *onigiri*'s power are not limited, however, to folktales and popular films. As a commercially mass-produced packaged food, the *onigiri* is one of the best-selling items in Japanese convenience stores. Beyond its material importance, the life of the *onigiri* as a processed industrial food is so closely tied to the growth of Japan's *konbini* industry that the development of some chains parallels advances in rice ball production and marketing. Japan's two largest convenience store chains, 7-Eleven Japan, the originator of the packaged *onigiri*, and its rival Lawson, are illustrative examples.

Onigiri, 7-Eleven Japan, and the Rise of the *Konbini*

Although not Japan's first convenience store, 7-Eleven Japan and its early success in localizing a new retail system through meeting consumer needs and satisfying franchisees made it a galvanizing force in the industry—the chain to watch and the chain to beat. A cornerstone of 7-Eleven's marketing strategy was to provide pre-prepared foods that appealed to the Japanese palate. The *onigiri* played a decisive part in this plan. 7-Eleven Japan introduced the *onigiri* to the marketplace of industrial cuisine in 1978 when it launched the industry's first line of packaged rice balls in a hundred of its fledgling franchises.

In 1978, the convenience store retail format was still a new phenomena in Japan. Only five years earlier, Tokyo-based retail corporation, Ito-Yokado, imported the American 7-Eleven name and store manual to Japan. Ito-Yokado used 7-Eleven's franchise system to "collaborate" with local merchants to modernize existing local,

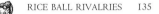

privately owned and operated establishments. The convenience store's small-scale format also gave Ito-Yokado a means for sidestepping restrictive legislation prohibiting big corporations from building large-scale outlets in residential neighborhoods and shopping districts. 7-Eleven's expansion was slow, fraught with logistical problems, store management missteps, product line failures, and resistance from shop owner associations. The Japanese company, conscious of the need to build a customer base for its stores, readily broke from the American marketing script of hotdogs and flavored Slurpee offerings and explored "new" types of convenience foods that would appeal to a hungry Japanese consumer. The *onigiri* was an obvious choice. Its size, relative ease of preparation, and the possibilities for value-added innovation through fillings, shapes, and flavors contributed to its strong potential as a *konbini* food. More critical still was the rice ball's social and symbolic standing in the Japanese diet. As a rice-based food, the *onigiri* was more immediately seen as a "meal" than a "snack" in the eyes of Japanese consumers (see Watson 1997). Furthermore, the *onigiri*'s long history and associations with the home, portability, and quick sustenance helped differentiate it from other "foreign" fast foods that required intense marketing efforts to win over public recognition and acceptance. The *onigiri* could be used to draw upon cultural associations and assist the *konbini* to convey a sense of care and familiarity, qualities that served to tone down the shop's American origins and its impersonal chain store image.

7-Eleven Japan oversaw the creation of its convenience store *onigiri* from ingredients and packaging to distribution and display. The first hurdle the company had to overcome was with production. 7-Eleven combed a Tokyo phone directory cover to cover before it was able to find a food maker willing to commercially mass-produce the rice ball (Yoshioka 2005:16). Despite the *onigiri*'s compositional simplicity, production still literally required many hands to pack and wrap the cooked rice. Most food makers were unwilling to add an additional production line for what was at that time a commercially untested product. Eventually, however, a producer was secured and the *onigiri* began to appear on store shelves in Tokyo neighborhoods.

The company's next challenge was the customer. Stores initially sold an average of five or six *onigiri* per day. "Everyone thought that the *onigiri* wouldn't sell," admitted Sawada Kazuhiro, 7-Eleven Japan's food product senior merchandiser, "but we recognized the latent potential of this product and we refused to give up" (Yoshioka 2005:16). The company fielded complaints ranging from the *onigiri*'s taste and the hardness of the rice to problems with product irregularity. In short, the convenience store *onigiri* was not quite "like mom's." 7-Eleven officials realized that "to capture the latent demand for such products it would need to improve their quality" (Bernstein 1997:514).

Over the next several decades, 7-Eleven Japan introduced numerous innovations in the *onigiri*'s display, packaging, and production to help broaden the product's appeal. The company placed open refrigerated cases in its stores so that *onigiri* could be stocked alongside *obentô* and other take-out foods. Initially, the triangular *onigiri* were covered in *nori* before being packaged, but between manufacture and sale the *nori* became soggy and sticky. In 1984, 7-Eleven developed a more advanced packaging system to deal with this problem. Referred to as the "parachute" wrap, an additional layer of plastic kept the seaweed crisp and separate from the rice until the *onigiri* was ready to be eaten. The purchaser removed the protective layer of plastic and manually enveloped the rice ball in seaweed, thus completing the final step in the process of making a homemade *onigiri*. In 1989, the "one hand" wrapping system replaced the parachute wrap. Pinching firmly on a colored plastic tab, the customer tears open the *onigiri* package with a single hand motion. The outer and inner layers of plastic are then removed by pulling on the corners of the package. 7-Eleven's innovations in packaging were mimicked by other convenience store and supermarket chains.

As part of an overall effort to standardize and improve the freshness of its pre-made food products, 7-Eleven reorganized the manufacturing and distribution processes. It established a cooperative association to help small firms with food production and management. Initially it contracted with ten smaller-scale makers to produce its rice-based foods. In exchange for their compliance with company standards like ingredients, cooking temperatures, and packaging requirements, 7-Eleven agreed to be the primary buyer of the group's output. By the 1990s the association had expanded to over one hundred firms with internal divisions overseeing such areas as bulk purchasing of raw materials as well as research and development of food products like *onigiri*. In 2003, this integrated association of food makers proved instrumental in launching 7-Eleven's "Rice Ball Revolution" (*Onigiri Kakume*). Under increasing competitive pressure by other convenience store chains, including Lawson, 7-Eleven developed a new mechanized system for creating *onigiri*. The focus was on preserving the softness of the rice and producing an *onigiri* that "tasted as if it was made by mother's own hands" (Yoshioka 2005:14). The "revolutionary" step is a specially designed heating unit that dispatches a quick blast of warm air into the hollowed out center of the *onigiri* before a filling, like pickled plum or cooked salmon, is added. The warm air separates the individual grains of cooked rice, preserves softness, and helps to capture the flavor of the filling.

From the beginning, producing a good-tasting product was not enough for 7-Eleven. Equally critical was improving ordering accuracy and speed through the development and implementation of an information technology system. The same year that 7-Eleven Japan launched its first *onigiri* line, it also initiated what would grow to become a powerful and comprehensive technological infrastructure linking the corporation with manufacturers, distributors, and corner stores. In its earliest stages, the system was simply handwritten order slips filled out by store owners and sent to 7-Eleven headquarters. The head office put together the orders and relayed them to the food manufacturers. The turnaround time between store order and delivery took a week or more. Upgraded eighty times, today the system is a store-based computerized network of Point of Sales (POS) terminals capable of seamlessly relaying sales information in real time. Turnaround times for most products have been reduced to just over twenty-four hours.

The POS terminal fuses the cash register with 7-Eleven's in-store product ordering system and a mainframe computer at 7-Eleven's headquarters. The system keeps track of what is sold and allows the store to gather consumer data with each transaction. While stocking the shelves, store clerks scan items into the system using a wireless, hand-held bar code reader. During checkout, product bar codes are again scanned at the register. This information is automatically combined with data such as the time, date, and weather conditions. By pressing a single key on the computerized register at the end of the sale, the store employee inconspicuously inputs the customer's gender and age category.[5] By the time the cash drawer springs open and the clerk begin to count change, the entire "transaction" has been electronically relayed as a complete data package to 7-Eleven headquarters where it is analyzed. An hour later the output is fed to manufacturers and back to store owners themselves, appearing as flow charts and graphs on the store computer located in the shop's back room. This system has proven invaluable in assisting manufacturers to create *onigiri* on demand. It has also enabled 7-Eleven Japan to generate customer profiles for its *onigiri* products. 7-Eleven Japan uses this data to advise store owners about how to adjust their offerings to suit the particular tastes of local consumers.

Today all of Japan's major *konbini* chains have followed 7-Eleven's lead by adopting and developing their own POS register systems. Consequently, a majority of the nation's forty-two thousand convenience stores are considerably more attuned to the purchasing habits of their customers. While the *konbini* is not a substitute for mother, the stores constantly strive to better predict what kinds of *onigiri* people will want and when they will want them. It is not uncommon to hear local residents living by themselves refer to *konbini* as "replacement refrigerators" (*reizōko no kawari*). Japan's convenience stores are oases of pre-prepared foods, like *onigiri*, for people without a mom around.

Onigiri continue to be one of the key products through which convenience store corporations seek to distinguish themselves and generate the kind of customer loyalty that will keep consumers flowing into their stores and not those of their rivals. Although 7-Eleven Japan played a considerable role in the initial mass production and marketing of the *onigiri*, Japan's second largest convenience store chain, Lawson, raised the bar of *onigiri* development a notch higher by using the *onigiri* as the flagship of its brand revitalization campaign.

Corporate Soul Food: "I Love Lawson *Onigiri* Project"

In 2001, the future of Lawson seemed uncertain. Its parent company, the large retail magnate Daiei, was on the verge of bankruptcy, individual franchisees profits were falling due to an increasingly competitive retail market, and the Lawson brand name image as a provider of safe food had been tarnished by a product scandal. The chain's restructuring began with the hiring of a young new company president and, under his guidance, the development, marketing, and launch of a gourmet line of rice balls under the moniker *Onigiri-ya* ("Rice Ball Shop"). In less than a year, the *Onigiri-ya* campaign netted the company a healthy profit and reaffirmed Lawson's image in the eyes of the consumer and its franchisees. The campaign defied the conventional wisdom at the time. Despite Japan's lackluster economy and depressed consumer spending, Lawson priced its *Onigiri-ya* rice balls ¥100 to ¥130 (approximately $1.00 to $1.30) above the national convenience store average. What seemed like a risky move was, in fact, a shrewd strategy for invigorating sales.

The *Onigiri-ya* campaign was the brainchild of Niinami Takeshi, a forty-four-year old executive from Lawson's new corporate retainer, trading company Mitsubishi Shoji. Wielding an MBA from Harvard, Niinami had proven his skill while serving as the marketing manager for Mitsubishi Shoji's Kentucky Fried Chicken account. Immediately after assuming his position as Lawson company head, Niinami set to work on an *onigiri* campaign that he hoped would rekindle Lawson's image as a name consumers could trust. On the eve of Niinami's appointment, a slice of flesh from a fingertip had been discovered in an *onigiri* purchased at a Lawson store in the northern Japanese city of Sendai. The media attention concerning this incident was swift and the consumer-related fallout immediate. Lawson food sales dropped and stock prices dipped while those of its major competitors, 7-Eleven and FamilyMart, rose. The incident was a harsh reminder of how carefully food quality was monitored and of the overnight impact that a mishap could have in a cutthroat retail environment where the competition was literally on the next corner.

For Niinami the rice ball project was as much a new business model as a product confidence campaign. *Onigiri-ya* had two interrelated goals: to please customers with a quality product and to reaffirm confidence among the members of the "Lawson family"—from company employees through to franchisees and manufacturers. The new Lawson image was not being constructed for either the public *or* the company's employees (Marchand 1998:44), but rather for both audiences simultaneously. In a TV-Tokyo interview, Niinami explained, "*Onigiri-ya* equals the 'New Lawson', that is the impression we are striving for. . . . If I can do all that then I will be happy with this as a business model" (TV-Tokyo 2003).

From its inception, the *onigiri* project was decidedly different from other product creation enterprises. The development portion of the *Onigiri-ya* campaign was titled "I Love Lawson Onigiri Project" and the development team consisted of product development division representatives as well as a cross-section of company employees from various other divisions and departments. Secretaries, middle management, and executives were included in the initial decision-making stages. For several months, the teams met on a regular basis. Lunch breaks became gastrointestinal overtime as members sampled different types of rice balls, ranked what they ate, and gave opinions on what needed to change in order to create an *onigiri* "with impact" (TV-Tokyo 2003).

Outside of the office, Niinami sold the *Onigiri-ya* project to the company's 7,600 franchisees as a way to reinvigorate profits. *Onigiri* are not only one of the best-selling items in convenience stores, but they also have one of the highest profit margins—on the order of 35 to 40 percent. In the case of Lawson, this profit is divided 40/60 between the company and franchisee respectively. A good tasting, more expensive *onigiri* that sold well meant more money for both the store owner and the corporation.

In November 2002, Lawson launched the new rice balls series under the nostalgic moniker *Onigiri-ya*. Like the *onigiri* varieties themselves, the project team also designed, voted on, and approved the campaign name and logo, a Japanese-style sliding door with a short blue curtain (*noren*) hanging just below the entrance's frame. The *onigiri* wrapping, a specially engineered rice paper, added an additional layer of distinction to the product. The wrapping paper also ensured that the *Onigiri-ya* products stood out from other rice balls offerings on the store shelves. While the price per *onigiri* was close to double that of the regular varieties, the *Onigiri-ya* product was noticeably larger in size. In addition, all *onigiri* in the series were made with one or more "name brand" regional food products. The base ingredient for all the rice balls was Niigata *koshihikari*, a well-known variety of rice from a region in Japan renowned for its rice production. The *onigiri* fillings included braised eel from Kyushu, pickled plums from Wakayama, and fish roe from Hokkaido. The *Onigiri-ya* selection represented the ultimate commodity frontier. The ingredients easily called forth popular destinations of travel (see Caldwell's chapter in this volume). For the salary men, office ladies, and retirees who bought the *onigiri*, their purchase became a means of traveling through taste without ever having to leave the confines of the office or park bench.

The *Onigiri-ya* products sold well. In the first several weeks of the product's launch, Lawson released a TV commercial featuring Niinami himself, dressed in a dark suit and looking out over an expansive array of *Onigiri-ya* rice balls.[6] The sentence *Onigiri wa nihonjin no sokojikara* ("Rice balls are the Japanese people's source of stamina") was spliced between the shots of Niinami pondering the selection and biting into rice balls he grasped in each hand. The decision to have Niinami appear on the commercial was doubly apt. The *Onigiri-ya* project represented Niinami's official debut as the new leader of Japan's second largest convenience store company, and the main purchasers of the *Onigiri-ya* product (according to POS data) tended to be white-collar company employees like himself, with more discretionary income than their younger colleagues (Murata 2003).

The Limits and Liability of Rice-Ball-Led Restructuring

Despite the success of the *Onigiri-ya* project as a whole, there were setbacks. On May 21, 2002, news leaked out that Lawson's banner Niigata *koshihikari* rice had been blended with rice from another area. Some 218 Lawson convenience stores in Miyagi and Yamagata Prefectures received *onigiri* made with the blended rice. The reason for the blending was never exactly clear, but some analysts suggested that the just-in-time production system was to blame. When producing more "generic" *onigiri*, blending rice was not an issue and thus cheaper grades of rice were acquired and mixed as needed, allowing for warehouse and storage costs to be kept to a minimum. But in turning to "prestigious" ingredients, whether *koshihikari* rice or fish roe, the just-in-time system left food producers in a risky situation. Unexpected spikes in demand and dwindling supplies due to weather, pollution, spoilage, or poor planning meant that not enough resources would be on hand to fill orders. Substituting inferior ingredients or "blending" was one solution, but it carried with it the danger of being exposed by consumer watch groups and housewife organizations that constantly keep an eye out for dishonest and deceptive practices. Blame strikes not just at the factory level, but at the company whose image is intimately linked to the product.

Lawson's head office reacted quickly when the rice-blending story broke. Niinami made an immediate decision not to hide the truth about the rice-mixing incident from consumers. Reversing mistakes made during the fingertip incident, Niinami ordered immediate disclosure of what had occurred. Within twenty-four hours, Lawson published official apologies in major national newspapers and on its website. A day later, Niinami met in person with the head of the factory that had produced the *onigiri* and made it clear that Lawson would not tolerate future missteps. Lawson's damage control appeared to work. *Onigiri-ya* products remain strong sellers. However, not long after the incident, Lawson's *Onigiri-ya* television ad campaign changed. Niinami's executive visage was replaced with that of the gray-haired, kimono-clad actress Ichida Hiromi, famous for her Kyoto dialect and numerous roles as devout wife and mother in Japanese period dramas (*jidaigeki*). Ichida continues to be the face of the *Onigiri-ya* brand, inviting television viewers to enjoy the old-fashioned goodness of the latest rice ball flavor. While the *onigiri* contributed to a corporation's reinvention, its public spokesperson returned to a recognizable matronly trope.

The Lawson *Onigiri-ya* case suggests paths for the *onigiri* and the limits and liabilities that accompany these trajectories. In moving outside of the home into a

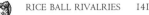

commercial sphere, the *onigiri* becomes more than a vehicle for cementing human-to-human relationships; it forges connections between individuals, stores, and corporations. But while the *onigiri* is offered as a kinder, gentler, more culturally recognizable fast food, it is not free from scrutiny. Problems with *onigiri*, whether the discovery of an unexpected gruesome ingredient or the blending of grades of rice, act as reminders to both the consumer and company of the limitations of corporate "maternalism" in mass food production. Products marketed as conveniences (*benrina mono*) in modern Japan have historically been accompanied by a social questioning of quality, health, safety, and even the possible deleterious impact that these technological and commercial advancements may have on people's lives. A matrix of organizations in Japan including active local, regional, and national consumer rights and housewife organizations, government agencies, and the media have contributed to distinctive social sensitivity toward and awareness of products. As *konbini* ad campaigns and company slogans push the *onigiri* further onto center stage, the product becomes a greater focus of attention for consumer advocacy organizations and the media as well. Newsletters, online forums, and newspaper articles are one counterbalance to intense product campaigns. By publicly examining and discussing the unhealthy dimensions of the convenience store, these sources embed the *konbini onigiri* in issues like the use of food additives and preservatives and the amount of waste that stores generate.

On yet another level, the ubiquity of the convenience store and the proliferation of *onigiri* consumption have led to cautionary tales and critical forms of moral discourse. Housewife logs from recent dietary surveys show that some mothers are now buying *onigiri* in *konbini* and supermarkets and these purchases are made to supplement family meals (Iwamura 2004). It is not uncommon to hear stories from frustrated mothers and grandmothers about children who will no longer eat their *onigiri* because the rice balls looked strange and tasted different than the store-bought varieties. Rather than being read as merely symptoms of the "commercialization of intimate life" (Hochschild 2003), these examples are important contributions to a collective consciousness about life in a commercial society.

Conclusion: The Category of *Konbini Onigiri*

The *onigiri* has not disappeared from people's diets; far from it. Its simplicity, nutritional value, and cultural cachet have allowed it to maintain its popularity as a food. While still produced by hand in homes and school cafeterias, the *onigiri* is also embraced by commercial enterprises and offered for sale to the Japanese consumer. Reinventing the convenience of convenience food in ways that benefit the bottom line and appeal to a consumer's changing needs, the convenience store has found a way to insert itself between reproduction of the family and the production of the market economy (White 2002). Corporate focus on the *onigiri* combined with public and consumer interest, both positive and negative, has led to the emergence of the *konbini onigiri* as a category of its own. In the course of my field research, informants and news sources increasingly use the term *konbini onigiri* to identify the commercially manufactured rice ball. The *konbini onigiri* is associated with certain shapes, flavors, and styles of packaging as well as a range of different practices introduced by the consumer rather than the producer. In Hokkaido and Okinawa, for example, customers prefer warmed *onigiri* and frequently ask clerks to microwave their purchases. Customers sometimes even instruct store employees on the exact number of seconds to warm the *onigiri*. *Konbini onigiri* are also integral ingredients in *yûshoku*, a new word used by young people to describe the practice of eating a quick meal with one's friends (*yûjin*) outside places like *konbini* rather than, or in addition to, consuming "dinner" at home with family. (The Japanese term for dinner is also *yûshoku*, however it uses a different Chinese character for the first syllable.) *Yûshoku* provides opportunities for young people to gossip about teachers, exchange information on part-time job opportunities, and even debate more efficient ways to open the *onigiri* wrappers (Utsunomia 2004:72).

Within the convenience store, the *konbini onigiri* blurs the distinction between gift and commodity. Despite company instructions to throw away all expired food items, convenience store owners frequently defy corporate orders by giving unsold *onigiri* and other expired food items to their part-time staff.[7] Clerks frequently mention the practice of food handouts as a critical bonus to their low-paying jobs. Said one informant, "You don't need to eat before going to work, particularly if you are on the morning shift." Clerks will even go as far as to encourage friends to apply for a job at a particular *konbini* because of the store owner's largess with unsold food. Even the *konbini onigiri* that get thrown in the trash have the potential to enter other systems of value and circulation. Well-wrapped and easily gleaned from the dumpsters behind stores, the *konbini onigiri* are a source of nourishment for urban homeless populations. According to one Osaka-based homeless research task force, convenience stores are ranked relatively high on the list of places to scavenge meals.

The *onigiri* is emblematic of the changes of comfort in "comfort food." Blurring the distinction between commodity and comfort, the rice ball assists in transition of family from home to workplace, helps corporations to post profits, and provides a means for convenience stores to ease into local communities. The rice ball is not merely the flagship for *konbini* chains like 7-Eleven Japan and Lawson, it is a metonym of the convenience store more generally. The time, effort, and attention paid to the commercialization of *onigiri* have not, however, emptied the *onigiri* of its value or meaning. Rather, they have contributed new meanings and practices to this historically fast, slow food. The category of *konbini onigiri* reflects the power, even magic, that food in a consumer society continues to posses. Although still able to resonate with notions of the home, motherhood, and comfort, the *konbini onigiri* is packed with a new set of associations and uses that extend beyond the label and logo that a corporation may try to give it.

Notes

Acknowledgments. This chapter is based on research conducted between 2002 and 2005 with generous support provided by various sources including Yale University's Council on East Asian Studies, the Program in Agrarian Studies, and a 2004–2005 Fulbright IIE Doctoral Dissertation Research Fellowship. I thank the Society for Economic Anthropology for allowing me to present a draft of this paper at the 2004 annual meeting in Decatur, Georgia. In addition I am grateful to Professors Richard Wilk, Bill Kelly, and Jean-Christophe Agnew for reading the paper and offering me their rich and thoughtful suggestions.

1. A housewife-initiated NGO, self-titled the "Japanese *Onigiri* Peace Corps" (*Nihon Onigiri-tai*), provides humanitarian aid in the form of rice balls. Each year they organize *onigiri* relief missions to disaster and famine-struck areas around the globe.

2. Ito-Yokado founded what became 7-Eleven Japan in 1973 through a licensing agreement with the convenience store chain's Texas-based American owner, Southland. The first 7-Eleven opened in 1974 in an industrial section of downtown Tokyo. By 1980, over one thousand 7-Eleven franchises were operating in Japan. 7-Eleven Japan purchased a controlling share of the U.S.-based 7-Eleven in 1991 when Southland filed for bankruptcy. In 2005, 7-Eleven Japan purchased the remaining shares of 7-Eleven from Southland, giving the Japanese firm complete control over 7-Eleven's global brand image.

3. The flavor of a woman's hands being transferred to the food she makes is a common theme in other cultural contexts as well. In reference to the magical associations that home-cooked food has, anthropologist Richard Wilk notes that in Belize people claim that each woman's handmade tortillas possess a distinct flavor.

4. The quote appeared on a packaged plastic model of Haku's *onigiri* that Hayao's Ghibli production company used to promote the video and DVD versions of the animated film. The life-size *onigiri* replica is hollow and can be opened by squeezing the toy's sides. The instructions explain that the toy rice ball is not for eating but for holding precious keepsakes. A color photograph of Hayao himself making *onigiri* appears on the toy's package. The plastic *onigiri*, however, is manufactured in China.

5. POS registers contain two vertical columns of color-coded keys. A light blue column is for male customers, and a light pink column for female customers. Each column is divided horizontally into four age brackets: adolescent (age fifteen and under), young adult (age sixteen to twenty-nine), middle-age adult (age thirty to forty-nine), and senior (age fifty and over). Some chains, including Lawson, separate the age categories into five groups: children (age twelve and under), teenager (age thirteen to nineteen), young adult (age twenty to twenty-nine), middle-age adult (age thirty to forty-nine), and senior (age fifty and over). For each sale, the machine will not calculate change and open the cash drawer until a customer data key is pushed.

6. In a later television interview, Niinami said he insisted upon being present at many of the rice ball taste testings and offered his own input. He admitted that the *Onigiri-ya* campaign added about eight pounds to his 6'2" frame.

7. A former Lawson employee explained that *konbini* corporations are as concerned about profit as health when insisting unsold food be thrown out and not given away. If employees are not provided with "free" meals, they are more likely to purchase store food and thus contribute to store sales. The corporations also warn store owners that giving away food may contribute to "bad employee habits" such as stealing.

References

Allison, Anne. 1996. Permitted and Prohibited Desires: Mothers, Comics, and Censorship in Japan. Boulder, CO: Westview Press.

Bernstein, Jeffery Richard. 1997. 7-Eleven in America and Japan. *In* Creating Modern Capitalism: How Entrepreneurs, Companies, and Countries Triumphed in Three Industrial Revolutions. Pp. 490–528. Cambridge, MA: Harvard University Press.

Hochschild, Arlie Russell. 2003. The Commercialization of Intimate Life: Notes from Home and Work. Berkeley: University of California Press.

Iwamura, Nobuko. 2004. Crisis in the Kitchen. JapanEcho 31(2):42–45.

Marchand, Roland. 1998. Creating the Corporate Soul: The Rise of Public Relations and Corporate Imagery in American Big Business. Berkeley: University of California Press.

Miyazaki, Hayao. 2002. Chi to Chihiro no Kamikamushi Onigiri ["Spirited Away" Kamimakmushi Onigiri], Tokyo: Sanrio.

Murata, Wahei. 2003. Ureru Netsuke [The Price that Sticks]. *In* Nikkei Business. Pp. 30–33.

TV-Tokyo. 2003. Kaikakuseyo! Konbini Shinjidai [Reform! The New Era of Convenience Stores]. *In* Gaia no Yôyake. Japan: TV-Tokyo.

Utsunomiya, Kentarô. 2004. Konbini Mae de Kyô mo Yûshoku. [Today, Again, Eating with Friends in front of the *Konbini*] *In* Aera. Pp. 72–73.

Watson, James L., ed. 1997. Golden Arches East: McDonald's in East Asia. Palo Alto: Stanford University Press.

White, Merry I. 2002. Perfectly Japanese: Making Families in an Era of Upheaval. Berkeley: University of California Press.

Yoshioka, Hideko. 2005. Motometa mono wa haha no te [Things Put Together Are by Mother's Hands], *In* Aera. Pp. 14–17.

Global Tastes, Local Contexts: An Ethnographic Account of Fast Food Expansion in San Fernando City, the Philippines

10

TY MATEJOWSKY

P OSSIBLY THE MOST WIDESPREAD manifestation of global consumer culture is the seemingly ubiquitous fast food restaurant. Its sleek design, standardized style of service, and distinctive menu has an appeal that resonates with millions the world over. These enterprises have become powerful agents in the spread of mass consumerism and Western values (Schlosser 2001:225–54; Stolicna 2000). Their proliferation outside of North America and Europe not only transforms notions of service, taste, and lifestyle, it also informs the built character of many urban environments (Matejowsky 2002). At a more personal level, it promotes eating habits and nutritional regimes that figure prominently in the rise of medical conditions like obesity, high blood pressure, and heart disease (Schlosser 2001:240–43).

Few contemporary societies remain beyond the global reach of the fast food industry. The spread of the political economy and institution of fast food occurs regardless of the specific content, nationality, or style of the food itself. The regimented service model on which fast food is based transfers easily to areas where conditions of free enterprise and neoliberalism have taken root. In many ways, it is the local variation of capitalism itself that influences the particular form and taste of the fast food that is eventually offered to consumers. The myriad fast food types available worldwide reflect the diverse ways in which contemporary capitalism manifests at the local level (Blim 2000).

The fact that corporate chain restaurants have successfully made inroads in so many parts of the world (Norton 2000; Downie 2000) is one of the reasons that anthropologists and others find fast food such an intriguing research topic. The empirical literature on fast food has expanded considerably in the last twenty-five years. Since the late 1970s, when social scientists first began to recognize fast food as a legitimate area of investigation (Kottak 1978), a growing body of work on fast food and its socioeconomic implications has been compiled (Fantasia 1995; Kincheloe 2002; Kruèsteva-Blagoeva 2001; Ritzer 1998, 2001; Talwar 2002).

When considered in concert this research has produced some revealing insights into the degree to which our social lives and consumer expectations have been shaped by fast food (Ritzer 2000; Stephenson 1989). Moreover, it has illuminated the transformative role ventures of this type bring to bear at the state and community level (Stolicna 2000; Watson 1997).

Not discounting the merits of these works, it would be erroneous to suggest that all aspects of fast food have received equal consideration from sociocultural researchers. Certain facets of this phenomenon appear to have captured more of the social scientific imagination relative to others. For example, nearly all of the anthropological literature on fast food deals with matters of consumption; that is, how consumers conceive of chain restaurants, utilize their products, and adapt to the contexts they create (Bosco 1999; Watson 1997). Less ethnographic attention has been directed toward the role of production or the ways in which fast food outlets emerge, operate, and engage local markets.

Equally, there tends to be a geographical predilection for researchers investigating the globalization of fast food. Most studies examining the sociocultural impact of fast food outside of the West focus on the developed nations of East Asia (Bosco 1999; Jing 2000; Noguchi 1999; Traphagan and Brown 2002; Zhongqiang 1999/2000). Anthropologists have especially trained their eyes on the growth of fast food in the region's major metropolitan centers (Watson 1997).

That so much interest is paid to the urban areas of Japan, China, South Korea, and Taiwan and not elsewhere is probably of little surprise. The Far East has undergone a sustained period of economic expansion over the last few decades that has created conditions favoring economies of scale. This growth, in turn, has facilitated the rise of national and multinational fast food corporations (Terry 2002). Such conditions have been absent in other regions until more recent times. The previously limited presence of chain restaurants in most non-Western societies has provided anthropologists with few real opportunities to study the effects of fast food away from East Asia's major cities.

So far, questions related to the spread of chain restaurants outside of the developed world have not been fully explored by anthropologists. While the urban populations of East Asia are still recognized as important fast food consumers, they no longer represent its only international market. Largely in response to an emerging middle class, quick service eateries are becoming pervasive features of cityscapes within less developed countries (LDCs) (Downie 2000; Lee and Karkoviata 2001; Norton 2000; Rai 2005).

As fast food begins to spread into LDCs, it is essential that the geographical scope of fast food ethnographies broaden. Such work will not only elucidate the various ways in which global trends affect local communities, it will also shed light on the increasing economic variability underlying local capitalisms worldwide.

Likewise, it will contribute to our understanding of how fast food operations first arise within non-Western contexts. Finally, it will provide an opportunity for exploring the marketing strategies and operating procedures of chain restaurants in societies with marked socioeconomic disparities.

This chapter examines the recent encroachment of fast food into the political economy of a provincial Philippine city—San Fernando City, La Union. The Philippines presents an ideal setting for this type of research. The 1990s witnessed accelerated growth in the country's fast food industry. By 2000, there were approximately two thousand fast food eateries operating nationwide with some sixty million regular patrons. Significantly, these consumers spent considerable amounts on fast food even when they had little discretionary income (Business Asia 2000).

By concentrating more on the production side of this phenomenon, it is my aim to draw attention to the underlying complexities of fast food within a developing context. The interplay between local entities and nonlocal corporate interests is of particular significance. The opening of an enterprise like McDonald's in communities outside of the developed West is often viewed as a form of "cultural imperialism" whereby more affluent countries impose their consumer tastes, market practices, and ideologies onto local populations (Friedman 1999:21; Ritzer 2000:174–76). Central to this assessment are the notions that (1) fast food inevitably gives rise to increased global cultural homogeneity; and that (2) developing communities are effectively powerless to resist or countervail the unrelenting forces of mass consumerism.

While this perspective is not unfounded, it should be pointed out that the establishment of a chain restaurant within the developing context rarely occurs without some degree of local receptivity or cooperation. Far from being a one-sided process, the opening of a modern fast food eatery at the municipal level normally depends upon the efforts of local individuals and groups. These interests often act as a driving force behind the spread of fast food into LDCs. Their contributions to this transnational trend underscore the various ways in which the standardized fast food model can be utilized to meet local market demands. Dealings between outside developers and local entities create a compelling framework for investigating matters of how the dual processes of globalization and localization interface and influence each other.

Issues and Objectives

Three major restaurant chains—McDonald's, Chowking, and Jollibee—opened outlets in and around San Fernando's central business district in 1996 and 1997. Details of fast food expansion and the influence of local interests over global processes are more fully understood by documenting their respective experiences in San Fernando.

After a providing a community profile of San Fernando City in the mid-1990s, I describe the development and organization of municipal trade over recent decades. Next, I consider the respective cases of McDonald's, Chowking, and Jollibee and examine the circumstances that allowed each to establish a presence in San Fernando. I then synthesize these accounts so that their individual experiences can be critically evaluated against one another. Finally, I summarize the findings of this chapter and relate San Fernando's experience to the spread of fast food in the Philippines and other LDCs.

Essentially, this work offers an anthropological account of (1) how rival fast food companies penetrate developing markets and (2) how their efforts are facilitated and modified by local interests. Information collected through intensive interviews, participant-observation, and other field methods adds ethnographic depth to a process that is transforming communities worldwide.

San Fernando: A Community Profile (1990s)

San Fernando is located on the main Philippine island of Luzon along the Lingayen Gulf some three hundred kilometers north of Manila. This bustling city operates as the primary trade, governmental, financial, health care, and educational center for the province of La Union. San Fernando's *poblacion* (city center) is composed of numerous mid-rise buildings and is bisected by a well-traveled highway known as the Manila North Road.

Most of San Fernando's hundred-thousand inhabitants claim an Ilocano ancestry. Ilocanos represent the third largest ethnic group in the Philippines and are traditionally recognized for their hard-working and enterprising tendencies (Pertierra 1992; Sawyer 1900; Scott 1986). So omnipresent are Ilocanos in San Fernando, in fact, that nearly nine out of every ten individuals classify themselves as Ilocano (National Statistics Office 1997). The city is also home to a small but powerful nonindigenous group that has figured prominently in local affairs since the midnineteenth century. San Fernando's ethnic Chinese community has contributed to the city's rise in numerous ways. Nowhere is this more evident than in matters of municipal trade. This tight-knit community has remained at the forefront of area commerce for generations even though they have never made up more than five percent of the total population. Broadly speaking, most large-scale commercial enterprises in San Fernando have owner-operators with a Chinese heritage.

Commercial Organization and Development

The basic morphology of San Fernando's commercial organization conforms to the dichotomous formal/informal economic model. Locals rely extensively on the informal sector to meet everyday employment and consumption needs. Over the years, the vendors and micro-enterprises that comprise this economic sphere have played an integral role in shaping and defining area commerce. In contrast, more expensive and value-added items are purchased from outlets within the town's formal trade sector. These ventures have proliferated in recent years as nonlocal corporate interests have stepped up their efforts to secure more of San Fernando's consumer market.

Formal sector operations maintained a rather limited presence in San Fernando until more recent times. From the end of World War II until the late 1970s, the formal sector encompassed just a few independently owned street stores, micro-groceries, service stations, and small family restaurants. These ventures were concentrated in the *poblacion* and maintained tenuous linkages with manufacturers and suppliers headquartered in Manila.

A notable shift in local commerce occurred in the late 1970s. This change came about gradually as market supply channels grew less fragmented and franchising and corporate dealerships became more prevalent. By the late 1980s, several modern supermarkets, department stores, and appliance/electronics showrooms were operating in downtown. It was also around this time that fast food made a modest appearance onto the local scene. Two multinational fast food companies (Dunkin' Donuts and Mister Donut) and one national chain (Cindy's) opened outlets within the *poblacion*. The latter, Cindy's, operated like an American diner but went out of business after a few years due to a lack of customers.

At the time, most San Fernandians viewed Dunkin' Donuts, Mister Donut, and Cindy's as little more than passing novelties. Several years would pass before this type of fare would catch on and fast food companies could begin expanding their San Fernando operations. Rather than ushering in a new period of fast food expansion, the arrival of Dunkin' Donuts, Mister Donut, and Cindy's merely hinted at what would later become a trend of chain restaurant growth.

San Fernando underwent a major surge of retail expansion in the mid-1990s. The opening of a bi-level strip mall along the Manila North Road just south of the *poblacion* in early 1996 marked a turning point for formal sector commercial growth. Known as the Christ the King College (CKC) Commercial Center since it was owned by the local Catholic diocese, the shopping center quickly became a focal point for fast food expansion at the local level. Two modern chain eateries—Mister Donut and Giacomino's Pizza and Pasta—were housed at opposite ends of the strip mall. The new Mister Donut outlet was virtually identical to the firm's downtown branch, while Giacomino's Pizza and Pasta operated as a modern pizzeria similar to Pizza Hut.

Fast Food Expansion

Following the launch of the CKC Commercial Center, three of the nation's largest fast food chains set up operations along the Manila North Road. San Fernando's commercial landscape came to include a McDonald's, Jollibee, and Chowking by the spring of 1997. With regard to service style, consumer amenities, sanitary conditions, and indoor setup, the restaurants were quite similar. They differed in terms of location, size, exterior design, menu selection, and primary clientele.

McDonald's

The Golden Arches first appeared over San Fernando in June 1997 with the opening of a McDonald's just opposite the CKC Commercial Center. The restaurant represented the company's first foray into La Union, although most locals were already familiar with the brand. McDonald's had been in the Philippines since 1981 and, thanks to a popular advertising campaign featuring Filipino celebrities dining on Big Macs, French fries, and Coca-Cola, had built up a significant consumer following. By the mid-1990s, the fast food giant had well over 150 outlets operating nationwide and several menu items developed specifically around Filipino tastes like McSpaghetti and Mango Shakes.

The events surrounding McDonald's appearance in San Fernando are much in keeping with the company's strategy of utilizing local partners as much as possible (Watson 1997:12). This approach entails McDonald's—through its overseas master franchise holder—entering into a franchise agreement with a local individual or firm for a contract period of no less than ten years. Under such an arrangement, the local partner puts up a substantial franchise fee and secures a property suitable for the restaurant facility. In some instances, a market feasibility study put together by the franchise applicant is required before contract negotiations can move forward.

Once the franchise agreement is finalized, the local operator takes charge of the restaurant's daily operations and pays the company an adjustable monthly rental. With at least a 40- to 50-percent stake in its international operations, the McDonald's Corporation is able to exact compliance from its franchise holders with regard to things like quality control and automated style of service. Yet, branch managers are able to exert considerable autonomy when it comes to advertising, distributing profits, and adapting to specific changes in the local market (Love 1986:431; Watson 1997:36–38).

The franchise for San Fernando's McDonald's was secured by a local ethnic Chinese family whose dealings in municipal commerce date back to the 1930s: the Tans. Although they have operated a number of successful wholesale and retail ventures over the years including the selling of tobacco, groceries, electronics, and appliances, the Tans truly made a name for themselves operating one of the community's most successful commercial firms—the Philippine Bazaar Corporation. The Tans' story exemplifies the dynamic role overseas Chinese family firms play in driving local commercial developments throughout Southeast Asia and beyond (Dannhaeuser 2004; Mackie 1999; Wong 1985).

Numbering a dozen or so, the Philippine Bazaar Corporation's board of directors is composed primarily of second-generation family members. The firm was officially formed in the early 1980s to consolidate the business holdings created by the first generation of Tan entrepreneurs. By the 1990s, this umbrella company had diversified into a number of specialized trade ventures within the greater San Fernando area.

Tapping into the local fast food market had been a move the Tans contemplated for several years. After carefully weighing their options, the family decided to approach McGeorge Food Industries Corporation—an ethnic Chinese business concern based in Manila that holds the master franchise for McDonald's operations in the Philippines—about opening a McDonald's in San Fernando. Their decision to go with McDonald's hinged on the fact that the chain was one of the few major fast food brands in the Philippines without a local branch.

As luck would have it, McGeorge Foods was also looking to put up a restaurant in La Union. The company was in the midst of expanding its McDonald's operations in northern Luzon when it received the unsolicited franchise proposal from the Tans (*Philippine Daily Inquirer* 1998). Their application met with enthusiastic support from company representatives. The family's high standing in area business, coupled with the connections they cultivated through their participation in the grocery trade and La Union Chinese Chamber of Commerce, worked to their advantage. Upon successfully completing the franchise application process, the Tans were approved as McDonald's operators in 1996.

Unlike its competitors, the new McDonald's does not occupy a space within a previously established commercial building but, rather, operates as a free-standing outlet. With a stand-alone restaurant, the Tans were required to pay more in construction costs. Their McDonald's franchise, thus, entailed a higher start-up investment (approximately P15 million) relative to San Fernando's other chain restaurants.

The local McDonald's lives up to the efficiency and standards that consumers expect from the fast food giant. Customers are greeted by a life-size Ronald McDonald replica as they enter the premises. The well-lit interior gives the place a family-friendly atmosphere. Beyond food, the restaurant also offers consumers amenities like an indoor playground, children's birthday parties, clean restrooms, and a stylish design. Approximately fifty workers, all of whom appear youthful and upbeat in their employee uniforms, make up the restaurant's staff.

The new McDonald's stands apart from other fast food eateries in San Fernando as it is geared mainly for those not living in the *poblacion*. The Tans made a special effort to attract those customers more inclined to make the short trip from downtown: namely, jeepney passengers and those with private vehicles. This orientation toward local commuters is reflected in a number of car-friendly features including a passenger drop-off area, a sizable parking lot, and—for the first time in this part of the Philippines—a drive-thru window. By offering these services, McDonald's was able to turn a healthy profit in its first year in San Fernando. So successful was the new McDonald's, in fact, that the Tans soon started plans for another free-standing outlet along the Manila North Road just north of the *poblacion*.

Chowking

Not enjoying the same level of success as McDonald's, although still quite popular with diners, is the local Chowking. The restaurant presents an alternative to hamburgers and French fries by offering selections of Chinese fast food. Consumers can select from a diverse menu with offerings like *mami* noodles, *siopao* (steamed bun filled with meat), and chicken and beef dishes served with rice. The chain eatery is the brainchild of Chinese-Filipino Robert F. Kuan, who entered the nation's fast food industry in 1985. Before being acquired by Jollibee Foods Corporation in 2000, his Chowking Foods Corporation had some 130 outlets (5,000 employees) in the Philippines (Quimpo-Espino 1998).

The Chowking in San Fernando was established in early 1997 within a downtown vendor complex not far from the Jollibee known as the Perez Galleria. The local franchise is operated by Raymond and Eduardo Perez, two brothers from a prominent Filipino family that has been active in area commerce and politics for generations. Like the Tans, the Perez family maintains various business interests in San Fernando including a bank, a bus line, an appliance store, and a movie house.

The circumstances behind how the Perez brothers secured the Chowking franchise owes as much to serendipity as it does to their business expertise. In the mid-1990s, Raymond was looking for a franchise venture of some kind to occupy the unused sections of the movie theater's lobby. At the time, he was not thinking specifically in terms of fast food but rather wanted something to capitalize on this vacant retail space. While he had some experience with enterprises of this type beforehand—he maintained the franchise for Mr. Quickee (a nationwide key and shoe repair company) in San Fernando since 1994—he was not having much luck tracking down other franchise opportunities. Things changed in 1996, however, after Raymond was put in touch with the Chowking Food Corporation through one of his film distributors.

Having dealt with Chowking on previous occasions, the film distributor, unbeknown to Raymond, invited company representatives to San Fernando to inspect the theater lobby. Impressed with what they saw, Chowking offered Raymond a franchise contract almost immediately. At the time, the standard Chowking franchise contract was for ten years and required a capital investment on the part of the franchise holder of approximately eight million pesos with an annual royalty fee of 6 percent of gross sales.

Initially, Raymond had difficulty meeting all of the franchise expenses on his own. Even though he would have minimal overhead because he already owned the property, Raymond did not have the start-up capital on hand. Thus, he brought in his brother, Eduardo, to be the restaurant's primary backer. With the Perez brothers' finances in order, the deal was finalized and, by late 1996, construction on the restaurant completed. The San Fernando Chowking had its official grand opening in January 1997.

Although the restaurant is smaller and has fewer employees compared to Jollibee and McDonald's, it does sport many of the same amenities as its rivals—a modern interior design and efficient service system. Significantly, the outlet is one of the *poblacion*'s few all-night eateries. The extended hours attract a pool of customers to Chowking not usually served by its fast food competitors. The restaurant's late night clientele includes jeepney drivers, movie patrons, and those disembarking from the nearby bus depot.

Perhaps more distinguishing in the case of Chowking compared to its rivals is its specialized Chinese menu. Chowking simply offers consumers fast food they cannot get at McDonald's or Jollibee. Especially popular with patrons is *Halo-halo*, a decidedly non-Chinese (read Filipino) layered dessert made of equal parts ice cream, condensed milk, crushed ice, diced gelatin, and an assortment of candied toppings. This traditional treat is often consumed at *merienda* (afternoon snack) and remains one of Chowking's most popular offerings. While features like extended business hours and a distinctive menu helped the restaurant earn a respectable profit in its first year, Chowking's success probably owes more to low overhead costs since the Perezes already owned the property.

Jollibee

The largest and most popular chain restaurant to open in San Fernando during the mid-1990s was the two-story Jollibee situated in a building complex directly across from the town plaza. The spacious eatery sports a red/orange color scheme with numerous images of the corporate mascot—a cartoon bee in a chef's hat—and the slogan *"Langhap Sarap!"* ("Smells Delicious!"). On the first floor, one finds a bustling eatery filled with customers. The lines to the service counter often extend as far back as the store's entrance during busy meal times. The upstairs contains restrooms, a playground, and a banquet room.

The Jollibee staff is composed mainly of wage-earners in their late teens and early twenties who provide a high level of customer service. The restaurant's menu-board offers a wide selection of Jollibee favorites like Champs (large hamburgers), Yums! (small hamburgers), Jolly Spaghetti, Shanghai Rolls (fried spring rolls), Jolly Hot Dogs, Burger Steaks, Fried Mango Pies, and *Palabok* Fiesta (traditional Filipino pasta lathered with a special pork-shrimp sauce).

The phenomenal rise of the Jollibee Food Corporation in the Philippines is the stuff of national legend. The fast food giant was founded by ethnic Chinese entrepreneur Tony Tan Caktiong and his brothers in the mid-1970s. Jollibee originally operated as a neighborhood ice cream parlor in Manila but quickly shifted focus to hamburgers and French fries. Over the course of two decades, the company established hundreds of Jollibee restaurants across the Philippines. By the 1990s, thanks to an aggressive marketing plan and the Tan Caktiongs' hands-on approach, Jollibee emerged as the top fast food brand in the Philippines. More remarkably, it also became one of Southeast Asia's most successful corporations. Jollibee maintains a commanding 55 percent share of the Philippines' fast food market. For 2002, the company posted upwards of P27 billion in corporate earnings, exceeding the previous year's high of some P24 billion. Notably, the Philippines is one of the few countries where McDonald's does not control the largest share of the fast food market (*Economist* 2002; McGurn 1997).

Part of Jollibee's success rests on its strategy of appropriating those techniques developed by rival firms, especially those of McDonald's. Early on, the Tan Caktiongs paid careful attention to McDonald's overseas operations. From a nearly duplicate color scheme to a food preparation system that is all but identical, the company has made a concerted effort to copy those aspects of McDonald's that have proven effective.

Even more integral to Jollibee's dominance, however, is the firm's intimate understanding of the Filipino palate. More so than its competitors, Jollibee has been able to develop products that appeal to local tastes. Most Jollibee menu items are notably sweeter and juicier compared to what is served at McDonald's and other modern fast food outlets (McGurn 1997). This ability to satisfy Filipino appetites, coupled with an efficient service model, has proven a winning formula for the company.

Unlike Chowking and McDonald's, the new Jollibee in San Fernando was launched as a branch outlet operated exclusively by the company. The prospect of minimizing financial risks by taking on a local partner was not a major concern for Jollibee given the growth in San Fernando's emerging fast food scene. This nonfranchise strategy did not really affect the interplay between outside corporate firms and local interests within the city's fast food sector. Area consumers were still able to influence Jollibee marketing efforts as the firm carved out its market niche in San Fernando.

For instance, the bi-level restaurant features a number of innovations designed with local families in mind. The eatery boasts an indoor playground and rents out sections of the second floor for children's birthday parties. The company is also a major supporter of local youth events. No less important to Jollibee's success in San Fernando is its free take-out service. The restaurant employs a number of uniformed drivers to deliver food orders throughout the city via motor-scooters. This service has made the eatery especially popular with downtown professionals who are unable to leave the office during lunch hours.

So well received was Jollibee on the municipal level, in fact, that by 1997 the company bought one of the *poblacion*'s few remaining large commercial lots. Located only three blocks north of its flagship restaurant at a major downtown intersection, the new Jollibee site was to serve as a multi-branch fast food complex. It will house another Jollibee as well as an outlet of its sister operation, the company-owned Greenwich Pizza.

Synthesis

The commercial landscape of San Fernando began to undergo a significant transformation in the mid-1990s. Soon after the CKC Commercial Center was opened in 1996, the municipal retail climate became increasingly favorable toward formal sector commercial enterprises. This new market orientation became most fully realized with the opening of a McDonald's, Chowking, and Jollibee along the Manila North Road.

A number of outside commercial firms (McGeorge Food Industries Corporation, the Chowking Food Corporation, and the Jollibee Food Corporation) were at the forefront of fast food expansion in San Fernando. All three restaurant chains are headquartered in Manila and are owned and/or managed by ethnic Chinese entrepreneurs. Significantly, these companies are able to access both Philippine financial institutions and overseas kin networks as sources of investment capital (Haley, Chin, and Haley 1998; Yoshihara 1988). However, they were not the only force helping drive fast food growth. Several area Filipino and ethnic Chinese business concerns (the Perez brothers and the Philippine Bazaar Corporation) and the town's Catholic diocese also contributed to establishing fast food outlets in and around the *poblacion*. Clearly, the emergence of quick service eateries in San Fernando would not have occurred as easily without the participation of key players in community life.

Differing fundamentally from more traditional retail ventures in terms of scale and that they set out to offer San Fernandians consumer experiences heretofore unavailable, the local McDonald's, Chowking, and Jollibee met with considerable success in their first few months of operation. So well received were Jollibee and McDonald's, in fact, that plans were initiated by both to establish additional outlets within and just beyond downtown. This intensification of fast food activity in San Fernando, in turn, helped stimulate growth in other areas of the municipal economy. Owner-operators of some of the *poblacion's* more substantial family restaurants, groceries, and street stores chose to either increase their respective floor space and/or refurbish their existing facilities during this time. By the spring of 1998, enough retail modernization had occurred locally to suggest that municipal commerce was advancing away from its more historical character.

Although San Fernando's three major fast food eateries display a number of similarities, they also differ in notable ways. The main difference distinguishing McDonald's, Chowking, and Jollibee from one another is that each sets out to serve a distinct segment of the local consumer population. In general, McDonald's is geared toward attracting commuters, tourists, and highway travelers; Chowking is outfitted primarily for night owls, bus travelers, and to a lesser degree Chinese-Filipinos; and Jollibee caters to families and those living and working in the *poblacion*. Beyond this, there are also less pronounced differences related to organizational styles (franchise versus corporate branch), menu items (hamburgers versus Chinese food), and degree of outside corporate oversight.

Conclusion

San Fernando's experience with fast food is not an isolated incident. It is merely one example of a local community confronting a trend that is spreading through many parts of the developing world (Miller 1997). To better understand the position of San Fernando within the larger context of fast food globalization, it is useful to consider how events leading up to and resulting from the arrival of McDonald's, Chowking, and Jollibee relate to the growth of fast food in the Philippines specifically and other LDCs more generally.

Dining out at chain restaurants has become an increasingly common aspect of Philippine life (Business Asia 2000). The rise of a new middle class has created conditions where Filipino households now have more discretionary income at their disposal and less time to prepare and cook meals at home as more women join the workforce. Domestic and foreign fast food firms have responded to this shifting demographic picture by expanding their presence in Philippine towns and cities. In many ways, this proliferation of quick service eateries can be viewed as a direct response to the demand created by middle-class families for pre-cooked meals that are convenient, affordable, and served in clean surroundings. Jollibee, McDonald's, and others have spent considerable sums advertising and marketing their products to this newly affluent segment of the population. Obviously, the fast food industry will continue to flourish as long as the purchasing power of the middle class remains strong.

Beyond the Philippines, fast food continues to make headway into the previously untapped markets of the developing world (Norton 2000; Downie 2000). The automated service model developed in the industrialized West has gained near-global acceptance even though significant differences still persist from society to society in terms of cultural traditions and norms. The success of this service strategy rests largely on its interchangeability. It can operate efficiently in a variety of retail formats irrespective of cultural context. As it relates to fast food, it lends itself quite well to capitalizing on local tastes to create menu items that are simultaneously novel and familiar. While the standard fast food fare of hamburgers, French fries, and soft drinks remains pretty much the same the world over, modifications that conform to regional tastes and customs are a key strategy for corporate chains expanding operations around the globe (Ritzer 2000:172–73).

Even in the face of these achievements, there have been some obstacles along the way. One of the challenges that fast food corporations typically encounter as they move into developing areas is a lack of sufficient market integration. Certainly, this complicates their ability to coordinate with suppliers and deliver products in an efficient manner. One way of coping with a fragmented market network is by relying upon local institutions (Watson 1997:12–13). The successful penetration of outside fast food brands requires assistance and cooperation from local firms and other interests at the community level.

Although the institution of fast food originated in the United States, it has become increasingly modified to fit local conditions as it penetrates developing areas. As the case studies from San Fernando illustrate, local firms and other interests play an active role in bringing these chain restaurants to area consumers. To varying degrees, this is accomplished through securing franchise operations, cultivating personal ties with company representatives, and adapting standard fast food fare to better correspond with local conditions.

Note

Acknowledgments. The material presented in this chapter was collected in the Philippines between 1997 and 1998. Part of the research was supported by a fellowship from the Leland T. and Jessie W. Jordan Institute for International Awareness, Texas A&M University. My research was also sponsored by the Institute of Philippine Culture, Ateneo de Manila University, Quezon City. In describing the franchise owners of San Fernando's McDonald's and Chowking, pseudonyms were used in place of actual family and business names.

References

Blim, Michael. 2000. Capitalisms in Late Modernity. Annual Review of Anthropology 29:25–38.

Bosco, Joseph. 1999. An Anthropological View of the Hong Kong McDonald's Snoopy Craze. Hong Kong Anthropologist 12:23–30.

Business Asia. 2000. Cashed-up Filipinos Feast on Fast Food. Business Asia, February 11.

Dannhaeuser, Norbert. 2004. Chinese Traders in a Philippine Town. Quezon City: Ateneo de Manila University Press.

Downie, Andrew. 2000. Barrio Burgers: McXperiment: Serving Billions in the Slums? Christian Science Monitor, January 26.

Economist. 2002. A Busy Bee in the Hamburger Hive. If McDonald's Is the Goliath of Fast Food, Tony Tan's Jollibee Is Its Filipino David. Economist, February 28.

Fantasia, Rick. 1995. Fast Food in France. Theory and Society 24:201–43.

Friedman, Thomas L. 1999. The Lexus and the Olive Tree: Understanding Globalization. New York: Farrar, Strauss, Giroux.

Haley, George T., Tiong Tan Chin, and Usha C. V. Haley. 1998. New Asian Emperors: The Overseas Chinese, Their Strategies and Competitive Advantage. Boston: Butterworth Heinemann.

Jing, Jun, ed. 2000. Feeding China's Little Emperors: Food, Children, and Social Change. Palo Alto: Stanford University Press.

Kincheloe, Joe L. 2002. The Sign of the Burger: McDonald's and the Culture of Power. Labor in Crisis. Philadelphia: Temple University Press.

Kottak, Conrad B. 1978. Rituals at McDonald's. Natural History 87(1):78–83.

Kruèsteva-Blagoeva, Evgeniia. 2001. Bulgarians and McDonald's. Bulgarska etnologiia 27(1):26–37.

Lee, James, and Leonie Karkoviata. 2000. Fast Track to Growth: Homegrown Enterprises Leverage on Proven Franchising Systems. Asian Business 37(12):29–36.

Love, John F. 1986. McDonald's: Behind the Golden Arches. New York: Bantam Books.

Mackie, J. A. C. 1999. Chinese Business Organization. In The Encyclopedia of the Chinese Overseas. Lynn Pan, ed. Pp. 91–93. Cambridge, MA: Harvard University Press.

Matejowsky, Ty. 2002. Globalization and Retail Development in the Post-Disaster Context: A Comparison of Two Philippine Communities. In Research in Economic Anthropology, vol. 21: Social Dimensions in the Economic Process. Norbert Dannhaeuser and Cynthia Werner, eds. Pp. 311–41. Amsterdam, Holland: Elsevier-JAI Press.

McGurn, William. 1997. Home Advantage: Local Chain Upstages McDonald's in the Philippines. Far Eastern Economic Review 160(47):70.

Miller, Daniel. 1997. Capitalism: An Ethnographic Approach. Oxford: Berg Publishers.

National Statistics Office. 1997. Census of Population. Report No. 2-49. Manila: A (La Union) Socio-Economic and Demographic Characteristics.

Noguchi, Paul H. 1999. Savor Slowly: The Fast Food of High-Speed Japan. Ethnology 33(4):317–30.

Norton, Michael. 2000. Today's Special: Happiness: New Fast-Food Joint in Haiti a Beacon Amid Gloom. Houston Chronicle, September 5.

Pertierra, Raul, ed. 1992. Remittances and Returnees: The Cultural Economy of Migration in Ilocos. Quezon City, Philippines: New Day Publishers.

Philippine Daily Inquirer. 1998. McDonald's to Pursue Expansion, March 21.

Quimpo-Espino, Margie. 1998. Local Chinese Food Chain Wants to Be in Every Nook and Cranny of the World. Philippine Daily Inquirer, March 20.

Rai, Saritha. 2005. India's Boom Spreads to Smaller Cities. New York Times, January 4:C3.

Ritzer, George. 1998. The McDonaldization Thesis. London: Sage Publications.

———. 2000. The McDonaldization of Society. Thousand Oaks, CA: Pine Forge Press.

———. 2001. Explorations in the Sociology of Consumption: Fast Food, Credit Cards and Casinos. London: Sage Publications.

Sawyer, Frederic H. 1900. The Inhabitants of the Philippines. New York: Scribner.

Schlosser, Eric. 2001. Fast Food Nation: The Dark Side of the All-American Meal. Boston: Houghton Mifflin.

Scott, William Henry. 1986. Ilocano Responses to American Aggression, 1900–1901. Quezon City, Philippines: New Day Publishers.

Stephenson, Peter H. 1989. Going to McDonald's in Leiden. Ethos 17(2):226–47.

Stolicna, Rastislava. 2000. Fast Food: The Global Phenomenon of Today's Eating Habits and Lifestyle. Slovensky Narodopis 48:305–13.

Talwar, Jennifer Parker. 2002. Fast Food, Fast Track? Immigrants, Big Business, and the American Dream. Boulder, CO: Westview Press.

Terry, Edith. 2002. How Asia Got Rich: Japan, China and the Asian Miracle. Armonk, New York: M. E. Sharpe.

Traphagan, John, and Keith Brown. 2002. Fast Food and Intergenerational Commensality in Japan: New Styles and Old Patterns. Ethnology 41(2):129.

Watson, James, ed. 1997. Golden Arches East: McDonald's in East Asia. Palo Alto: Stanford University Press.

Wong, Siu-lun. 1985. The Chinese Family Firm: A Model. The British Journal of Sociology 36(1):58–72.

Yoshihara, Kunio. 1988. The Rise of Ersatz Capitalism in South-East Asia. Oxford: Oxford University Press.

Zhongqiang, Jin. 1999/2000. Kentucky Fried Chicken, McDonald's and Chinese Drama. Chinese Sociology and Anthropology 32(2):35–7.

TRANSFORMING MARKETS AND RECONNECTING WITH CONSUMERS

IV

From the Bottom Up: The Global Expansion of Chinese Vegetable Trade for New York City Markets   11

VALERIE IMBRUCE

N EW YORK CITY presents an enormous and ever-changing market for a vast diversity of food products. In New York you can indulge your senses in sticky Jordanian pastries made with pistachios imported from Afghanistan, Amazonian *açaí* whipped into shakes, and a steaming bowl of Vietnamese *pho* with a fresh sprig of Thai basil floating atop. New York City prides itself on the ability to offer authentic tastes from distant corners of the world. This joy of urban life depends on a global order of trade. Traditional food products increasingly come from nontraditional places.[1] Chinese okra is grown in Honduras, rambutan in Guatemala, and longan in Mexico. New York, like most other cities, contributes to a supposedly efficient, industrial, and corporately controlled food system. Such agribusiness developed in part to feed burgeoning urban populations. Yet within the same cities that support industrial agriculture, other systems are defined and redefined every day. The many spaces of New York City offer opportunities for alternatives to the seemingly dominant political economic reality of corporate globalization. Multilingual, transnational peoples find ways to use spaces not appropriated by corporate interests to create their own international systems of capital exchange.

Immigrant populations develop alternative food systems, yet they have not been adequately analyzed, empirically or theoretically, in the food system literature. Studies have analyzed the ethnicities of farm workers highlighting otherwise invisible aspects of production systems (Wells 1996). Ethnicity, however, has not been considered in studies of marketing and distribution (Friedland 2001). Researchers are finding that the activities of once seemingly ephemeral immigrant communities are playing an important and unnoticed role in global political and economic restructuring, particularly in New York City (Stoller 2002; Guest 2003), and that global circulation is not just the rhetoric of corporate expansion (Tsing 2000). The complexities and dynamism of cities in particular present a multitude of opportunities for activities alternative to dominant structures (Harvey 2001).

In this chapter I begin to sketch what I see as an alternative food system in New York City, the Chinatown food system. The Chinese control their own distribution networks, moving thousands of boxes of fruits and vegetables a day through warehouses in Manhattan and Brooklyn to be sold by independent greengrocers and street vendors in the city's multiple Chinatowns. While some Chinese merchants use Hunt's Point Terminal Market, the city's main distribution point and the country's largest terminal market for conventional fruits and vegetables, the vast majority of Asian products are traded by Chinese brokers outside of Hunt's Point.

The practice of fruit and vegetable exchange in Chinatown has historical roots. Since the development of a Chinese enclave in lower Manhattan over one hundred years ago, the Chinese have created their own networks of exchange. Local farms in New Jersey and Long Island operated by Chinese families grew and trucked fruits and vegetables preferred by the urban Chinese to be sold in Chinatown markets.

Currently Chinatown's fresh fruit and vegetable markets are part of a highly complex, global system of production and distribution. Fresh food products now come from New York state, New Jersey, Florida, California, Mexico, Honduras, and the Dominican Republic as well as Taiwan, mainland China, and other places. Although Chinatown's food system is undergoing rapid geographic expansion, it does not display the hegemonic tendencies of global agro-food systems (McMichael 1994; Lyson and Raymer 2000; Goodman and Watts 1997; Bonnano et al. 1994; Barndt 2002). The industry is neither vertically nor horizontally integrated, nor has it been subject to corporate appropriation. From farm to retail level, businesses are individually owned and operated. Transport is contracted by independent trucking companies, and as many as three brokers may be involved in international commodity chains. Individuals who grow, sell, import, and export Chinese fruits and vegetables employ their cultural knowledge about food preferences, language skills, and kin and ethnic ties to develop a food system to meet the demands of Chinese, other East Asian, and Southeast Asian ethnic groups.

Can a Global Food System Meet the Goals of "Alternative" Food Systems?

Food systems that contest, resist, and oppose global agro-food systems share a political agenda for ecological sustainability, economic viability, and social justice. Alternatives are united in the practice of reconstructing a locally situated, decentralized food system (Kloppenburg et al. 1996; Hinrichs 2000), or in the commodification of ecologically and socially responsible food production and trade (Guthman 2000; Murray and Raynolds 2000). Tensions between local and global processes are constantly negotiated and it is clear that the local-global binary is problematic. Although it has been recognized that the ideology of alternative food systems has been better theorized than the practice itself (Allen et al. 2003), the tensions between the local and global have not been reconsidered in theory or in practice. The commitment to the relocalization of agriculture is indeed an important one, but I am afraid that it may obscure merits of other systems, particularly systems that feed people across class boundaries. We cannot ignore that farmers' markets, artisan slow foods, organic, and fairly traded foods can often be prohibitively expensive, and they may only appeal to certain demographics as well as class sensibilities. We continue to face the challenge of defining the many manifestations of "alternativeness" (Watts et al. 2005).

If we compare part of the mission of slow food and its sister alternatives—to conserve agricultural diversity and protect traditional foods—to Chinatown's food system, there is a clear commonality. Supplying a market with over one hundred types of fresh, culturally specific ingredients year round, as Chinatown's food system does, can very much help conserve biodiversity as well as gastronomic traditions. *Cittaslow* (slow cities), according to their website, seek to promote something "less frantic, yielding, and fast—no doubt more human, environmentally correct and sensible." Chinatown at any given moment is often frantic, but when you step back and think about how the community has retained so much of its cultural tradition while the city is constantly changing and hybrid cultures are constantly forming, you recognize the "slowness" of New York's Chinese community. The pace of immigration and trade may deliver change, but it can also slow change. New immigrants sustain old habits, and old habits are sustained by trade.

This chapter seeks to bring the global into the alternative food system discussion by exploring what Chinatown's food system looks like. While the Chinatown food system *in practice* displays part of the vision of alternative food systems, it does not share in its political agenda. The global expansion of the food system follows processes outside of the dominant industrial and corporately controlled food system, but not by consciously resisting it. I argue that Chinatown's food system constitutes an alternative global food system in which individual entrepreneurs are making new spatial connections through their lived experiences, and that this system contributes biological diversity to produce stands of the city, as well as helping sustain cultural practices of new and old urban inhabitants.

The Development of Chinatown's Food System

The development of Chinatown's food system is intertwined with the history of Chinese immigration and the development of the Chinese enclave in lower Manhattan. The first major wave of Chinese immigration to the United States was from Canton Province (now Guangdong) and began over one hundred years ago. Until this migration, only small populations of Chinese sailors, cooks, and others involved in U.S.-China trade were living in lower Manhattan in the mid-1800s in the multiethnic Five Points area. After the British forced open the ports of southeastern China in the Opium War (1839–1842), Chinese laborers from the port city of Canton (now Guanzhou) were transported to California to mine in the Gold Rush. They later went on to build the western spur of the transcontinental railroad. At this time Chinese "coolies" were also sent to the Caribbean and South America, and many Chinese immigrated to locations through Southeast Asia initiating the Chinese diaspora. As a result of these labor migrations, New York's Chinese population expanded steadily in the late 1870s.

An economic recession heightened antipathy toward the Chinese. Many Chinese departed from California back to China or to the East Coast to escape California's racially charged environment. Anti-Chinese sentiments were codified with the passage of the Exclusion Act in 1882. Chinatowns along the East Coast grew both involuntarily and voluntarily. Because they were denied structural assimilation, the Chinese developed enclaves for self-protection as well as social and economic improvement (Zhou 1992).

The food system arose out of the desire to preferentially feed the enclave. Like much of Chinatown's social and economic activity, the food system operated outside of the mainstream food system in New York. Restaurants were one of the first business sectors to develop in Chinatown. Restaurants catered to Chinatown's bachelor society. Tea houses and "chop suey" houses were places where men could get hot, homemade meals and socialize with others. Typical Cantonese dishes (which would come to be known as Chinese-American food) like chop suey, lo mein, chow mein, and fried rice were served because they were quick and inexpensive mixtures of meats and vegetables (Zhou 1992). The demand for basic Chinese vegetables like bok choy, *lo bak* (Chinese radish), *ong choy* (water spinach), and *dau mui* (snow pea shoots) encouraged Chinese farms to develop in the agricultural areas outside of New York City.

Much like the dominant food systems of the time, Chinese fruits and vegetables were grown in New Jersey and Long Island and trucked into Manhattan. It was also reported that greens for winter trade and some subtropical items were supplied from gardens in Florida and even Cuba (Porterfield 1951). Records of Chinese crops in the United States date back to the nineteenth century. The prominent American horticulturalist Liberty Hyde Bailey wrote about Chinese crops in the United States in 1894 and their great potential for assimilation into the American diet. Mainstreaming "ethnic" crops is a preoccupation of those interested in the economic potential of new crops. The Chinese cabbages (*Brassica spp.*) were among the earliest cultivated Chinese crops in the United States, possibly because they were regarded in this way. It is no wonder that bok choy and napa cabbage are seen on almost every supermarket shelf today. There were many more food items of less interest to agronomists but regularly sold in Chinatown. In 1937 over forty types of plant foods were available in Chinatown, including dried items like fungus, fruits, and lily flowers in addition to fresh roots, tubers, fruits, and leafy vegetables (Porterfield 1937).

The First Chinese Farmers

> A few of the vegetables sold, such as cabbage, found their way into Chinese markets in the United States many years ago, but a large number, because they do not appeal to American palates, because of difficulties raising them as agricultural crops or perhaps merely because they are as yet unknown to the American farmer, are cultivated for Chinese use, that is for their own benefit or for Chinese-American restaurants. (Porterfield 1951:5)

In Porterfield's musings over why many Chinese plants were not more popular crops there is affirmation that the Chinese were not only selling and buying a wealth of crops but growing them as well. The first Chinese farm on Long Island, Sang Lee Farms, was founded by the Lee family in 1948.[2] The Lees were part of the Cantonese migration to New York City in the early 1900s. They ran a laundry business in which their son helped after school. After returning from World War II, George Lee, father of the current owner of Sang Lee Farms, went to the State University of New York at Farmingdale to study agronomy. His parents, immigrants from Canton, approved of his career choice. In an interview with the *New York Times*, George Lee's wife said, "In those days, being a farmer was different than in China, where it was considered low. Here, they knew you had to have an education and know what you're doing" (Toy 2003). George Lee and his cousin began Sang Lee Farms. At this point Chinese farms were well established in southern New Jersey, but the Lees preferred Long Island because of its extensive underground aquifer. Southern Jersey has a longer growing season, but the aquifer promised a competitive advantage during dry periods.

The Lees' intuition was right. Sang Lee Farms quickly became the main supplier of Chinese vegetables for New York, Philadelphia, and Boston, as far north as Montreal, west as Detroit, and south as Miami. They established a reputation in Chinatown among wholesalers as well as market shoppers. The farm expanded to Hobe Sound, Florida, to produce during winter months in the late 1950s. At the peak of production the farm was double cropping six hundred acres in East Moriches, Long Island, and several hundred in Florida during the winter. Half of their acreage was bok choy, and the other half was a mix of about two dozen types of vegetables.

The farm grew alongside the immigration rates of the Chinese. The mid-1960s saw a boom in Chinese immigration. Although sixty years of Chinese exclusion ended in 1943 when China became allied with the United States in World War II, it was not until the year 1965 that there was a turning point in U.S. immigration history. In 1965 the United States government abolished nation-of-origin quotas that had favored immigration from northwestern Europe for eighty years. Whereas the first half of the twentieth century saw 85 percent of its immigrants from Europe, the second half saw the reverse: 85 percent from Asia, Latin America, and the Caribbean. Between 1961 and 1970, the number of Chinese immigrants to the United States was just over 100,000, more than four times that of the previous decade, and from 1971 to 1980 the number jumped to roughly 240,000 (INS Statistical Yearbook 1950–1988).

Chinese growers followed the Lees to Florida. Tommy Yee, the son of a New Jersey farmer, established a 110-acre farm in Loxahatchee in 1974.[3] His father farmed in Warren County, New Jersey, during the summer and bought vegetables from Florida in the winter to hold over their New York and Boston customers until the next season (Snyder 2004). Prior to the establishment of his farm, Tommy drove a truck between Florida and New York for his father. During this time he gained a valuable insight. He noticed a broken link in the commodity chain. Brokers (wholesalers, also called jobbers) in New York could not supply a steady product, and farmers in Florida didn't have consistent buyers. He wondered why there was no stability, so he developed a business solution to this problem. Tommy found that "as long as I could supply an above average product, it didn't have to be superior, and the market was good, the wholesalers would consistently buy." He used independent truckers since they were fairly priced and reliable. Now 95 percent of his business is repeat business. He has worked with the same two wholesalers in New York since 1978. He attributes the longevity of his success to his business philosophy. He believes that "one hand washes the other."

One Hand Washes the Other: The Business of Expansion

Tommy's attitude toward the business of agriculture is one I have heard espoused numerous times from other successful farmers in Chinatown's food system. Trust and mutual respect in addition to a quality product (from the farmer) and a good price (from the broker) are necessary ingredients for long-term success. Getting paid, of course, is also crucial. Farmers are very vulnerable to market conditions because they sell highly perishable goods. Chinatown brokers in New York City work on consignment, which means they don't pay until after shipment is received. Farmers have to ship their product in good faith that they will get paid. From the brokers' perspective, they don't want to pay for a product that they haven't yet seen. If it is of poor quality, they lose, plus they have to pay for disposal. Just about everyone has a story about how they were never paid by so-and-so, with whom they never worked again. The only way to survive in this type of market is to find buyers and sellers that can be trusted.

Some who have achieved stable business relations have done so by trial and error, taking risks and taking losses, but most have tried to preempt this gamble by partnering with trusted friends or family members. As agriculture in general has become a global system, and imports from Mexico, Latin America, and the Caribbean have challenged American farmers throughout the 1980s and 1990s, actors in Chinatown's food system have used social networks and practiced the philosophy of give and take to become global players.

Double Green

Double Green,[4] for example, began with international ambitions. Double Green Farm, Inc.; Double Green Produce, Inc., in Florida City; and Double Green Wholesales, Inc., in New York City, were born out of the same idea: to supply the rapidly growing Chinese population in Flushing, Queens. From 1980 to 2000, the number of Chinese inhabitants in New York City grew by almost 250 percent (New York City Department of City Planning, 2000 Census). The rapid growth led to the development of satellite Chinatowns in the outer boroughs of New York City, the largest located in Flushing, Queens. Flushing was economically depressed in the 1970s and offered many opportunities for those with the capital to start their own businesses. Chinese investment turned the community around. Laura Huang, a Taiwanese immigrant and resident of Flushing, seized a rather serendipitous business opportunity to co-found Double Green.

Laura Huang's family fell from high society to the farming peasantry under wartime suspicions in Taiwan. Laura worked on her family's farm until she immigrated to New York in the 1970s. Through her church Laura met a Taiwanese family living in Haiti who was looking for a good school for their children in New York. Laura took it upon herself to help them. Laura took Mrs. Li and her children to get the appropriate forms for student visas, which must be acquired at the school one intends to attend. She also found them an apartment. The Lis were so appreciative that Mr. Li flew from Haiti himself to thank Laura. When they met, Laura and Li discovered that they were both interested in going into business. Li suggested importing fish from Haiti because it was plentiful. Laura saw the need for vegetables for the growing Taiwanese population in Flushing. Since Li had expertise in agriculture (at the time he was an agronomist in Haiti), Li and Laura decided that they could open a production and distribution business. Li would run the farm and Laura would run the wholesale warehouse in Chinatown's distribution hub of lower Manhattan.

Li scouted locations where he could establish a farm and packing operation. He decided on southern Florida because it has the humid climate he likes and is accustomed to in Taiwan and Haiti. He drew confidence about his choice of location from seeing the other successful Chinese farms in Florida. Li, however, decided to go further south in Florida than the other farmers, like Yee, where more subtropical and tropical fruits and vegetables could be grown. He believed that he would have an advantage that way.

Li and Laura opened Double Green in 1985. They decided on a name that means "very lucky" in Chinese, yet they were quite unlucky in the beginning. The first year they lost money. The second year they also lost on many crops but made some money on papaya and bitter melon. However, it was not enough to keep them together. It was more difficult than Li expected to farm Chinese vegetables under Florida's ecological and economic conditions. In China, agriculture is very labor intensive. In Florida, however, it is too expensive to use the same labor dependant methods Li knew from China. He was forced to develop new techniques and needed time to learn how to farm in Florida City. Laura felt that she could not wait, so she went on to find new farmers. Although the partnership dissolved, Li and Laura helped one another realize their goals of opening a business. They both went on to build successful businesses.

Li used his experience and contacts in Haiti and Honduras to develop export agriculture. He was chief agronomist of the Taiwanese Mission to Agriculture in Haiti. There is also a Taiwanese Mission in Honduras. These missions began with the sole purpose to aid in rice production but have since diversified their interests. In Honduras, the mission is a key part of the Chinese vegetable industry. Haiti has more infrastructural challenges to exporting goods than Honduras, and Li's production there has waned. Production in Honduras, on the other hand, is growing. Li remains in close contact with both missions. Since he has established himself as a successful businessman and farmer in Florida he has been recommended as an importer and a consultant. The Honduran mission put a new exporter of Chinese vegetables in contact with Li. Now Li is importing three to four container loads of produce per week from Honduras. Li was recently invited to Honduras in October of 2004 to give a workshop to agronomists from all over Central America on growing Chinese vegetables for U.S. markets. Li also hosts his colleagues at his house in Florida and shows them his business. One Taiwanese colleague who was visiting while I was interviewing Li was interested in retiring from the mission in Haiti and beginning his own farm in Florida. Perhaps he will represent a new generation of Chinese agriculture in Florida.

After Laura left Li she took extraordinary risks to find new growers. She believes that it is important to take a chance with new growers. She looks for potential business partners through her social networks. Friends would go into partnership with her, or introduce others to her. If the grower turned out to be good, then she would take care of them. By taking care, Laura means giving her farmers a good price and keeping them aware of exactly what the market wants. Both of these aspects are critical to a farmer's and wholesaler's success. Ironically, while Laura has a wonderful reputation with "her" farmers, she has a terrible reputation with other farmers. Those who have tight relationships get paid, those who do not experience a cutthroat, perhaps unethical way of doing business. The famous line in Chinatown upon the receipt of a shipment is, "quality no good!" Farmers know that this means they are going to get paid poorly. Even if the quality is good, unless the farmer can get on a plane and fly to New York that minute (and that does sometimes happen), there is nothing they can do to prove it.

One of the growers with whom Laura took an extraordinary risk is Jack. Jack was up from Florida visiting his New Jersey farmer friend Johnny. Jack was a conventional grower.[5] He had a good contract to grow chili peppers for Pace foods. Johnny, on the other hand, grew Chinese vegetables for a woman in Chinatown. Jack had no interest in this, although he did have experience with Chinese growers. Besides Johnny, Jack was also a friend and neighbor of Tommy Yee in Florida. Jack spent a lot of time hanging around Yee's packing house because he borrowed the vacuum cooler to pack his peppers. Inadvertently, he was learning about farming Chinese vegetables at the time.

Johnny worked with Laura. Laura was looking for a new grower, and requested to meet Jack. Jack, being a courteous fellow, agreed to the meeting, but his immediate reaction to Laura's request was "No way!" He knew nothing about Chinese vegetables and could not afford to take the risk, nor did he have the capital to expand. He gave Laura his ear until he could not listen anymore. He said straight out, "Laura, I am absolutely not interested. I don't know these vegetables and frankly I don't trust Chinese people." Laura calmly replied, "What would it take for you to trust a Chinese person?" Jack sarcastically said, "Laura, in America we have an old saying. Shit walks and money talks." Laura reached into her pocketbook and asked, "How much do you want?" Jack left that meeting with a $25,000 check and a verbal agreement that he would learn to grow Chinese vegetables for Laura. Now he owns seventeen hundred acres on the south banks of Lake Okeechobee and packs a semi-truckload a day for Laura. He is the largest and only farmer of European descent to farm Chinese vegetables in Florida and it is because of Laura's leap of faith.

In Jack's opinion, the advantage of working with Laura is that she really knows the market, what people do and do not like. She is an avid cook and high-quality produce is of paramount importance to her. Jack says, "Laura taught me about the place of vegetables in the Chinese diet. If I can understand that, then I can understand how to grow and sell them." Once, she was complaining about a little sand on the cut end of the bok choy. She wanted to be able to open a box and see perfectly neat and clean bok choy ends. The Chinese pick many of their thick-stemmed vegetables by the quality of the cut end. The cleanliness of the cut that Laura was demanding was impossible, given the price the market was willing to pay for the vegetable. Laura did not understand the real production cost; she thought it was simple to change the harvest technique. She flew down to the farm to show Jack her idea. Jack recalls, "She opened a box of bok choy and started furiously pulling the vegetables out of the box, pulling off old leaves and cutting the butts. She cleaned off one-third of the box." Laura said, "For this type of packing job I would give you double the previous price, $18 a box." Laura thought that sounded like a very attractive offer. Jack was still skeptical. He said, "Laura, that is still not worth it for me. Let me show you how we pack."

Jack took Laura out to the field, where his workers harvest and pack the bok choy. It took them one labor hour ($6.00) to pack one box the way Laura wanted it. "Maybe my good pickers can do it in less time, for $4.00, about two-thirds an hour of labor." Jack broke down the math on this new procedure for Laura. With all other costs the same (cost of the crate, postharvest cooling and shipping), the labor cost for the new approach increases from $1.75 per box to $5.00 per box, almost by three. The sales price doubles per box and the profit margin increases from $4.65 to $10.40. However, with the new procedure, fewer boxes are harvested per acre. In the end, the new way made only a little bit more per acre, much less than what Laura first perceived to be doubling Jack's profit. Jack would not honor Laura's request. He does not make agreements he does not believe in, but he does believe in open communication, as illustrated by this story. Because Jack and Laura have been able to have detailed interchanges like this, it has benefited both of their businesses. They keep each other aware of their strengths and shortcomings.

Yi Jen

The relationships I continue to find within Chinatown's Food System never cease to amaze me. In part it may be because the ominous term *globalization* once seemed so nameless and faceless. Or it may be that the environmental destruction and human exploitation associated with the globalization of agriculture has been so well documented. One of the most inspirational stories I was told comes from a now successful distributor in Homestead, Florida, who sells locally grown produce and imports produce from Honduras. Yi Jen[6] used to be a farmer herself, so she understands its hardships, the insecurity of the harvest and the exhaustion that comes with the work. However, she was not a farmer by choice. Yi Jen was forced to work on a farm in China during the Cultural Revolution. Someone in her family had to, and she was not going to permit her younger sister to do it. So she went, and she persevered. She found a way to study and get out of an imprisoned farm life. She left China when her grandfather gave her the chance to immigrate to the Dominican Republic, and she helped him open a hardware store. Yi Jen became familiar with business and recalls that she learned "mainly how to fight and not be afraid of people." Aspiring to open her own business, she got her grandfather's permission and moved to Florida.

Yi Jen worked for Li at his packing house, where she learned the ins and outs of the business. When she was ready to go out on her own, she raised $70,000 in cash from friends and family and went into business packing and shipping produce. She had a friend in the Dominican Republic who had moved to Honduras to export vegetables. She began to work with him. They have been working together for over ten years, and they have the most stable export business in Honduras.

Yi Jen does not work with many people. Rather, she builds strong relationships with the few she does work with. Yi Jen treats her business relationships like long-term investments. She says, "one penny today is worth ten tomorrow." She has even gone so far as to take a loss so that her farmers could turn a profit. She has a handful of growers in Florida, one that credits her as the only reason he makes money on his longan harvest. Last summer there was a glut of longan on the market from Florida and prices bottomed out. Yi Jen took a smaller cut on her share of the longan sales so that her farmer, who depends on longan for his primary income, could make a more respectable profit. Yi Jen says, "after all, what was one season's loss on one crop with one farmer, when you have had that farmer working with you for many seasons and you will have them for many more?" Yi Jen has not only built a stable business, she has the best reputation for quality produce in Chinatown.

Changing Times, Changing Practices of Chinatown's Farmers

These examples show how entrepreneurs in Chinatown's food system have established and expanded their businesses. Through social networks they meet potential partners, and they strengthen and expand relations that prove to be mutually beneficial. These stories bring out the human side of trade relations. But I do not want to mislead you into thinking that relations never change and trust is never broken. Some observers perceive Chinatown's food system as insular and difficult to penetrate. This may be true in some cases; however, it is not a niche system immune to the challenges of international competition. There are many farmers and distributors who have sought to duplicate the business success achieved by entrepreneurs in the system, but who have failed. There are constantly new farmers and brokers coming in and out of the system, and at some points there are more than the market can bear. This pressure can cause once stable businesses and business relations to crack.

Sang Lee Goes Chi-Chi

Sang Lee Farms has a new shingle outside the farm gate. It announces Sang Lee's positioning in the farm-chic rurality of the north fork of Long Island. On their website they boast "over 250 varieties of naturally grown produce"; *naturally* meaning "utilizing sustainable agricultural practices and integrated pest management." Their competitive advantage is their Chinese twist. On-line or at the farm stand you can buy premium baby greens like mini bok choy and shanghai choy for premium prices ($4.50 for 12 ounces and $5.99 for 24 ounces, respectively). Bok choy is usually $1.00 per pound in Chinatown! Or how about purple opal microbasil for $6.99 a quarter ounce? They claim that it will add intense flavor to any recipe! The farm, and its image, has drastically changed since its inception as the first Chinese farm on Long Island in 1948. But of course, agriculture on Long Island has changed. Now it is an industry that fosters agrotourism and caters to the elite summer lifestyles of Long Island's East End.

Fred Lee, son the founder of Sang Lee Farms and current proprietor, just gave up their last account in Chinatown. It was a hard decision, he says, but he could not emotionally or financially stand having truckloads of harvest returned, unpaid. This practice became more and more frequent when Fred's wholesaler could not sell his produce; it was simply too expensive in the face of Mexican-grown products. Fred's long-time associate offered him the chance to go to Mexico and set up a farm, but it was against Fred's own idea of farming. He wanted to stay on Long Island, so he did what the other farms around him were doing. He began to diversify his product line and market directly to restaurants, consumers, and caterers. He went into baby vegetables, herbs, cut flowers, and heirloom tomatoes. He kept his array of Chinese vegetables, and now assembles bags of ready-to-cook stir fry greens and sauce. He set up a farm stand and began to advertise his own organic philosophy (he did not want to bother with certification; too much bureaucracy). Maybe Fred and his wholesaler no longer shared the same goals or vision of agriculture. But one thing was definitely true: internationally grown produce was undercutting Fred's business, and he had to change.

Losing Faith in Chinatown Markets

Jack was also getting restless. His relationship with Laura lasted for ten years, but it has come to a close. When I last visited him, Jack told me the news. He said, "I had a divorce with my Chinese broker!" In Jack's opinion, Laura lost her aggressiveness in the market. It may be because she has realized that her son will not take over the business. Without Laura fighting for a good price for him, working closely with him to understand his needs, and keeping him informed about market demands, Jack could not continue to work with her. Jack clearly emphasizes that the Chinese vegetable market is not a niche market. There is no added value in growing Chinese vegetables, and competition is growing every day, particularly from Mexico, where high-quality vegetables can be grown at a fraction of the cost. If he does not have a broker working for him, pushing his product and demanding the prices that he needs to make a profit, then he will not continue growing Chinese vegetables. In fact, in the 2003–2004 growing season Jack lost money on his Chinese vegetables. The other vegetables he grew carried his farm. Jack's divorce with Laura, however, did not end his tenure as a grower of Chinese vegetables. Jack's decision to leave Laura was provoked by a common event in Chinatown markets: Jack was offered better prices by another broker. Because Jack had been growing tired of working with Laura, the offer helped him make up his mind to leave her. As Jack believes in honesty and integrity, instead of deceiving Laura and selling to another broker behind her back (a more frequent practice), Jack flew to New York to settle the divorce in person.

Conclusion

There are over one hundred fresh fruits and vegetables for sale in New York City's Chinatown year-round. Old and new Chinese immigrants, as well as Vietnamese, Thai, Malaysian, Cambodian, and Laotian immigrants make a living within China-town's food system. Countless other first-, second-, and multi-generation Americans patronize Chinatown's shops and street vendors. The cultural heterogeneity of the system is iconic of New York City. The abundance, freshness, and cost of produce in Chinatown are unrivaled in the city. Where else can you get a pound of baby bok choy or Chinese eggplant for a dollar?

The marketing channels that deliver the great diversity of products to Chinatown are constantly growing and changing. Entrepreneurs continually enter and leave the system and continually look for new suppliers as well as new products. Thai guava is the new popular fruit among Florida growers, and longan, available practically year round, was once only available in July. The shift in product availability is as much a result of international competition as it is inter-regional competition. When a product grows well in an area, others also want to grow it. Because of this dynamism and competition, the successful farmers as well as brokers are always experimenting with new items and new places. Brokers do not shy away from global trade but use their social networks to develop new trade relations. The globalization of Chinatown's food system has happened like a groundswell, in a bottom-up rather than a top-down fashion.

Chinatown's food system exemplifies an alternative globalization that some scholars call globalization or transnationalism from below (Glick Schiller 1999; Basch et al. 1994), globalization from the margins (Appadurai 1996), or transnational urbanism (Smith 2001). As a process it is not something extrinsic to daily life, or imposed by regulatory bodies, but rather it is a result of new spatial arrangements made by individuals. Globalization, in this sense, is the means of conducting business over widening distances and distended social relations (Flusty 2004). As Smith (2001) points out:

> Specific collectivities—local households, kin networks, elite fractions, and other emergent local formations—actively pursue such strategies as transnational migration, transnational social movements or transnational economic or cultural entrepreneurship to sustain or transform resources, including cultural resources, in the face of the neoliberal storm. (167)

Chinese immigrant entrepreneurs have indeed transformed their cultural as well as economic resources in a way that has led to globally distended networks of trade. What remains exceptional is that they have done so in a way that *remains* outside of the dominant modes of food trade.

There is no single explanation for this; rather, there are several contributing factors that begin to explain Chinatown's food system as it exists today. The people who control access to the markets are the wholesalers based in urban Chinatowns. As Chinese people they fully understand the food preferences of their community. Some non-Chinese people have told me they would like to deal in Chinese vegetables but are unknowledgeable about them. The wholesalers also largely do business in Chinese. Of course many are multilingual, but I have often seen Chinese wholesalers hide behind feigned language difficulties as a way to protect themselves from people to whom they are not interested in talking. The closed ethnic character of the entrepreneurs, whether created or real, may have protected the food system from appropriation by American and European food giants.

Extreme competition, particularly on the retail end, keeps companies within the system from getting too big. It also keeps quality high but prices low. In Manhattan's Chinatown alone there are eighty-five small vendors (greengrocers and street vendors) and eight wholesalers. An informal system of apprenticeship serves to sustain this tradition of doing business. Many "new" entrepreneurs have gotten their start by working for others in the system, are family members sent to open an independent branch of the business at another point in the commodity chain, or are children who inherited the family business. Finally, Chinatown wholesalers and Florida brokers, as we have seen, drive expansion of the system by networking, rather than through buy-out and consolidation. They have set an example that is in perpetuation.

The global, fast-food systems that most slow food advocates oppose are not the only global food systems in existence. Far from leading to simplification and loss of diversity, global trade can help preserve traditions as well as foster innovation. New business ambitions can thrive without inevitable cooptation or appropriation by larger, more powerful global giants. Variety and diversity can exist in a food system at competitive prices, and without the sophisticated rhetoric that many people are unaware of, disenfranchised from, or completely skeptical about.

Notes

Acknowledgments. This research has been completed through the support of the New York Botanical Garden and the NSF Doctoral Dissertation Research Improvement Award 0425734. Fieldwork could not have been undertaken without the help of Louis Putzel, Andrew Roberts, and Karen Jiron, who not only assisted in interviews but helped in the conceptualization of the project. Most invaluable has been the academic advice of Christine Padoch, Charles Peters, and Roberta Balstad, and the editorial advice of Richard Wilk.

1. The production of nontraditional agricultural exports (NTAEs), also known as high-value exports, is an economic development strategy prevalent in Latin America. NTAE refers to those products that (1) were not traditionally produced in a particular country for export (traditional exports are soybeans, sugar, bananas, and coffee); (2) were traditionally produced for domestic consumption but are now exported; (3) are traditional products now exported to a new market. NTAEs are generally high-value or niche products. Fresh fruits and vegetables and fair trade coffee are examples of NTAEs (Thrupp 1995).

2. I conducted an interview with Karen Lee in July 2003. She is the wife of George Lee, the son of the founder of Sang Lee farm. Karen now works full-time with her husband on the farm. About a month after the interview an article on the farm came out in the Long Island section of the *New York Times,* covering much of what Karen had told me in addition to other things. I use my interview data supplemented with the *New York Times* article in this chapter.

3. I had the fortunate experience of visiting Tommy, his wife, and most of his nine fields in February 2004 with Ken Schuler. Ken used to be the vegetable specialist at the Palm Beach County Agricultural Extension Office and was especially active with the Chinese vegetable growers. Although he is now retired, he works as a pest scout for Tommy, visiting his fields once a week. He invited me along and shared much of his expertise about Chinese vegetable farming in Florida. He also created a very comfortable interview atmosphere for Tommy, who needed reassurance of the validity of my study.

4. All of the individuals discussed in this section are protected by the use of pseudonyms. They were interviewed between August 2003 and October 2004. Li was interviewed on two occasions, once in Florida and once in Honduras. I also interviewed his son, who

now runs the packing house. In addition to Laura, I interviewed her long-time employee. Because all of these people have worked together and remain in contact, it was very easy to cross-reference data.

5. Laura put me in contact with Jack. On my second trip to Florida in February 2004 I visited his farm and interviewed him.

6. Yi Jen is also a pseudonym. My first try at interviewing her in August 2003 failed; she flat out refused. Fortunately I subsequently interviewed her friend, a fruit grower who had been supplying her for several years and largely attributes his financial success to her. When I told him that Yi Jen refused to speak with me, he called her and told her I was harmless. That afternoon I had a four-hour interview with her.

References

Allen, Patricia, Margaret Fitzsimmons, Michael Goodman, and Keith Warner. 2003. Shifting Plates in the Agrifood Landscape: The Tectonics of Alternative Agrifood Initiatives in California. Journal of Rural Studies 19:61–75.

Appadurai, Arjun. 1996. Modernity at Large. Minneapolis: University of Minnesota Press.

Bailey, L. H. 1894. Some Recent Chinese Vegetables. Cornell University Agricultural Experiment Station, Horticulture Division Bulletin 67:177–201.

Barndt, Deborah. 2002. Tangled Routes: Women, Work, and Globalization on the Tomato Trail. Boulder, CO: Westview Press.

Basch, Linda, Nina Glick Schiller, and Cristina Szanton-Blanc. 1994. Nationals Unbound: Transnational Projects and the Deterritorialized Nation-State. New York: Gordon and Breach.

Bonnano, A., L. Busch, W. Friedland, L. Gouvia, and E. Mingione. 1994. From Columbus to Con-Agra: The Globalization of Agriculture and Food. Lawrence, KS: University of Kansas Press.

Flusty, Steven. 2004. De-Coca-Colonization: Making the Globe from the Inside Out. New York: Routledge.

Friedland, William H. 2001. Reprise on Commodity Systems Methodology. International Journal of Sociology of Agriculture and Food 9:82–103.

Glick Schiller, Nina. 1999. Who Are These Guys? A Transnational Reading of the U.S. Immigrant Experience in Identities on the Move. In Transnational Processes in North America and the Caribbean Basin. L. Goldin ed. New York: Institute for Mesoamerican Studies.

Goodman, David, and Michael Watts, eds. 1997. Globalizing Food, Agrarian Questions and Global Restructuring. New York: Routledge.

Guest, Kenneth J. 2003. God in Chinatown: Religion and Survival in New York's Evolving Immigrant Community. New York: New York University Press.

Guthman, Julie Harriet. 2000. Agrarian Dreams? The Paradox of Organic Farming. PhD Dissertation. Department of Geography, University of California, Berkeley.

Harvey, David. 2001. Spaces of Capital: Towards a Critical Geography. New York: Routledge.

Hinrichs, C. 2000. Embeddedness and Local Food Systems: Notes on Two Types of Direct Agricultural Markets. Journal of Rural Studies 16(3):295–303.

INS Statistical Yearbook. 1950 to 1988. Statistical Yearbook of the Immigration and Naturalization Service. U.S. Department of Justice.

Kloppenburg, Jack, J. Hendrickson, and G. W. Stevenson. 1996. Coming into the Foodshed. Agriculture and Human Values 13:33–42.

Lyson, Thomas A., and Annalisa Lewis Raymer. 2000. Stalking the Wily Multinational: Power and Control in the US Food System. Agriculture and Human Values 17:199–208.

McMichael, Philip, ed. 1994. The Global Restructuring of Agro-Food Systems. Ithaca, NY: Cornell University Press.

Murray, D., and L. Raynolds. 2000. Alternative Trade in Bananas: Obstacles and Opportunities for Progressive Social Change in the Global Economy. Agriculture and Human Values 17:65–74.

New York City Department of City Planning. 2000. Census, Demographic Profile of New York 1990–2000.

Porterfield, W. M. 1937. Chinese Vegetable Foods in New York. Journal of the New York Botanical Garden 38:254–57.

———. 1951. The Principle Chinese Vegetable Foods and Food Plants of Chinatown Markets. Economic Botany 1(5):3–37.

Smith, Michael. 2001. Transnational Urbanism, Location Globalization. Malden, MA: Blackwell Publishers.

Snyder, James. 2004. Black Gold and Silver Sands: A Pictorial History of Agriculture in Palm Beach County. Historical Society of Palm Beach County.

Stoller, Paul. 2002. Money Has No Smell: The Africanization of New York City. Chicago: University of Chicago Press.

Thrupp, Lori Ann. 1995. Bittersweet Harvests for Global Supermarkets: Challenges in Latin America's Agricultural Export Boom. Washington D.C.: World Resources Institute.

Toy, Vivian. 2003. East End's Lost Link to Agriculture. New York Times. August 31: Long Island Weekly Desk.

Tsing, Anna. 2000. The Global Situation. Cultural Anthropology 15:327–60.

Watts, D. C. H., B. Ilbery, and D. Maye. 2005. Making Reconnections in Agro-Food Geography: Alternative Systems of Food Provision. Progress in Human Geography 29:22–40.

Wells, Miriam. 1996. Strawberry Fields: Politics, Class, and Work in California Agriculture. Ithaca, NY: Cornell University Press.

Zhou, Min. 1992. Chinatown: The Socioeconomic Potential of an Urban Enclave. Philadelphia: Temple University Press.

The Role of Ideology in New Mexico's CSA (Community Supported Agriculture) Organizations: Conflicting Visions between Growers and Members 12

LOIS STANFORD

Introduction

Despite national declines in agricultural land and total numbers of farmers, some subsectors in the U.S. agricultural system provide alternative directions in food production and marketing that support sustainable agricultural development. The 1990s witnessed a dramatic increase in organic food production and product sales (CCOF 1990; Andreatta 2000). As well, alternative forms of marketing and farm organization, such as Community Supported Agriculture (CSA) organizations and farmers' markets, began to develop in certain U.S. regions. These alternative forms of food production and distribution comprise a dynamic and emergent movement within the United States. Food activist scholars contend that these new organizational forms bring together different groups of people within a local food system, constructing new networks that can lead to social and political change in the food system (Allen 2004; Clancy 1997; DeLind 1993; and Kloppenberg, Hendrickson, and Stevenson 1996). As direct agricultural markets, these new types of farmer-consumer organizations are based on personal links that bypass existing commercial market channels and integrate local food systems in new ways that are more resource conserving than conventional agricultural marketing systems (Cone and Myhre 2000: DeLind and Ferguson 1999; and Sharp, Imerman, and Peters 2002). For small farmers unable to compete effectively in large commercial markets, alternative organizational forms can provide market niches, increased income, and income security.

Alternative farming presents a series of options that require construction of new linkages between producers and consumers: (1) farm-to-restaurant; (2) farm-to-school; (3) farmers' markets; (4) cooperatives; (5) value-added products; and (6) community supported agriculture (CSAs). Farm-to-restaurant and farm-to-school comprise the establishment of contracts between small growers and food institutions, thus guaranteeing small growers a secure income and the consuming institution a guaranteed supply of locally grown produce. Farmers' markets create a social and economic place within which small growers can sell their produce, yet they require that farmers incur all financial risks without any guarantee of consumer purchase. Cooperatives have a long history in U.S. agriculture, reflecting the legacy of family farming and agrarian ideologies. Value-added products involve the production of processed foods that take advantage of local and regional efforts to market local farmers, cultural traditions, and/or heritage tourism. These new forms share a common purpose of developing alternative food institutions within a local food context and promoting local food systems (Allen 2004:65–66). As well, they form the basis for constructing new kinds of social and economic relationships among producers and consumers; however, they differ in the nature and permanence of these linkages. As an example, in the case of farmers' markets, consumers do not invest up front in the farmer and may change producers spontaneously. In contrast, CSAs require the construction of both ongoing relationships between producers and consumers and a formal organization. For the purpose of clarifying new organizational relationships, this chapter focuses on new community supported agriculture organizations, or CSAs.

The CSA movement emerged in Japan in the early 1970s, based on these ten principles:

mutual assistance
intended production
accepting produce
mutual concession in the price decision
deepening friendly relationships
self-distribution
democratic management
learning among each group
maintaining the appropriate group scale
steady development (Main and Lawson 1999)

In 1982, the first U.S.-based CSA was established in Massachusetts, and by 2003, the CSA Center listed over nine hundred CSAs operating in the United States (Center for CSA Resources, n.d.). In principle, the CSA operates to bypass the market, forging direct linkages between the producer and consumer. Logistically, CSA consumer members invest in the CSA grower by purchasing shares at the time of planting, both providing critical income for the grower and assuming some of the risks associated with production. In return, the CSA grower provides an allotment of fresh produce at weekly intervals throughout the growing season. The quantity and quality provided will vary according to growing conditions, and CSA members assume some of the production risks at the distribution end as well. Across the United States, as well as in New Mexico, CSA member responsibilities vary, and some CSAs require greater member involvement in harvesting, distribution, recruitment, management, and publicity. In addition to the economic feature of bypassing established markets, there is an implicit community-building dimension, through which consumers develop and direct connections to the farmer, farmland, and rural lifeways (Sharp et al. 2002).

Fundamentally, CSAs can differ along organizational goals and principles, ranging along a set of dimensions, and these underlying objectives ultimately shape the respective CSA vision, ideology, and social relations within the specific organization. Understanding consumer choice and membership retention has emerged as an important theme in CSA research. Studies have identified a cluster of factors that affect consumers' decisions to join and to retain membership in a CSA, identifying a desire for local produce and commitment to local food systems as being critical considerations (Goland 2002; Kodolinsky and Pelch 1997a, 1997b; Stafl and O'Hara 2002). Understanding member retention is critical, given that many CSAs experience a 50-percent turnover rate each season, and consumers have driven the development of alternative food systems (Kloppenberg et al. 2000). Complementing these sets of values and preferences is the vision and ideology of the CSA grower himself or herself. Farmers often express strong motivations and values that lead them into establishing a CSA (McIlvaine-Newsad 2002). These goals often emerge from the CSA leadership, that is, the grower, thus structuring the nature of social and economic relations between grower and members within the organization. Growers have different visions of how they want to develop their own CSA.

At one end, the CSA can be conceptualized as an alternative system of production and marketing, through which producers can continue to grow local agricultural products and consumers can acquire locally grown, pesticide-free, safe food. In this respect, consumers demonstrate their commitment to local food systems and growers through their financial investment in the farm. The degree of their commitment to the farm and this new bypass system may be temporary, limited, and subject to unforeseen expectations. At the other end of the dimension, CSAs represent an arena within which to construct new forms of social community, forging linkages between grower and consumer that lead to greater commitment from consumers and consumer involvement in the vision, operations, and long-term strategies of the CSA farm. Drawing on the ideas espoused by Steiner and Robin Van En, the original leaders of the U.S. CSA movement envision a CSA organizational structure that ultimately reformulates direct, permanent ties between producer and consumer and forms the economic and political base for creating social justice, re-establishing rural community, and undermining the power of large-scale agricultural corporations.

When these two differing, yet overlapping, visions clash, underlying differences in the mission between growers and consumers can lead to tensions between the two parties (DeLind 1999, 2002; Lamb 1994). In the words of one New Mexican CSA grower,

> The CSA movement is successful, and we need to pay attention. The corporations will take over. There will be franchise CSAs, and employees distributing vegetables, and there are all kinds of iterations of that. There are hints of that already around here. Cooperative CSAs are the first step towards corporatizing CSAs. I hate to say it. It does not have to lead to that, but it probably will. See, I think there is nothing wrong with these other ideas. They just need to be clear on what they are. It is such a disservice to use one name to describe such a range of activities.

In this chapter, I examine the role that these conflicting ideologies can play in the construction and maintenance of the CSA organization, focusing on the narratives and interpretations of the CSA growers and leaders. Managing these differences and constructing some degree of consensus are critical to the long-term organizational cohesiveness of these alternative farm organizations.

Setting: New Mexico Agriculture

In the U.S. Southwest, agriculture and rural lifeways still comprise an important component of states' economies, although this region remains marginal to the U.S. commercial agricultural industry. In New Mexico, out of 77 million acres total land area, 45 million acres are dedicated to farmland, predominantly ranching. Despite New Mexico's heavy dependence on agriculture and ranching, the state's agricultural industries contribute relatively little to U.S. commercial agriculture and ranching. In 2002, New Mexico's total value of agricultural commodities only reached an estimated $1.7 billion, out of the U.S. total market value of agricultural products of $200.6 billion. That is, New Mexico agriculture contributes approximately 1 percent of the U.S. market value in agricultural commodities. While the cattle industry contributes 44 percent of the state's agricultural value, New Mexico cattle industry receipts only represent 2.3 percent of the national cattle sector. As well, dairy products represent an important component of state agricultural commodities, contributing 30 percent of the state's value in agricultural receipts; yet New Mexico's dairy industry only contributes 3 percent of national value (NASS/USDA 2002). New Mexico remains rural and agriculturally based but hardly a mover in the national agricultural commodity scene.

Despite these challenges, many New Mexican residents continue a rural and agricultural livelihood. Across the state, 50 percent of New Mexico's population resides in nonmetro areas, in contrast to 1.4 percent of the total U.S. population

in non-metro areas. Unlike other U.S. agricultural regions, farming is not generally concentrated in the hands of large agribusinesses and/or landowners. Out
of 15,200 total farms in New Mexico, family farms comprise 89 percent, while
only 0.7 percent are represented by nonfamily corporations. Within the family
farm sector, 58.7 percent are full owners, while 30.7 percent are part owners. New
Mexico farmers also face financial challenges. Of all farms, 81 percent of farms
report less than $50,000 by sales annually, while only 3 percent report annual farm
sales greater than $500,000 (ERA/USDA 2002). New Mexican small farmers do
not compete effectively in the U.S. commercial agricultural sector, yet farmers and
rural residents continue to hold onto their land and reside in rural communities.
Sustainable development and alternative food markets could provide these farmers
with new options, ones that would allow them to remain in their home communities
(Stanford 2005).

New Mexican food and food policy activists recognize that these new forms
of marketing and farm organization could enable New Mexican small farmers to
bypass commercial markets and integrate local food systems in new ways. Despite
this acknowledgment, a cultural chasm exists between this new food movement and
the economic reality of small New Mexico growers, ranchers, and consumers. There
are currently twenty-five CSAs scattered throughout different counties across New
Mexico, but only four CSAs are managed by minority farmers. There are thirty-
six New Mexico farmers' markets, and the most famous, the Santa Fe Farmers'
Market, generated gross sales of $1.25 million in 2001. Yet, New Mexican con-
sumers are relatively poor and face constraints in purchasing fresh produce. In New
Mexico, a new WIC Farmers' Market Nutrition Program now provides subsidies
for participating women and children to purchase fresh produce. In the Santa Fe
Farmers' Market, WIC sales comprise 1 percent of total sales, while WIC sales
make up 73 percent of farmer sales in farmers' markets in Albuquerque's South
Valley. Whether or not the new food movement provides options for poor, His-
panic growers and consumers requires both a clear recognition of this cultural and
economic chasm and a concerted effort to bridge this gap (Stanford 2001).

In this chapter, I examine the challenges to constructing and maintaining a
New Mexico CSA from the perspective of CSA growers. This chapter draws on
a statewide survey of New Mexico CSAs[1] and taped ethnographic interviews
conducted with a small group of CSA leaders and members throughout the state.
These interviews walked the leaders and members through a personal narrative of
the history of their CSA, probing for their insights into challenges and concerns
at different stages in the life cycle of the organization. The themes and issues
identified here represent an attempt to develop a more systematic methodology for
comparing different (and often contradictory) visions and expectations within the
organization.

For New Mexico small farmers, CSAs provide new opportunities at the same time these transitions pose great challenges. There are currently twenty-five CSAs scattered throughout different counties across the state. New Mexico CSAs are small, averaging five acres, and tend toward organic production, although half are not yet organically certified. This reflects the higher consumer demand for organic produce in Taos and Santa Fe, where most New Mexico CSAs are geographically concentrated. The small size compares with a U.S. average of 6.92 acres for CSA farms.[2] In most cases, CSAs are initiated by the grower as an alternative to traditional farm production and a complement to small-scale vegetable production for farmers' markets. In a few cases, organized consumer groups, such as a church or alternative school, have approached a grower about starting a CSA. Most recently, in 2002, a group of Santa Fe food activists established a cooperative CSA, made up of a group of producers furnishing a wide range of fresh products for CSA members. Another CSA has been formed by university faculty and represents a pilot demonstration project (Licona 2003 and 2004). The New Mexico CSA movement is relatively new, dynamic, precarious, and autonomous. Independent CSAs may form and develop on their own, while contact between growers is informal and sporadic.

Reflecting the relatively harsh growing conditions that characterize New Mexico, all CSAs regularly use compost, adding manure and/or organic fertilizers as needed. During the off-season, cover crops provide additional soil enrichment. The growing season extends from mid-March to early fall, with an average of thirty-two weeks of distribution, although some CSAs may extend production and distribution up to forty-eight weeks with the use of greenhouse production to extend the growing season. New Mexico CSAs are relatively small with an estimated forty to fifty full share equivalents per season, and the average price of a full share equivalent is $470.[3] New Mexico CSA share prices tend to be more than U.S. average ($409.78 for a full share).[4] The New Mexico CSA movement is a relatively recent phenomenon, and only one CSA has been operating for longer than fifteen years; the remaining CSAs have been in operation for four to five years.

These small organizations face great external challenges that affect their continued operations and long-term sustainability. First, harsh growing conditions impinge on the survival of agriculture in the state. In 2003, New Mexico faced the fourth year of a sustained drought, and two of the CSAs surveyed did not even plant during that summer. As well, market constraints confront CSA growers. Since most New Mexico CSAs are relatively small, all growers depend on additional income sources to supplement the CSA operations. Most CSA growers cannot depend completely on their CSA operations and also market their product in other markets, including regional farmers' markets, wholesale markets, and institutional contracts. The CSA and farmers' market movement has been most successful in Albuquerque and Santa Fe, where wealthier customers comprise an important market for organic, locally grown, fresh, and exotic produce. In contrast, CSA growers face great economic and cultural constraints extending this new movement into rural communities throughout the state.

Within the conditions imposed on CSAs by the natural environment, state policy, and regional markets, CSA growers also face the challenges of maintaining and running their farm organizations. Half of New Mexico CSAs are family managed farm operations, and partnerships comprise another 25 percent of regional CSAs, much greater than the national average. The brunt of organizational management also falls to the grower and his or her family. Confounding this challenge, New Mexico CSAs also report an average retention rate of 64 percent, with reported retention rates ranging from a high of 80 percent down to 45 percent. New Mexico CSAs annually confront the problem of replacing between 40 and 50 percent of their membership in order to survive. Facing and resolving critical issues of membership retention, involvement, and commitment are critical to the long-term survival of New Mexico CSAs. Given the CSA movement's recent expansion in New Mexico, the involvement of members also remains problematical. In general, CSAs rely substantially on the active involvement of the core group, that is, members who assume an active role in the management, operations, and planning of the respective CSA. In New Mexico, less than half of existing CSAs report a core group, and only six CSAs require members to contribute field labor. Members assist with distribution, publicity, and newsletters. Three CSAs report reducing the costs of shares for those members who regularly volunteer to work in the field. Throughout this recent evolution, growers and members have renegotiated their relationship with each other, reflecting an ongoing dialogue about what constitutes duties, responsibilities, and loyalties toward each other. The dynamics of this dialogue pose questions and challenges for the construction of this "shared community" that CSA activists envision. In the words of one CSA grower, if this discussion is not made conscious and reflective, New Mexico CSAs run the risk of becoming "food buying clubs," not agents for social and economic change.

Bridging the Gap Between Grower and Member/Consumer

Exploring these themes covers four stages in the life cycle of a CSA: establishment, incorporation, institutionalization, and future vision for the CSA. Within this framework, I recognize that, as a constructed community, these organizations inherently contain a life of their own. CSA growers draw on a range of motives in starting a CSA, reflecting, in part, their own socioeconomic origins. In New Mexico, about half of CSA leaders do not come originally from farming families; they chose the CSA path because they express a commitment to social change, alternative forms of farming, and sustainable development. Other CSA leaders emerge from small growers who express both an interest in new types of agricultural production and viable alternatives to traditional small farm production. These closely linked goals of both environmental and economic sustainability comprise the motivational base of growers' ideology in creating a CSA, yet they equally reflect ideological differences, as noted previously. Other CSA scholars have noted the "hybrid nature of the CSA as an institution, since it encompasses both a market instrument for small diversified farmers and a place...upon which shared sense of purpose and community can emerge" (DeLind 2002:194). Others have commented on the inherent tension between a market orientation and a philosophical ideology that sees the CSA as a catalyst for profound social change (Cone and Kakaliouras 1995). These different visions clearly influence growers' efforts to construct and maintain CSA organizations, yet they do not give rise to permanent, separate organizational *types*. Differences in ideologies and expectations create challenges within organizations, but the CSA leaders themselves vary to the degree that they reconcile the tensions, and their own ideologies may shift over time. Despite espoused differences in organizational ideology, CSA growers share a common goal of building on the cultural and agricultural traditions of rural New Mexico and forming new linkages with consumers to thwart the deterioration of New Mexico agriculture. Identifying both common themes and diverse ideologies provides insights into the social and political complexity of embedding these new linkages in local food systems.

Establishing the CSA

In New Mexico, most CSAs originated in an informal manner. The growers recognized a shared vision of an alternative agricultural system, they were aware of what CSAs were, but they often embarked on this adventure without much long-term planning or foresight. In several cases, a group of potential members approached the respective grower, introducing and advocating for the CSA operation. As one grower recalled, in the initial establishment of his CSA,

> They interviewed several farms, and they came down to visit us, and they really liked what we were doing. We were growing produce in the winter is what we were doing. They agreed as a group to support Santa Cruz Farms as a CSA sponsored by the Unitarian Church, so that's kind of the way the CSA started.
>   The first few years, they did all the recruiting, they did the membership drives. The first two years they even took care of the finances. You know, the books and everything. It started, I think, we had 35 members the first year during the summer, then it went up to fifty during the summer.

In all cases, growers cite noneconomic factors and/or personal experiences that motivated them to embark on an alternative production system. They see the CSA model as not just another form of farm operation but as an alternative strategy to preserving a rural and communal way of life. The motivational force described is a powerful factor, one that in some cases approximates a transformational experience, as recalled by another CSA leader,

> They [members] came looking for me. They volunteered, "Well, why don't we start the CSA on his land? He probably won't mind." And so they came back up here and they said, "Our school wants a farm and the school doesn't have the correct kind of land for it. What if we do it here?"
>
> I said, "I think it's too soon. We don't have the infrastructure in place for it. We can't just start farming." "Oh, yeah, we can," they said. "Here, read this book, *Farms for Tomorrow*." And I read it. And it talks about, it's not like just being a farm out there in the market, and there's some unity to the communities that are supporting the farms. And then they got me this other book, called *Towards Social Renewal*, and it's about another way of organizing society different than capitalism, that wasn't anti-capitalist.... The other thing that is in that book is the idea of the three elements of human society. In human beings, Steiner is always talking about thinking, feeling, and willing and accepted methods that guide the human individuality.... So, I read that one, too. And when I read it, I thought, "He's got it! He's dead on! This is what we need to understand." ... What I saw community supported agriculture as was the implementation of the balancing of the realms Steiner described in a world that doesn't have very many working examples of that. So, I was totally excited about CSA. I realized we didn't have the resources, but we started anyway.

All growers interviewed reflected on their lack of preparation for starting a CSA. Despite their inexperience with CSAs, they cited their willingness to experiment, to try out something new when they had little idea where it would lead them. The endeavor is described almost as an adventure that unfolds over the course of the first few seasons. The contrast between CSA leaders lies in their respective vision for the CSA. Many of those involved in the alternative food movement in New Mexico come from the outside, drawn to the state because of its rich cultural traditions and alternative lifestyles. These CSA growers, identified as the "visionaries" in table 12.1, often emphasized their political philosophy and environmental concerns as motivating their establishment of a CSA, while other growers, identified as the "pragmatists," cited personal experience, particularly in relation to pesticide use, or alternative marketing niches as the factors that led them to seek farming alternatives.

As well, contrasts between grower and consumer expectation are evident from the beginning. Most CSAs across the United States draw on a membership base from the upper socioeconomic bracket, and New Mexico is no exception. In an ethnographic study of one New Mexico CSA, new members repeatedly remarked on the importance of freshness, taste, and safety, at the same time that they cited

Table 12.1.   Concerns and Issues Identified by New Mexico CSA Growers and Members

	Establishment	Incorporation	Institutionalization	Future Plans
Growers				
'Pragmatists'	income	leadership	loyalty of members	certified organic
	new people	dependence on core	member as priority	pass land to children
	experiment	ability to respond	solve problems quickly	regional linkages
	personal experience		cultivate consumers	
'Visionaries'	income	member relations	raise consumer consciousness	fear of organics' success
	environment	ability to respond		creating new community
	organic political philosophy		distinguish members question commitment	broader linkages

the importance of their political commitment to the organization (Licona 2003 and 2004). In contrast, lower socioeconomic consumers may obtain food subsidies, such as food stamps or WIC coupons, that enable them to purchase fresh produce at a farmers' market, but the high costs of the initial payments often prevent them from joining a CSA.

Incorporation of the Organization

Yet, by the end of the first few seasons, growers recognized that running a CSA required a kind of leadership and action that went far beyond the farm. When asked what he thought was the most important lesson he had learned in his first season as a CSA grower, one farmer reflected,

> Self-promotion. You've got to be self-promoting. You've got to get out there, and you've got to put out the word. You've got to get out there and talk to as many people as you can, you might get one or two. But, if they're core members, they'll recruit a couple more members. And it's an on-going thing. It's not just, "I'm going to do this for a couple of months, and then it'll be good." You've got to follow through on your promises.

Other growers cited the importance of maintaining good relations with members through newsletters, visits, and the like, often commenting that they had never envisioned that there would be so much work involved in the social relations of the organization. As well, they described the constant effort required to maintain good relations, in part reflecting the periodic problems that often developed in CSA operations and distribution. As another grower reflected,

> At the beginning, I think, there's been challenges, but they haven't really been disastrous. One of them was the pricing and distribution. We couldn't figure out what we were doing wrong, and the people were dropping out. People would come in and you'd hear a lot of grumbling about the prices and stuff. But, we've kind of settled down.

Given that most growers initiated their CSAs with a general vision but little experience, periodic problems developed through the course of the first few seasons. The CSA's survival past the first season reflected the ability of the grower to respond quickly to these problems, to learn from mistakes, and to develop his/her own capacity in running the day-to-day operations.

In successive seasons, growers described a delicate balance between cultivating the farm and cultivating the members. Despite lack of involvement by members in many CSAs, most growers recognized that they depended highly on the members. In some cases, growers described their relationship with members almost as if it were a marriage, repeatedly referring to the importance of trust, obligation, loyalty, and commitment. They recognized that they had a window of opportunity with the members, a short honeymoon period in the beginning, during which they needed to resolve minor problems, develop the operations, and retain members. As one long-time CSA grower reflected,

> I've seen a lot of CSAs start, and they do good their first year, two years.... I think you've got to follow through on your promises. You've got to really follow through. Because the first year, they [the growers] go, "Oh, yeah, the drought, man, I couldn't get my chile out of the field." Okay, that's okay the first year. The second year, the members start to question it. The third year, man, I've seen CSAs that just don't pull out of that second or third year.
>
> They see the CSA members as like a second-class marketing tool. Instead of, "This is my CSA member. This is who I have to please." A lot of people have the mentality that "whatever I have left over, I'll give to my CSA members".

Critical to the long-term survival of the CSA is the grower's ability to rescale operations to tailor to the preferences of members and to creatively engage his/her members (see table 12.1).

Being a CSA member requires shifts in consumer consciousness. Rhetoric about farmland preservation and romantic notions of connections to the farm must be backed up by a willingness to accept imperfect produce, new kinds of product, and periodic differences in produce volume, reflecting changes in field conditions.

Those CSA growers who recognize the "personality" of the consumer can play on these tendencies, cultivating their membership at the same time that they solidify and institutionalize their CSA as an organization. In one case, one CSA grower recalled the changes he initiated when members initially balked at the limited choice available to them in their weekly CSA delivery. In response, he developed an alternative distribution method, as he describes:

> We don't make a central delivery to our CSA members. They go to the farmer's market, and we have everything laid out on the table at the farmer's market. Everything that we're doing, that we're selling that day. And the members can go and choose whatever they want. We have a credit card system. The total starts here at $330, and we have the dates they're supposed to pick up during the week. Then we put the amounts of what they took for that day.
>
> So, whenever they run out of their credit, we tell them, "This is your share, and we really thank you." And then, "Oh, by the way . . . We had such a bountiful year, you're going to get another 15 percent added on to that." So, they'll get another delivery, or two more, so that makes them feel like they're getting a bonus for it.

Yet, underlying resentment develops when the grower senses that he/she is losing influence over the CSA's direction and becoming the servant of the CSA member (see DeLind 1999). Growers also express frustration as the CSA develops and they become increasingly aware of the discrepancy between membership rhetoric and romantic visions of the CSA, on the one hand, and membership unwillingness to assume work responsibilities, on the other. Growers may recognize that the members do not really share the same vision of what a CSA can represent and that these ideological differences ultimately undermine the organization. In response to a question about how to solicit "good" members, one grower explained,

> What I would like is a set of questions that a potential member should answer. If these questions, such as "Who owns the farm?" "Who owns the land?" "What provisions are made for the retirement of the farmers?" "How is the next generation of farmers going to be able to afford it?" "What is your source of soil fertility?" "How much extra land is there to feed the wild communities?" "How much water do you use?"
>
> If those kind of questions mattered as much as, "How much is your share?" "When does it start?" "What do I get?" then, the people would be making a conscious choice, and we would not be selling the seeds of gross ambiguity and reaping the harvest.

From this grower's perspective, CSAs as organizations often encompass a wide range of different kinds of relations between growers and members. When discrepancies exist between the grower's vision and that of many members, the lack of clarity and consensus of vision undermines the CSA. For growers who initiate CSAs as instruments of social change, it is frustrating to deal with the reality of members who conceptualize their CSA as a food-buying club. However, as an organized social group, the CSA is a community, and the different visions of what constitutes a CSA are part of constructing that community. Yet, for growers who have their own vision and have invested their own sweat and labor, it is disheartening to lose control of their CSA's direction. At times, the CSA dynamics result in shifts in grower-member relations over time. Even under ideal conditions, these changes in social relations can require adjustments and reflection on the part of the grower. In one case, where a church group had initiated the CSA, the member group oversaw the business operations and promotions during the first few seasons in order to get the CSA off the ground. By the third year, they began to cede power and responsibility to the grower, something that he wanted, but at the same time he regretted the loss of their active presence. As he recalled the transition,

> They kind of stepped back. I know they kind of really stepped back. I know that at one time, they had pretty hard discussions about how they were going to handle our CSA. . . . Their plan was just to empower people and show them how to do it and let the people go loose and do it themselves. I was never invited to the discussions, so we've kind of taken over the whole process.

Institutionalization

As CSAs continue to operate over the course of several seasons, they evolve as organizations internally, reflecting shifts in member-grower relations and member ideology. Other CSA studies have noted changes in membership motivation and priorities as the CSA develops, recognizing that values such as civic responsibility and spirituality can exert greater influence over time (Cone and Myhre 2000). Those CSAs that survive the early seasons of production and distribution mistakes, unforeseen natural disasters, and recalcitrant members begin to witness changes in the social organization of their "community." As one long-time CSA member explained,

> There has got to be an evolution of consciousness. You always have to start with where people are. You start with where they are, just so you can take their money? Or do you start with where they are so that you can furnish them with the tools to facilitate their own evolution? Then, they begin to evolve on their own initiative. They are not going to get involved because we want them to. If they do not have the desire or initiative to receive information, nothing you can do is going to change them.

At the same time that New Mexico CSA growers look to the few success stories for guidance, they watch with unease at the failures of other CSAs and expansion of the commercial organic industry in the United States. They recognize that they are engaged in a social experiment in these alternative organizational endeavors and that each failure undermines the survival of rural lifeways in New Mexico. For those growers who have been involved for many years in community development and social justice issues in New Mexico, the lessons of failed organizations provide insights and guidance not only for the local grower. As one long-time community activist commented with regard to the legacy of failed cooperative organizations in New Mexico,

> The larger corporate world has a field day. They just sit out there and watch us doing this, and they lick their chops. They let us do the research and development and spend the years of losing and creating worlds of possibilities, so they can take them over and make them into something.

Planning the CSA Future

New Mexico lags behind other U.S. regions, such as California, the Pacific Northwest, and the Northeast, where CSAs have a longer, more established tradition. New Mexico CSA growers and members see themselves and their alternative farm sector at a crossroads, one holding great promise at the same time that risks loom ahead. On the one hand, the U.S. government now recognizes the viability or attractiveness of the sustainable farming movement, and there are more government programs and financial support for alternative farming projects. As well, the New Mexico farm sector is still dominated primarily by *nativo*/Latino farmers. In recent years, following a number of lawsuits against the USDA, the federal government has targeted more programs and funds toward minority farmers and rural communities. These growers themselves recognize that these changes present them with opportunities to expand and broaden this movement in New Mexico. As one Latino grower commented,

> Now, when you go to the national conferences, that's all you hear about. Small farms, small family farms, community, those are what's successful. Big agriculture is all minimalized, and they're shipping it off to other countries. In the future, big agriculture isn't going to be in the U.S.; it's not profitable enough. So, it'll go to Third World countries. That's already the way I see it, the way it's happening. And the only future we have here is small farms for our communities. CSAs are an important part of that because it goes directly to the farmer to help support the small farms. Even, Anne Fuerman, Secretary of Agriculture, in one of her reports, mentioned the sustainability of small farms are critical to the community and food security. With the Secretary of Agriculture talking like that, I know it's small, it's only like one percent, but it's already being heard, it's already being talked about. I think there's a shift occurring, slow, but it's a shift that people are thinking differently.

At the same time, CSA growers and members recognize the general trends in U.S. agricultural production and marketing, as reflected in the growing centralization of large commercial operations. New Mexico presents critical challenges to the CSA movement. Expanding CSA organizations requires resolving local challenges posed by a high number of low-income consumers, lack of nutritional education, and lack of grower experience and knowledge of alternative farming practices. Those growers who have been successful in organic production, CSA organizations, institutional contracts, and/or production for farmers' markets recognize that the expansion and institutionalization of these local food systems as alternatives must be carried out in a timely manner. In part, this reflects increased concern by CSA activists, generally outsiders, about the growing interest in the organic food movement by the commercial food industry. In discussing the various retail market options in Santa Fe, one organic grower referred to Whole Foods as the "Wal-Mart of the organic food industry."

Increased federal regulation of organic production presents opportunities for small growers in New Mexico, yet it also ushers in increased bureaucracy and paperwork. Small growers see themselves being left out of a movement and a market that they themselves have fought hard to establish. Within these conditions of increased regulation and market competition, CSA growers also turn back to their own membership and organizations, recognizing the need to develop consensus, strong ties, membership loyalty, and collective consciousness, all ideological components of the shared community that CSAs will need to fend off the advances of organic Wal-Marts. This battle is not just economic; it is political, bitter, and personal. As one CSA grower reflected,

> People who are using CSA as a marketing technique are using my efforts personally to build meaning around a word, CSA. They are stealing my efforts to use it to develop members for their marketing techniques. I sort of take offense at that. You know, it hurts because I need the money, but they [those members] probably were going to quit here, anyway....
>
> There is not only one answer. I just think it is so frustrating to see a movement go this way. Basically, we are doing with CSAs exactly what we did with organics. We are setting ourselves up to get ripped off. And then we sit around and bitch and whine about it when it happens....And it will happen.

Looking back over these four stages of organizational evolution, certain contrasting patterns appear to emerge from the narratives. In no way do these differences represent distinct and bounded contrasts; rather, they point to the challenges of bridging cultural divides in constructing new organizational forms and including new groups of consumers. The narratives emphasize the dynamic nature of these organizations and the evolution of the new relationships that are constructed between growers and consumers. Clearly, if alternative farm organizations are to survive in the long run, they must address the changing needs, perceptions, and constraints faced by both members and growers over time. Equally important is the diversity among both growers and members. In states such as New Mexico, where the general population reflects a great cultural and economic diversity, growers and members bring with them very different sets of expectations about the nature of these organizations and how they should function. Failing to address these differences and balance the contradictions will inevitably undermine the cohesiveness of the organization.

Conclusion

CSA growers and members face great challenges in the market and external environment as they attempt to establish and maintain these alternative forms of direct marketing. While other studies have identified the concerns that affect members' interests in joining a CSA, equally important is the construction and maintenance of organizational cohesiveness that forms the basis of dependable, dedicated social relations that would characterize a CSA community. Concerned with production, distribution, and management of operations, growers also have to maintain social cohesion and organizational loyalty. The narratives presented here provide a structure within which future research needs to examine the evolution of growers' missions, ideology, vision, and relations with members. The narratives reveal a complex and often contradictory relationship between ideology, as expressed through these narratives, and practices, expressed through growers' and members' behavior. Examining how these ties evolve over time, how they change, and how they contest one another, among other features, will provide critical insights into the social construction of new forms of community in the alternative farming movement. In these narratives, several emergent themes stand out.

First, farmers initially establish CSAs for a variety of reasons, embedding from the start the ideological conflicts expressed in other studies (Cone and Kakaliouras 1995; DeLind 2002). Instead of expressing an abstract tension within the CSA as an organizational concept, these leaders themselves expressed a series of different motivations for starting the CSA. They also embark on this new effort with relatively little foresight and experience. Some CSA leaders are familiar with the movement and clearly understand the complexities of these new organizational forms; others respond to market opportunities or ideological reasons almost as an act of faith. While scholars may use analysis to tease out these inherent contradictions, the CSA leaders interviewed recognize the necessity of addressing both market concerns and social transformation; their challenge is maintaining a delicate balance between these two poles.

Second, from the first season, CSA growers recognize the tremendous effort and time that they must devote to cultivating their own membership. In addition to agricultural production, they work to address the concerns of their members and to foster membership loyalty. They recognize the dynamic nature of CSAs as organizations and the critical nature of building membership support during the early stages, usually in the first season. Unforeseen events, such as miscalculations in productivity or problems in distribution, all present challenges to the CSA grower that must be resolved quickly before members complain. Addressing these issues in a timely manner in turn builds the trust and loyalty of members that, in the long run, eases the burden of maintaining the organization.

Despite the CSA literature on core groups and membership activity, growers still assume the overwhelming leadership responsibility of maintaining the CSA organization at the same time that they work in the fields. Their commitment to their CSA is deep-rooted and emotional, and frustration develops when leaders perceive that their effort to carry out the vision is diverted by recalcitrant members who do not share that same vision. It is the sense of losing control, of working for their own members, that drives growers to resent and criticize the CSA members. Yet, most CSA growers recognize that the CSA can encompass different visions and ideologies. The challenge is to identity those members who share a broader vision, to construct some consensus and commitment among the core group, and to figure out the limits of membership commitment. As well, the CSA leaders recognize the dynamics of ideology within their own organizations. Through their efforts to institutionalize their organization over time, they foment the membership loyalty and engagement in the CSA that they hope will gradually effect changes in membership ideology. Members join CSAs themselves for a range of reasons, many grounded in a sense of commitment to local food systems and farmers. The CSA grower's success in instilling membership loyalty forms the base for nurturing members' expressions of ideological commitment to a local food system into long-term commitment to the organization.

Finally, CSA growers recognize the emerging competition within the alternative industry and the important role that ideology plays in fostering membership loyalty. They recognize that the long-term success of CSAs in New Mexico requires extending the model beyond a membership composed of upper middle-class "yuppie" consumers to lower income consumers. In this way, they also consciously link an alternative food movement to the challenge of food security of rural communities. At the same time, they look nervously over their shoulders at the rapid commercialization of the organic foods industry and expansion of retail markets into organic food distribution. Their long-term survival depends on their success in both broadening the movement to include different types of consumers, inevitably bringing with them differences in ideological visions, and instilling a shared vision among existing members, whose loyalty will thwart the expansion of commercial organic operations.

Notes

Acknowledgments. Appreciation is expressed to Le Adams, Don Bustos, Connie Falk, Felicity Fonseca, Jeff Graham, Dan Hobbs, and Steve Warshawer for their insights and ideas. Funding for this exploratory field research was provided through the NMSU Southwest Borders Cultural Institute faculty research grant, supported by the National Endowment for the Humanities. The author assumes full responsibility for any errors in data and/or in interpretation of the interviews.

1. The statewide survey was conducted by Joaquin Gallegos as an undergraduate research project.

2. See the CSA Center Organization website at: http://www.csacenter.org.

3. The average price of a full share was $470, although membership costs ranged from $275 to $750. Average price of a half share was $288, with a range from $150 to $387. Variations in price shares often reflect distribution periods of different lengths of time.

4. See the CSA Center Organization website at http://www.csacenter.org.

References

Allen, Patricia. 2004. Together at the Table: Sustainability and Sustenance in the American Agricultural System. University Park: Pennsylvania State University Press.

Allen, Patricia, M. FitzSimmons, M. Goodman, and K. Warner. 2003. Shifting Plates in the Agrifood Landscape: The Tectonics of Alternative Agrifood Initiatives in California. Journal of Rural Studies 19(1):61–75.

Andreatta, Susan. 2000. Marketing Strategies and Challenges of Small-Scale Organic Producers in Central North Carolina. Culture and Agriculture 22(3):40–50.

California Certified Organic Farmers (CCOF). n.d. http://www.ccof.org/.

Center for CSA Resources. n.d. http://www.csacenter.org/.

Clancy, Kate. 1997. Reconnecting Farmers and Citizens in the Food System. In Visions of American Agriculture. W. Lockeretz, ed. Ames: Iowa State University Press.

Cone, Cynthia, and A. Kakaliouras. 1995. Community Supported Agriculture: Building Moral Community or an Alternative Consumer Choice. Culture and Agriculture 51/52:28–31.

Cone, Cynthia, and Andrea Myhre. 2000. Community-Supported Agriculture: A Sustainable Alternative to Industrial Agriculture? Human Organization 59(2):187–97.

DeLind, Laura. 1993. Market Niches, Cul de Sacs, and Social Context: Alternative Systems of Food Production. Culture and Agriculture 47:7–12.

———. 1999. Close Encounters with a CSA: The Reflections of a Bruised and Somewhat Wiser Anthropologist. Agriculture and Human Values 16:3–9.

———. 2002. Considerably More than Vegetables, a Lot Less than Community. In Fighting for the Farm: Rural America Transformed. Jane Adams, ed. Pp. 192–206. Philadelphia: University of Pennsylvania Press.

DeLind, Laura, and Anne Ferguson. 1999. Is This a Women's Movement? The Relationship of Gender to Community-Supported Agriculture in Michigan. Human Organization 58(2):190–200.

Durrenberger, E. Paul. 2002. Community Supported Agriculture in Central Pennsylvania. Culture and Agriculture 24(2):42–51.

Economic Research Service, United State Department of Agriculture (ERA/USDA). 2002. Statistical Data.

Feenstra, Gail. 1997. Local Food Systems and Sustainable Communities. American Journal of Alternative Agriculture 12(1):28–36.

Fieldhouse, P. 1996. Community Supported Agriculture. Agriculture and Human Values 13(3):43–47.

Gallegos, Joaquin. 2003. Where Farmers and Consumers Meet: A Survey of CSAs in New Mexico. Unpublished paper, New Mexico State University, Las Cruces, New Mexico.

Goland, Carol. 2002. Community Supported Agriculture, Food Consumption Patterns, and Member Commitment. Culture and Agriculture 24(1):14–23.

Hendrickson, J. 1999. Community Supported Agriculture: Growing Food and Community. Madison: University of Wisconsin, Center for Integrated Agriculture Systems. Research Brief #21.

Hinrichs, C. Clare. 2000. Embeddedness and Local Food Systems: Notes on Two Types of Direct Agricultural Market. Journal of Rural Studies 16:292–303.

Kloppenberg, J., Jr., J. Hendrickson, and G. W. Stevenson. 1996. Coming into the Foodshed. Agriculture and Human Values 13(3):33–42.

Kloppenberg, J., Jr., S. Lezberg, K. De Master, G. Stevenson, and J. Hendrickson. 2000. Tasting Food, Tasting Sustainability: Defining the Attributes of an Alternative Food System with Competent, Ordinary People. Human Organization 59(2):177–86.

Kolodinsky, Jane, and Leslie Pelch. 1997a. Factors Influencing the Decision to Join a Community Supported Agriculture Farm. Journal of Sustainable Agriculture 10(2/3):129–41.

———. 1997b. Who Leaves the Farm? An Investigation of Community Supported Agriculture (CSA) Farm Membership Renewals. Consumer Interests Annual 43:46–51.

Lamb, Gary. 1994. Community Supported Agriculture: Can It Become the Basis for a New Associative Economy? Biodynamics November/December:8–15.

Licona, Laura. 2003. Locating the Critical Connections in Community Supported Agriculture: A Case Study of OASIS CSA. Paper presented at the meetings of the American Anthropological Association, Chicago, Illinois, November.

———. 2004. OASIS: An Ethnographic Study of a New Mexico CSA. Unpublished undergraduate honor's thesis, New Mexico State University, Las Cruces, May.

Main, A., and J. Lawson. 1999. Returning Relationships to Food: The Teikei Movement in Japan. In Sharing the Harvest. E. Henderson and R. Van En, eds. Pp. 214–18. White River Junction, Vermont: Chelsea Green Publishing Company.

McIlvane-Newsad, Heather. 2002. Direct from Farm to Table: Community Supported Agriculture in Western Illinois. Paper presented at the American Anthropological Association meetings, New Orleans, November.

National Agricultural Statistics Service/United States Department of Agriculture (NASS/USDA). 2002. Census of Agriculture. National Agricultural Statistics Service, United States Department of Agriculture.

New Mexico Farmers' Market Association n.d. Statistical data. Santa Fe: New Mexico Farmers' Market Association.

Ostrom, M. R. 1997. Toward a Community Supported Agriculture: A Case Study of Resistance and Change in the Modern Food System. Unpublished Ph.D. dissertation, Institute for Environmental Studies, University of Wisconsin, Madison.

Sharp, Jeff, Eric Imerman, and Greg Peters. 2002. Community Supported Agriculture (CSA): Building Community among Farmers and Non-Farmers. Journal of Extension 40(3):1–7.

Stafl, Sigrid, and Sabine O'Hara. 2002. Motivating Factors and Barriers to Sustainable Consumer Behavior. International Journal of Agricultural Resources, Governance, and Ecology 2(1):75–88.

Stanford, Lois. 2001. Negotiating Niche Markets: The Challenges of Small Farmers in Northern New Mexico. Paper presented at the American Anthropological Association meetings, Washington, D.C., November.

———. 2005. Sustainable Farming in the Southwest: Challenges and Alternatives. Paper presented at the, Saving the Wide Open Space: How to Conserve Biodiversity and Sustainable Ranching, Forestry and Farming in the American West conference, Tucson, Arizona, 13–15 May.

Wells, Betty L., and Shelly Gradwell. 2001. Gender and Resource Management: Community Supported Agriculture as Caring-Practice. Agriculture and Human Values 18:107–19.

Artisanal Cheese and Economies of Sentiment in New England

13

HEATHER PAXSON

IN THE PAST TWO DECADES, new American cheeses with such names as Humboldt Fog and Hooligan have cropped up in specialty shops and farmers' markets, signaling producers and consumers keen to cultivate novel tastes. Consider Vermont Shepherd: a 2000 American Cheese Society Best of Show winner, it is among America's most distinguished cheeses. "With its golden brown rind and rustic shape," quoting from the farm's brochure, "every wheel of Vermont Shepherd is distinctive. The texture is smooth and creamy. The flavor is sweet, rich and earthy, with hints of clover, wild mint and thyme." The Vermont Cheese Council website adds: "it is only made during Vermont's warmer months, when our sheep are grazing the pastures and fields." The makers' website offers serving suggestions— "As a dessert, pair with a cherry preserve (a French Pyrenees classic)"—and adds a democratic reassurance that the cheese goes well with just about any wine.[1] Not only are we tantalized by the epicurean experience of a slice of Vermont Shepherd, we are invited to imagine the flavors distinctive to this cheese emerging from equally distinctive clover-filled pastures, locating the cheese, and its makers, in the pastoral landscape of Vermont.

It might be easy to dismiss this synesthetic appeal as a mere marketing tool, selling the consumer, at over $20 a pound, a value-added fantasy of clean rural living with a classy Europhilic twist. One might level at America's artisanal cheese renaissance a critique aimed at Whole Foods Market and the Slow Food movement, that it represents the profit-driven creation of an elite niche market (e.g., Wurgaft 2002:87; Gaytán 2004; Pilcher this volume). In fall 2003, Slow Food USA inaugurated an American Raw Milk Farmstead Cheese Presidium to support makers of cheeses, like Vermont Shepherd, "who face the daily challenges of maintaining their farms, tending to their animals, and finding the time to make cheese."[2] But critique of such announcements as mere marketing itself rests on a "corporate vision of food as pure commodity"—precisely what the founders of Slow Food hoped to overcome with their "manifesto in defense of pleasure" (Parasecoli 2003:35). As

Melanie Du Puis (2002) notes, academic food fights over value-added agricultural products like organics often come down to how each side views the consumer: as agent of change leveraging the power of market demand, or as corporate dupe animated by a feel-good false consciousness that good shopping can save the family farm and the environment from globalization and agribusiness. Without ignoring the class differentials of taste and purchasing power central to food marketing and consumption, I show here what is missed when analyses, like the Slow Food movement itself, neglect to consider how *all* foods produced for market, "capitalist" and "noncapitalist," are embedded in cultural and moral economies.

Critics and champions of alternative foods have often assumed that only desire for profit drives the owners of the means of food production. Despite Sahlins's attempt in *Culture and Practical Reason* (1976:169) to get us to think of capitalist production as "something more and other than a practical logic of material effectiveness," many of today's substantivists, speaking of cultural capital if not cultural reason, focus on consumption as a site for cultural production and class differentiation, a location of resistance or complicity. When scholars overlook production in searching for food politics, they may assume capitalists lack not only political goodwill but also "cultural intention" (1976:169). A parallel trend in anthropology, however, has linked cultural histories of production to meanings and operations of "the market" (e.g., Mintz 1985; Carrier 1997). In development studies, scholars employ variations of commodity network analysis to study how Third World production and First World consumption of agricultural products, like specialty horticulture, are linked by codes of conduct (e.g., Barrientos and Dolan 2003; Friedberg 2004). Labelle (2004) entertains Slow Food as a "recipe for connectedness bridging production and consumption." Bestor, in his study of Tokyo's fish market, details how "the idiom in which [wholesalers] speak of credit, labor, or capital" is a distinctly cultural one of "kinship, personal connections of mutual obligation, apprenticeships, and myriad ties of self-interest embedded in communal . . . affiliations" (2004:219–20). In *Producing Culture and Capital*, Sylvia Yanagisako proposes "a cultural theory of economic action that treats all social action—including capital accumulation, firm expansion, and diversification—as constituted by both deliberate, rational calculation and by sentiments and desires" (2002:21).

Social relations of small-scale agriculture and food production in the United States are driven by sentiment, affiliation, and politics as well as by economic rationality (Barlett 1993; Jarosz 2000; Duram 2000). Cabot Cheddar, the industry giant of the Vermont Cheese Council, is a widely distributed, plastic-wrapped supermarket cheese available in such flavor-added varieties as "pizza cheddar cheese with pepperoni"—*not*, perhaps, a slow food. However, the Cabot cheese factory has been farmer owned since 1919, merging in 1992 with Agri-Mark, New England's

largest dairy farmer cooperative. Milk from Agri-Mark's owner farms is collected daily and pasteurized collectively to be marketed as fluid milk or to be sent to a processing plant, including the Cabot cheese factory. This is far from farmstead production, but neither is it corporate buy-out. Grafton Cheddar, another Vermont cheese sourced from a dairy cooperative, is produced in a factory owned by the not-for-profit Windham Foundation. Established in 1963 by an investment banker with local family roots, the foundation is devoted to the historical restoration and economic revitalization of Grafton village and to "the general welfare of Vermont and Vermonters." Ben and Jerry, finding in their premium ice cream another value-added product to support Vermont's dairy farmers, did not invent the sentiment of worker-owned, local-minded, philanthropic capitalism.

Farmstead cheeses—handcrafted in small batches from milk produced from a herd on the same farm as the cheese—are located in this cultural economy. Who *are* the new cheesemakers, producers of this slow food? What are the kinds and sources of affiliation through which cheesemakers develop their product and bring it to market? I am interested in how the cultural capital of socially conscious or gastronomic foods is not exclusive to consumers. The values that make artisan cheeses taste "good" are related to those values that make such cheeses "good" to make. "Taste" is relevant to production, economic efficiency is a consideration in consumption, and in both, class difference is reproduced while individual class mobility remains a possibility.

This chapter reports from fieldwork undertaken in spring and summer 2004 to chart the cultural economies of New England artisanal cheese production and consumption. Drawing from interviews with cheesemakers and purveyors, I offer examples of how the sentiments of New England small-scale family farmers are variously attached to the cultural capital generated by the artisanal products of their labor.

The Rise of American Artisanal Cheese

Vermont supports more farmstead cheesemakers per capita than any other state (Howland 2004), selling itself as a "green mountain" state of rocky hills and open pastures that depend on grazing sheep and cows. Across the country, the development of commercial dairying has meant fewer and larger farms are producing more milk, sold at cheaper prices (Lyson and Gillespie 1995). Smaller operations have been forced out of business owing to increasing health regulations (e.g., 1950s mandates for concrete-floored milking parlors and replacing metal milk cans with bulk tanks), higher production and equipment costs, and decline in milk consumption. In 1953, at the time of the first bulk tank, Vermont had 10,637 dairy farms with an average herd size of 25 milking cows yielding a total production of 1.5 billion pounds of milk. By 1999, Vermont had only 1,714 dairy farms, with an annual production of 2.6 billion pounds of milk (Albers 2000:278). But rocky New England farms cannot compete in today's fluid milk economies of scale, calibrated to California's vast valleys, mild winters, and pro-agribusiness political climate (Du Puis 2002:202). In 2002 half of Vermont's dairy farms held seventy cows or fewer. Their survival is said to lie in niche farming—instead of selling commodity [fluid] milk to agribusiness dairies, state legislators and academic consultants encourage farmers in Vermont and Maine to add value to their milk by processing it for specialty markets (Albers 2000:281–84). But it is reductionist to explain that Vermont leads the dairy niche market *because* rocky hillsides are not accessible to large machinery (Hall 2001). This answer, to begin, cannot account for why another state where artisanal cheese is flourishing is California, home to the very largest industrial dairy farms.

Indeed, a bit of state rivalry may inspire Vermont Cheese Council founder Alison Hooper's declaration of Vermont as "the Napa Valley of artisanal cheese." Likening the blossoming of American artisanal cheese to the California wine revolution of the 1970s, industry experts and journalists assert that growth in cheese, particularly strong since the middle 1990s, has been fueled by *nouvelle cuisine* chefs and consumers with a taste for locally sourced, nonindustrial foods such as those found at the country's increasingly popular farmers' markets (Berry 2003; Burros 2004; Howland 2004). Tasting booths promoting local cheeses are appearing at New England fairs, like Brattleboro, Vermont's annual "Strolling of the Heifers," following a long tradition of American boosterism celebrating local food specialties (e.g., Gilroy, California's famous Garlic Festival). But the connection between California cuisine and today's artisanal cheese movement runs deeper than cultivation of taste for fresh, unprocessed foods with known origins.

The California culinary movement epitomized by Alice Waters and her Berkeley restaurant, Chez Panisse, shares with the Slow Food movement political beginnings in 1960s leftist student movements (Belasco 1993; Kuh 2001; Parasecoli 2003). Similarly, Vermont's self-proclaimed eccentric values—small government and homesteading individualism combined with ecological sensibility—are conducive to artisan farmstead production. Compared with Wisconsin, another state with a significant history of cheese production (and boosterism), Vermont legislators stipulate less demanding regulations for farmstead cheese facilities. Rural Vermont is also within a few hours of metropolitan Boston and New York, key markets for high-end niche products. Formaggio Kitchen early on promoted regional farmstead producers; the cheese shop is located in Cambridge, Massachusetts, home to elite institutions of higher education that nurture political liberalism and a Europhilic palate. In 1995, owner Ihsan Gurdal was the first cheesemonger in the United States to create a French-style cave, a damp basement room for ripening cheeses.

I spoke with Gurdal about the growing interest in artisanal cheese. From his perspective, it began with the strong economy and dollar of the 1990s, which encouraged weekend trips to Paris. In Europe, "people were exposed to cheese" and to the way Europeans eat cheese, as a course in itself. Meanwhile, they realized the 1980s "cholesterol scare was overdone." Restaurant diners started requesting cheese plates. Middle-class consumers have since flocked to educational cheese-tasting workshops. Cheese is becoming the new wine—a mark of educated, yet wholesome, good taste. The recent low-carb diet craze has done more for hedonistic cheese consumption than news of "good" cholesterol. Awake to this new market, New England state legislators and agricultural activists herald artisanal cheeses as value-added commodities that might save small dairy farms from collapse or consolidation.

Gurdal grew animated talking about new American cheesemakers, and he revealed that the majority are *not* traditional farmers making the transition to niche-market production but successful businesspeople who retired early, bought land in the country, and started making cheese. Among the earliest were Miles and Lilian Cahn, former owners of Coach Leather, who bought farmland in New York's Hudson River Valley twenty years ago and make Coach Farm goat cheese. At a New York City Slow Food event in 2001 I heard Miles Cahn tell his story, retold in the photo-filled *Perils and Pleasures of Domesticating Goat Cheese* (2003): "We had this idea about moving to a farm. We were Manhattanites. I definitely had a particular image of a farm in my head. I had seen this cartoon, with a red barn and a silo and Farmer Brown on his tractor, talking to a cow. And that's how I thought of it, as me and the animals talking to each other." Behind this playfulness is a successful businessperson who brought a wealth of economic and cultural capital to farmstead cheesemaking. Cahn is not the only millionaire cheesemaker. Tom Clark, behind Old Chatham Shepherding Company and their exceptional ewes' milk Camembert, remains president of an equity investment firm in Greenwich, Connecticut, and commutes to his Hudson River Valley farm. The newest of this cohort is David Muller, who has a Wharton MBA and chemistry PhD and made a fortune selling medical equipment in Cambridge before moving to Vermont, where he has invested $1.5 million, plus an additional million loaned by the state, in a farmstead water buffalo mozzarella operation, Star Hill Dairy. These stories map a möbius strip of upscale urban consumers and producers, suggesting a translation of the family farm into a sustainable retirement project.

Gurdal pointed out that these pioneering cheesemakers have made a name and market for American farmstead cheeses, paving the way for newcomers with less start-up capital. Some of the younger urban transplants, he said, really are "becoming farmers," invested in their land and local communities. If the native farmer is not the average cheesemaker, neither is the former CEO. I traveled to Vermont and visited (among others) two cheesemakers whom Gurdal singled out to me as exemplars of this new cottage industry, and whose cheeses he sells at Formaggio. Like these two, the majority of New England's artisanal cheesemakers are college graduates who either have returned to family land with new class dispositions and business sensibility, or have adopted Vermont as a land of ecologically sound economic opportunity.

Vermont Shepherd

My first stop was Major Farm in southern Vermont, a region of rolling hills, quaint general stores, and cozy B&Bs. David and Cindy Major, makers of the award-winning Vermont Shepherd, are often cited as the vanguard of New England's farmstead cheese movement. Arriving shortly after 1:00 P.M., I roused David from a nap. It was lambing season and he had been spending nights in the barn, ready to assist difficult deliveries.

David, forty-three, grew up in a farmhouse across the road that his parents bought when they started a family and where they live still today. David's family raised sheep for meat and wool, but the farm wasn't "sustainable"; his mother taught kindergarten and his father, while serving as state legislator, sold real estate. David and his three siblings were well educated. David graduated from Harvard, where he studied international development and engineering. In 1983, he returned to his parents' farm with the goal of making it economically sustainable. He was working in the wool industry when he met Cindy. It was Cindy's father, owner of a dairy processing plant in Queens, New York, who suggested the newly married couple milk the sheep—this had never occurred to the Majors, who regarded sheep as meat, wool, and pets. With a USDA grant and financial support and encouragement from Cindy's parents, they built a cheesemaking facility next to their new farmhouse. By 1993 Cindy and David were making Vermont Shepherd, a value-added product that now sustains their family of four and a handful of paid, mostly part-time or seasonal, employees. In summers their children help on the farm. The operation includes a barn and milking parlor on David's parents' property and a larger barn and parlor on an adjacent farm that Cindy's parents bought. In terms of capital investment it is an extended family farm.

David Major is a sheep dairy farmer who also makes cheese. He does the shearing. During lambing season he sleeps in the unheated barn. He takes shifts in the milking parlor. The Majors cut and bale their own hay, family and neighbors pitching in, and nourish the pastures with composted manure and whey. Following his politically active parents, David serves as a farmer representative on numerous local and state agricultural committees.

During my initial visit David led me on a tour of the cheesemaking facilities before crossing over snow-covered fields, trailed by a pair of working border collies, to feed sixty-five ewes at his parents' barn. For David this is not foremost about the cheese. Cheese is what allows him to spend his days on the land and with the sheep. His favorite part of the enterprise is grass pasturage, maintaining clover, wildflowers, and grasses through rotational grazing. As I learned during a two-week stay on Major Farm, moving into the barn apartment as resident anthropologist/volunteer laborer, a significant portion of the day-to-day work on a sheep dairy farm entails "making pasture" by moving electrified plastic fencing to create fresh grazing zones. The Major family is fond of the sheep, direct descendants of animals David helped tend as a child. He pointed out to me ancestral traits, like a brown speckling on some of the ewes' faces. This sentimental focus on the origins of the milk, rather than the eventual product of the milk, may help explain why in more than a decade Vermont Shepherd is the only cheese they make from their sheep's milk.

Today, three days a week, David makes most of the Vermont Shepherd while Cindy oversees accounts and shipping, but it was Cindy who first applied her energy to cheesemaking, experimenting with recipes before seeking the advice of British cheese writer Patrick Rance. One stormy evening over a cup of tea, Cindy showed me Rance's handwritten reply to her initial plea for help. He suggested the family travel to the French Pyrenees, where climatic and geographic conditions were similar to Vermont, to learn about making sheep's milk cheese and to solve their "crust problem," a difficulty they were having with their rinds. Cindy safeguards this letter along with photographs of the Basque cheesemakers who generously took the Majors under their wing and taught them their craft.

In Europe the Majors picked up more than cheesemaking skills; they were drawn to the regional designation and collective sentiment of a cheese consortium. Sandra Ott (1981) describes one such consortium in her ethnography of a Basque shepherding community. Indeed, when I first explained my ethnographic project to David Major, he replied, "You mean like Sandra Ott?" and pulled down from a kitchen shelf, near the *Moosewood Cookbook*, a copy of Ott's (1981) *The Circle of Mountains*. Inspired by France's cheese guilds, in the late nineties Cindy and David developed a consortium of neighboring farms "hooked together for curing and marketing." With funds from a federal grant they established a residential internship program. American bureaucrats, unlike those in Europe (Terrio 2000; Herzfeld 2004), do not view artisans as "backward" obstacles to modernization; here, artisans are figured as harmless hobbyists or as quintessentially American entrepreneurs. Cheesemakers like the Majors have won educational grants to train others in craft skills that might translate into economic capital. But if the *cultural* capital of artisan cheesemaking is subsidized, the economic capital of farmstead production is not. Indeed, the strong dollar that helped develop an American palate for artisanal cheese also made it difficult for American cheeses to compete with state-subsidized European originals—the cheeses Americans were adopting and adapting for new geographical, economic, and gastronomic realities.

David and Cindy Major trained cheesemakers who went off to milk sheep on their own farms, craft Vermont Shepherd, and send the "green" wheels to Major Farm to be collectively aged, labeled, and marketed. Nine farms have been involved in the Vermont Shepherd guild. Most of those interested in learning to make cheese were themselves entrepreneurial types. Once they got the hang of Vermont Shepherd, they developed their own cheeses and labels. Although the consortium has dissolved, it was instrumental in training nearly all of Vermont's ewes' milk cheesemakers.

Jasper Hill Farm

The second farm Gurdal pointed me toward represents this young entrepreneurial spirit. Engaged in collective enterprise, Mateo and Andy Kehler are brothers who think big. To reach the Kehlers' Jasper Hill Farm, I drove north through economically depressed areas. Many farms up there, at least when covered with spring snow, seem more desperate than quaint. Lacking a major waterway, the Northeast Kingdom, a trio of optimistically named counties, missed out on the region's logging boom and remains a land of struggling farms and open frontier. I was greeted by Andy, the brother in charge of the cows, and directed to pull on hospital booties before entering the stainless steel cheesemaking room where Mateo, his wife Angie, and Andy's fiancée Victoria—all in their early thirties—were at work. They were in the cheddaring stage of a cheese they call Aspenhurst, fashioned after an English Leicester. They make cheese every other day, alternating this variety with Stilton-style Bayley Hazen Blue and a luscious mold-ripened cheese called Constant Bliss.

Mateo pitched me his vision: "We wanted to make some money and live in Vermont, the most beautiful place in the world" and where the brothers used to visit their grandmother during childhood summers. After studying international development at Friends World College in New York, Mateo became committed to sustainable agriculture. Googling Mateo, I found him pictured at an anti-globalization rally with Public Citizen's Global Trade Watch. Vermont, he told me, is in need of agricultural development the same as any struggling farming region. The brothers' first business model explored the market potential for organic tofu. But then they looked around and said, "Why not cows?" Cows, they explained, are not only part of the existing landscape but are central to Vermont's identity. As with the Majors, artisanal cheese has provided the Kehlers with a means of becoming rural entrepreneurs; it is not the reason for it.

What sentiments motivate this economic action: buying land in an isolated, depressed rural area, mortgaging it to add to an old barn a new cheese room, working seven long days a week, and giving up any social life? It is the sentiment of left-leaning college graduates who have developed a business model, as they call it, that I view as a hybrid of an ecologically minded critique of capitalism and a middle-class family ethic. Andy, a University of Vermont graduate, told me that after years in carpentry he realized the only way he could make a decent living was as a contractor. But then, he said critically, "You make money off of other people's labor." With the aim of supporting two families without engaging in exploitive labor relations (since our initial meeting, Angie has birthed a baby), the brothers turned to cheese. As they have calculated it, "A family here can make a good living with twenty-five cows" *if* they make artisanal cheese. The Kehlers plan to expand their herd of twenty-eight to fifty because "we're two families." While the brothers initially intended to go it alone, Victoria and Angie left their jobs to work full-time in the new family business.

The Kehler brothers, in keeping with an ethical business sentiment, are committed to "keeping the money in town."[3] They buy hay from a neighbor and wooden packing crates from a local carpenter instead of "getting on the Internet" to find the cheapest price. This is why they are not organic; to be organic they would have to bring in hay and grain from further away. They also keep the price of their cheese within reach of local consumers. At the Greensboro general store Bayley Hazen Blue sold that spring for seven-fifty a pound (it went for more than twice that in Cambridge). Thanks to networks of personal affiliation (Victoria made Vermont Shepherd as part of the Majors' guild and Mateo interned at London's Neal's Yard Dairy during a college year abroad) and to exposure afforded by Slow Food, their product is sold at a larger profit margin to restaurants from Atlanta to San Francisco.

Mateo and Andy are young entrepreneurs who speak of business models; their vision includes developing northeastern Vermont's economy without compromising the "working landscape" or local "culture." As we lunched on grilled sandwiches Mateo made with their Bayley Hazen Blue, English chutney, and Angie's homemade bread, he told me Vermont lost four hundred dairy farms last year, exclaiming "That's more than most states have!" The problem, as he sees it, is that Vermont will not abandon fluid milk, important to the state's self-image. "To do so would be to admit that it's a failed industry. But we can't compete with the economies of scale in California." Mateo cited a dairy farm in Barstow with ninety thousand cows and predicted, "California is going to bury Vermont in a tidal wave of cheap milk."

Their project is to demonstrate how Vermont dairy farms can prosper by making cheese. Dairy sheep and goats are on the rise, and the state is providing economic support to try llamas, ostriches, and buffalo. But at the moment, Mateo said, the notion that traditional farms are being "saved" through cheese is more ideal than reality. Most Vermont cheesemakers are, as he put it, "like us"—well educated, not truly local. According to Mateo, this is because local farmers are not comfortable taking risks, a distinction he identified as a matter of "class" disposition. Their neighbors would never do what they are doing because it is too risky economically. He gestured out the window, "That farm is just scraping by. The land they own is worth a bundle because it's near a resort lake, but to them it's not worth that because it's not for sale." While annual income may not be a pressing concern for his immediate neighbors, who own their farm outright and have low overhead costs, Mateo is convinced that struggling farmers could go from poverty level to earning $100,000 a year if they crafted artisan cheese from the milk they are already producing from the animals they already own.

Sustainability for the Kehlers, as for the Majors, means not only living independently on land they love, it refers to the economic and cultural viability of a region. This is neither romantic nostalgia—the Kehlers want to change how Vermont dairy farms are conceived—nor the forced change of classic development. Mateo is applying the lessons of a liberal arts education. From his perspective, the Majors' consortium ran into difficulty because David and Cindy imported from France a social model based on a sentiment of collectivity and shared tradition that does not exist in Vermont. It produced what he sees as a "culture clash" among dairy producers. I would elaborate that while *dairy* collectives, like Agri-Mark, have long operated in New England, artisanal *cheese* collectives are different in organizational and economic ways. More, the craft fashioning of cheese is imbued with sentiments of proprietary pride that may not obtain with fluid milk. This may lead American cheesemakers to want not only to mark the products of their labor with traces of personal identity—wheels of Vermont Shepherd, like the Basque cheeses the Majors studied, are stamped with the logo of their maker—but to develop and name their own distinctive recipes. "Culture" is productive of economics, and vice versa; it is not merely a "viewpoint" from which to describe and value economic processes (Wilk 1996).

Motivated to show their neighbors how to exploit a niche market without compromising a sense of independence, the Kehlers' long-term plan is to help reverse engineer a kind of regional appellation for the Northeast Kingdom through which producers could collectively benefit from regional branding without having to conform to a particular product. In just forty years California's wine industry went from churning out undifferentiated "tank car wine" to cultivating a patchwork of renowned valleys celebrated for particular varietals. In developing a sense of Californian *terroir*, or place, bottles were reduced in size and relabeled to feature place-names rather than name brands. Evoking place "gives the drinking of that wine an emotional dimension" (Kuh 2001:144). If the California wine industry is precursor to American artisanal cheese, it is no surprise that discussions have begun in the cheese community regarding *terroir* (Binchet 2002). Cheesemakers like the Kehlers, and consultants like Vermont Institute for Artisan Cheese's Jeff Roberts, are considering which elements of the European Union's Appellation of Origin Control may, or may not, translate to the United States, where innovation rather than tradition is the national value embodied in artisanal cheeses.[4] Grounded in the pragmatics of local cultural economies, the producers of American artisanal cheeses deploy economic, social, and political knowledge that overlaps with, but extends beyond, that of their consumers, who are freer to romanticize "local imaginaries" for foods (Gaytán 2004).

Neighborly Farms

New England farmstead cheeses encompass European-style cheeses, like Vermont Shepherd and Bailey Hazen Blue, requiring months of care to ripen (what the French call *affinage*), but also "everyday" cheeses (Colby, Cheddar, Jack, Feta) that are vacuum-packed and sold soon after manufacture. The former, with labor-intensive "natural" rinds and strong, distinctive flavors, are sold at high-end shops and appear on restaurant cheese carts; they retail as high as $29 a pound. The second type is sold at farmers' markets, food co-ops, and local groceries; they retail at $6–9 a pound. A third Vermont family cheesemaking farm I visited turns out "everyday" cheeses in a variety of mild flavors. Linda and Rob Dimmick made the transition from dairying to cheese. Their story reveals sentiments that overlap with the Majors' and Kehlers' but that are not backed by the same economic and cultural capital.

Fourteen years ago, Linda and Rob bought the picturesque farm in Randolph Center, Vermont, where Rob grew up and his parents raised dairy cows. The farm grew to 180 milking cows but, Linda told me, "it burnt the family out," and in 1986 Rob's family sold the farm. In 1990, as Rob and Linda were starting a family of their own, Rob grew determined to give his three children the kind of childhood he enjoyed, on a working farm. They bought back the farm and tried to make it as a traditional dairy, selling milk, but the commodity price was too low to turn a profit. They sold the cows and Rob started a waste disposal business. In 2001, after Linda attended a state-sponsored workshop on cheesemaking, they decided to give cheese a try. They bought a new herd. Rob sold his business and, with federal grant money to support agri-tourism (again, while the federal government subsidizes the economic capital of agribusiness, it subsidizes the cultural capital of small-scale farming), in 2001 they built a cheese facility with a public viewing area. "My mother in Michigan thinks we're nuts," Linda confided. "Normal people wouldn't sell their life savings and put it into a failing business." But for her husband, "not farming was not an option."

A long corridor runs alongside the sterile cheese room partitioned by a glass wall through which visitors can watch production. On the facing wall hang framed photographs of the Dimmicks' kids showing cows at county and state fairs. Each child has raised a pet calf from birth. Linda and Rob hope their eldest son might eventually take over the farm. In addition to several flavor-added varieties of cheddar, Neighborly Farms makes Monterey Jack and Feta. With the exception of a raw milk cheddar, they pasteurize their milk because it provides quicker cash flow. While the FDA requires raw milk cheeses to be aged at least sixty days before sale, pasteurized cheeses can go on the market immediately. The Dimmicks package their cheese the day after it is made. All the cheeses are organic. Like deciding on which varieties to make, choosing to go organic was a "business decision, not out of a philosophy"; market research revealed an unmet demand for raw milk, organic cheddar, and this has become their best seller. Impressed by reductions in their veterinarian bills since the cows have been "eating well, with no chemicals and antibiotics," Linda has been converted to the virtue of organics; "seeing is believing." Each year has seen a 300 percent growth in production. They milk forty-eight cows.

Linda started out as the cheesemaker, but in 2004 they paid five full-time employees, including a cheesemaker and a farm manager, who is Rob's brother. Linda spends much of her time on the phone with retailers, arranging deliveries and securing new accounts, but she enjoys the escape of the cheese room, finding the physical labor distracting: "You're not taking any calls, not worrying about the grain bill that's due." They do their own packaging and sell everything cryo-vacuum packed, with one exception: every two weeks someone from the farm drives more than five hours each way to deliver forty-pound blocks of Monterey Jack to an organic Mexican restaurant in Manhattan. When they started, Linda visited delis and supermarkets and was appalled at how cheese was handled. Before she married, she worked as a dental hygienist and so she's "picky about germs" and sells her cheese pre-packaged because she's "picky about who touches my cheese." She admires the work that the Majors and Kehlers do to age cheese, work she likened to "babysitting." Natural rind cheese tastes wonderful, she said, but she is not going to do it. It's too labor intensive. "In every way we're a little guy," she said—then added, "but then in some ways we're like a big guy," pasteurizing and packaging.

Linda feels the tension between little guy/big guy status in marketing and distribution. With Whole Foods she has "run up against a corporate wall." The national chain carries the corporate Horizon brand organic cheese and, in competition, their own private label. Linda has been working to convince the Whole Foods buyers of the distinction of her cheese, which is not only organic but farmstead, but to no avail. Trader Joe's, meanwhile, drives down retail prices so low she would be left without "wiggle room"; it has no place for "little guys." Dimmick is already selling her cheese as low as she can, at the $7–8 per pound at which they calculate they will need to sell to turn a profit once they are up to full production and selling their entire inventory. Linda finds herself caught between two sentiments. On the one hand, she and her husband share with the Majors and Kehlers a love for the land, for farming. But on the other, she is a populist who wants to make cheese for people who do not think of food as a marker of social distinction. As she put it to me, "We're an everyday cheese."

In many respects, Linda and Rob Dimmick are taking precisely the path Mateo Kehler hopes to encourage: they are a family dairy farm that, after failing with milk, turned to cheese. But when Mateo speaks of farmers making significant money with just twenty-five milking cows, what he has in mind is upscale "boutique" cheese representing American innovation on European themes, not the "everyday" cheese Linda wants to make. Linda, struggling to find a market niche to sustain their suite of sentiments with forty-eight cows, is finding it difficult to be a farmstead *and* a quotidian cheesemaker, to be "little guys" catering to customers (and tastes) often served by "big guys." Consumers who are happy eating a mild pre-packaged cheddar or Monterey Jack may not go out of their way to buy an organic farmstead version—at least that is what the big retailers assume. Meanwhile, consumers who care about organic farmstead production might also favor—and be able and willing to pay for—the stronger, sophisticated taste of a cured cheese: a Slower cheese.

As of May 2004, the Dimmicks made 1,600 pounds of cheese a week and sold to regular clients 1,000 pounds. Underselling their product, they had yet to turn a profit. And while Rob is the one who really wanted to work the land as a farmer, it is Linda who works full-time with the cheese. Five months after opening the cheese plant, their one-year grant ran out, and Rob was forced to return to his outside business to subsidize the farm. They hope the cheese will make the farm self-sufficient—"all we want is for it to support itself"—so Rob can return full-time to farming. Despite their financial difficulties, Linda Dimmick is committed to keeping her cheese affordable. She does not want people to "wait for the holidays" to buy her cheese as a "treat." Linda sent me off with a gift assortment of eight-ounce packages of cheese to enjoy at home.

Conclusion: Sentiments and Their Limits

While it is true that most, although not all, new cheesemakers are sophisticated urban transplants bringing bourgeois economic and cultural capital to farmstead production, this should not stymie us as social analysts, for their sentiments are far from uniform. Some are engaged in politically conscious rural revitalization.

Others are "hippie" homesteaders working modestly out of their kitchens, making only as much cheese as they feel like, even when the market could absorb more. Some are really into the cheese. Mark Gillman, a young Connecticut cheesemaker I visited, is having fun experimenting with a dozen cow's milk cheeses, including the delicious washed-rind Hooligan.

Examining the sentiments that, alongside profit motive, mold small-scale cheese production, promises to enrich our understanding of family farms and artisanal foods. Juxtaposing just three Vermont farmstead cheesemaking concerns reveals varied configurations of sentiment and capital: with the support of extended family, makers of Vermont Shepherd milk family sheep to produce a single high-end cheese while training new cheesemakers and engaging in farm politics. Jasper Hill Farm is the collective enterprise of two brothers and their spouses working from a business plan to provide for their growing families as well as to revitalize local economies. Neighborly Farms is a resurrected dairy turned cheesemaking enterprise catering to popular tastes that, through the exercise of economic reason, has discovered the virtues of organic farming. Clearly, farmstead cheesemakers "engage in both the deliberate, calculative pursuit of profit and the fulfillment of other culturally meaningful desires" (Yanagisako 2002:21).

What can attention to moral economies linking production and consumption tell us about artisanal foods? To begin, we must realize that the economies at issue are capitalist ones (socialist economies might entail a different suite of sentiments). Insofar as farmstead cheesemakers are usually landowners and employers as well as farmer-craftspeople, this produces the sort of embodied contradictions anthropologists have documented for French winegrowers (Ulin 1996) and chocolatiers (Terrio 2000). Individualistic sentiments of greed and pride are a lurking worry, with their potential to undermine community, locality, and neighborliness. Finally, success in craft production entails, in part, the successful selling of sentiment: images of the bucolic family farm help sell high-end cheeses. Success thus runs the risk of "selling out" one's values—ecological, anti-corporate, "little guy." That organic milk and produce are being mainstreamed at levels of production and marketing raises concern that the community-focused values that instigated the organic movement will be swamped by rationalized industrial practices (Allen and Kovach 2000; Klonsky 2000; Campbell 2001; Guthman 2004). Corporate consolidation of organics calls into question the long-term viability of niche-market production as a means not only of alternative agriculture, but of alternative sociality, an organizing sentiment for many cheesemakers.

If success runs the risk of compromising sentiment, the Dimmicks' story raises the inverse question: What are the limits of sentiment in driving market success? Opening up picturesque, organic, family-owned and -operated Neighborly Farms to visitors is proving insufficient to sell their "everyday" cheese to retailers catering to foodies.[5] The Dimmicks are in search of a market to sustain what Sidney Mintz calls in this volume a "food of moderate speed." Ethnographic attention to sentiment in practices of production and consumption over the span of social reproduction will reveal how elastic "sentiment" might be in social action and, therefore, how explanatory it might be in social analysis.

Notes

Acknowledgments. Many thanks to my interlocutors at the 2004 Society for Economic Anthropology meetings, and to Rick Wilk for his insightful comments on an earlier version of this chapter. I am grateful to Ihsan Gurdal; David and Cindy Major; Mateo, Andy, and Angie Kehler; Victoria Von Hessert; and Linda Dimmick for their willingness to share with me their stories, and for reading over excerpts of this chapter. Stefan Helmreich gave his critical reading.

1. http://www.vtcheese.com/vtcheese/vtshepherd/vtshepherd.html and http://www.vermontshepherd.com/. Accessed 4/19/05.

2. http://www.slowfoodusa.org/ark/farmstead_cheese.html. Accessed 8/7/04.

3. There is a long history of ethical business models in British and American capitalism, going back to eighteenth- and nineteenth-century Quaker building of iron bridges in lieu of casting cannonballs and producing "non-slavery" sugar. But utopian thinkers who go into business to do socially beneficial work have often been accused of "selling out" when they attain financial success. Philadelphia Quakers who grew wealthy on family businesses that succeeded owing to thrift and a reputation for trustworthiness have been popular targets for derision—as if ethical business must preclude the possibility of profit.

4. One possible model they are developing is a regional trust charged with overseeing that standards of quality and possibly some elements of artisan technique are met, as well as providing technical assistance and the marketing umbrella of a regional appellation. The trust could be funded by a percentage of gross sales from member producers.

5. At the 2006 American Cheese Society competition, Neighborly Farms won two second place awards, for Monterey Jack made from cow's milk, and for flavor-added cheddar. These awards may well boost Neighborly Farms' visibility among retailers and, hence, their sales.

References

Albers, Jan. 2000. Hands on the Land: A History of the Vermont Landscape. Cambridge, MA: MIT Press.

Allen, Patricia, and Martin Kovach. 2000. The Capitalist Composition of Organic: The Potential of Markets in Fulfilling the Promise of Organic Agriculture. Agriculture and Human Values 17:221–32.

Barlett, Peggy F. 1993. American Dreams, Rural Realities: Family Farms in Crisis. Chapel Hill: University of North Carolina Press.

Barndt, Deborah. 2002. Tangled Routes: Women, Work, and Globalization on the Tomato Trail. Boulder, CO: Westview Press.

Barrientos, Stephanie, and Catherine Dolan. 2003. A Gendered Value Chain Approach to Codes of Conduct in African Horticulture. World Development 31(9):1511–26.

Belasco, Warren J. 1993. Appetite for Change: How the Counter-culture Took on the Food Industry. Ithaca, NY: Cornell University Press.

Berry, Donna. 2003. Cheesemaking Highlights: Farmstead Cheese Movement Shows Dynamic Growth in California, while Wisconsin Remains the Leading Cheese Manufacturing State. Dairy Foods, August:1.

Bestor, Theodore C. 2004. Tsukiji: The Fish Market at the Center of the World. Berkeley: University of California Press.

Binchet, Maria Lorraine. 2002. The Terroir of Cheese. Wine Business Monthly 9(2).

Burros, Marian. 2004. Say Cheese, and New England Smiles. New York Times, Wednesday, June 23.

Cahn, Miles. 2003. The Perils and Pleasures of Domesticating Goat Cheese: Portrait of a Hudson Valley Dairy Goat Farm. New York: Catskill Press.

Campbell, David. 2001. Conviction Seeking Efficacy: Sustainable Agriculture and the Politics of Co-optation. Agriculture and Human Values 18:353–63.

Carrier, James G., ed. 1997. Meanings of the Market: The Free Market in Western Culture. Oxford, UK: Berg.

DuPuis, E. Melanie. 2002. Nature's Perfect Food: How Milk Became America's Drink. New York: New York University Press.

Duram, Leslie A. 2000. Agents' Peceptions of Structure: How Illinois Organic Farmers View Political, Economic, Social, and Ecological Factors. Agriculture and Human Values 17:35–48.

Freeman, Carla. 2000. High Tech and High Heels in the Global Economy: Women, Work, and Pink-Collar Identities in the Caribbean. Durham, NC: Duke University Press.

Freidburg, Susanne. 2004. French Beans and Food Scares: Culture and Commerce in an Anxious Age. Oxford: Oxford University Press.

Gaytán, Marie Sarita. 2004. Globalizing Resistance: Slow Food and New Local Imaginaries. Food, Culture & Society 7(2):97–116.

Guthman, Julie. 2004. Agrarian Dreams: The Paradox of Organic Farming in California. Berkeley: University of California Press.

Hall, Ross Hume. 2001. Will Fears of Germs Stymie a Small Farm Revival in the U.S.? The Ecologist, June.

Herzfeld, Michael. 2004. The Body Impolitic: Artisans and Artifice in the Global Hierarchy of Value. Chicago: University of Chicago Press.

Howland, Daphne R. 2004. Say Cheese, Say Flavor. Flavor & the Menu, Pp. 60–66. Winter.

Jarosz, Lucy. 2000. Understanding Agri-food Networks as Social Relations. Agriculture and Human Values 17:279–83.

Klonsky, Karen. 2000. Forces Impacting the Production of Organic Foods. Agriculture and Human Values 17:233–43.

Kuh, Patrick. 2001. The Last Days of Haute Cuisine: America's Culinary Revolution. New York: Viking.

Labelle, Julie. 2004. A Recipe for Connectedness: Bridging Production and Consumption with Slow Food. Food, Culture & Society 7(2):81–96.

Lyson, Thomas A., and Gilbert W. Gillespie. 1995. Producing More Milk of Fewer Farms: Neoclassical and Neostructural Explanations of Changes in Dairy Farming. Rural Sociology 60(3):493–504.

Mintz, Sidney. 1985. Sweetness and Power: The Place of Sugar in Modern History. New York: Penguin Books.

Ott, Sandra. 1981. The Circle of Mountains: A Basque Shepherding Community. Reno: University of Nevada Press.

Parasecoli, Fabio. 2003. Postrevolutionary Chowhounds: Food, Globalization, and the Italian Left. Gastronomica 3(3):29–39.

Petrini, Carlo. 2001. Slow Food: The Case for Taste. William McCuaig, trans. New York: Columbia University Press.

Sahlins, Marshall. 1976. Culture and Practical Reason. Chicago: University of Chicago Press.

Terrio, Susan J. 2000. Crafting the Culture and History of French Chocolate. Berkeley: University of California Press.

Ulin, Robert. 1996. Vintages and Traditions: An Ethnohistory of Southwest French Wine Cooperatives. Washington, D.C.: Smithsonian.

Wilk, Richard R. 1996. Economics & Cultures: Foundations of Economic Anthropology. Boulder, CO: Westview Press.

Wurgaft, Benjamin Aldes. 2002. East of Eden: Sin and Redemption at the Whole Foods Market. Gastronomica 2(3):87–89.

Yanagisako, Sylvia Junko. 2002. Producing Culture and Capital: Family Firms in Italy. Princeton: Princeton University Press.

Fast and Slow Food in the Fast Lane: Automobility and the Australian Diet 14

CATHY BANWELL, JANE DIXON, SARAH HINDE, AND HEATHER MCINTYRE

T HE CAR, COURTESY OF BRITISH AND AMERICAN FIRMS, has been a presence on the Australian landscape for almost half of our colonial history. The automobile, which began as a novel, eccentric, and somewhat inconsequential technology has, in fact, transformed society to the point where life without cars in Australia is nearly unimaginable. Australia's reliance on cars has made a major contribution to structuring the lifestyles and social practices of increasing numbers of Australians.

This chapter arises out of our study of the contribution of car-reliance to the rise in obesity. We report on the ways in which car-reliance structures dietary patterns including the provisioning and preparation of food, consumption practices, and the products consumed. By becoming indispensable in dietary practices and physical activity regimes, the car assures its own reproduction. We discuss some of the many discourses and practices that constitute the Australian fast and slow food car-centered diets, based on fieldwork in rural areas of New South Wales (NSW), in Sydney, and in Australia's national capital, Canberra. We begin by briefly amplifying what we are calling car-reliance, or the way in which the automobile structures, and is structured by, the social practices of Australians.

Car-Reliance

In 2003, we conducted a cultural economy audit of car-reliance in Australia and systematically explored car availability, acceptability, and the actors involved in those two processes (Hinde and Dixon 2005). Availability was interrogated through the production, distribution, accessibility, and uptake of cars, and other commodities or structures that facilitate car use (often referred to as transport infrastructure). We judged the car's acceptability, which is the value and meaning society attaches to cars and the "normal" patterns that embed car use into our daily lives. And we identified the actors, namely the organizations, groups, and individuals within the state, market, and civil society, who benefit from contributing to or resisting the availability and acceptability of cars and their use.

To summarize, we note that Australia is an extremely car-reliant nation, close behind the United States in the extent of car ownership and use. Along with the United States, we have an enormous amount of infrastructure devoted to the car compared to other developed countries. There are an extensive network of roads (Austroads 2000), plenty of car-parking spaces (Laird et al. 2001), and among the cheapest petrol prices after the United States and Canada (Austroads 2000). At the same time, the public transport system in Australia does not compete with cars in terms of average speed (Laird et al. 2001) and perceptions of access (Australian Bureau of Statistics 2000). In turn, the vast majority of the population travels in a motor vehicle to work, education, or shopping (Austroads 2000). In one year, Australia's vehicles together travel "the equivalent of going to Pluto and back 23 times" (Australian Bureau of Statistics 2003).

Car ownership has increased steadily over the second half of this century. Fifty years ago, the rate of car ownership was 1 motor vehicle per 7.8 persons, but by the end of the century it had increased to 1 per 1.6 persons (Australian Bureau of Statistics 2002). In Australia in the year 2000 there were around twenty million people, twelve million registered motor vehicles, and twelve million licensed drivers (Austroads 2000).

This extensive use and support of the car arises from a deep acceptance of its role in our lives. The Australian Treasurer reported "all time bumper record [car] sales for 2003" which he said was "good for the manufacturers, it is good for the people who are employed in the retail end of the car industry, and best of all it is good for consumers who have bought more cars than have ever been sold in Australia before" (Commonwealth Treasurer 2004).

Our research supports the definition of car-reliance as "a set of institutional policies and practices wherein the use of the car is embedded in the ways in which we organize our lives" (Urmetzer et al. 1999:355). It shows that there are numerous physical, economic, and cultural processes that reproduce car-reliance in everyday life. Beckmann (2001) states that "modern cultures are moving cultures" (594) and describes how the car becomes a structuring force: "The automobile turns into a structural prerequisite for the organisation of everyday life, while at the same time the variety of forms of everyday action becomes the structural prerequisite for the expansion of the automobile" (Beckmann 2001:595).

The car provides us with the means to live our lives across more and more distant destinations, in turn reproducing the demand for cars to get there. It is woven into all aspects of Australian life. For example, some Sydney mothers base their definitions of themselves as good mothers on their complex lives chauffeuring children and husbands, doing shopping, and socializing. The multiple demands on their time cut across various locations and necessitate the ownership and daily use of a motor vehicle (Dowling 2000).

Fast Food

Much has been written about fast food, which is characterized among other things by its uniformity of ingredients used to make food that is convenient, quick, and portable no matter where it is purchased (Noguchi 1994). In academic and popular literature, the car and fast food go hand in hand. Jakle and Sculle (1997), for example, argue that fast food, mass produced, was a response to fast cars, mass produced. In their history of *Fast Food, Roadside Restaurants in the Automobile Age*, the rise of the quick-service restaurant (the soda fountain, luncheonette, main street café, and diner) pre-dated mass car production, but the arrival of customers by automobile led to new demands on eating establishments and new possibilities. "The auto promised not only speed of movement, but the convenience of door-to-door travel, something that the railways could not provide" (Jakle and Sculle 1999) (although trains prefigured eating-on-the-move courtesy of their dining cars). The car altered perspectives on time, space, and freedom while contributing to new entrepreneurial opportunities, including fast-food chains, which as Marvin Harris observed "were spin-offs of the auto age. They catered to motorized families who preferred to take their meals inside chromium and glass, high finned living rooms on wheels, rather than round the kitchen table" (Harris 1985). Some fast foods, such as McNuggets, were designed to be purchased and eaten in the car, and the first KFC outlets were built next to petrol stations.

In very different cultural contexts the car is associated with a range of similar psycho-social states of being. In the United States, the auto offered privacy in travel, a prized possession, and freedom from the tyranny of the corporate railway timetable; while in Japan, the automobile serves as a metaphor for self-expression and individualism in contrast to the collective thought and action of train travelers (Noguchi 1994). In Australia, individualized self-expression is displayed through the type of car one uses, its color and ornamentation, and its specialized forms (for example, utilities, four-wheel drives, and accessories such as tow bars and "roo" bars [to minimize the damage to the car if a kangaroo is hit while driving], spotlights, mag wheels, and surfboard racks and internal decorations). Accounts exist of similar gendered forms of self-expression through automobility, linked to subcultural, transgressive practices among young women in Norway (Garvey 2001) and in young Swedish men's displays of working class mobility, virility, and rebellion (O'Dell 2001).

Ironically, the individualized self-expressing car is frequently linked with fast food, which itself is a product that stresses uniformity in ingredients (which do not vary across great distances) (Noguchi 1994). The uniformity of the product negates the individuality of the chef. As Shelton points out, everyone can have a burger made of 100 percent beef, but you cannot ask for it to be made by any particular individual (Shelton 1990).

Slow Food

The Slow Food Movement famously was established in 1986 by Carlo Petrini in response to the opening of a McDonald's fast food outlet next to the Spanish Steps in Rome (Leitch 2000). Ever since then, Slow Food Movement adherents have highlighted their distinctive identities through opposition to fast food. The official movement, whose symbol is a charmingly depicted snail, aims to protect and promote local customs in relation to food, local production techniques, and the agriculture products themselves. The Slow Food Movement website states,

> Let us rediscover the flavours and savours of regional cooking and banish the degrading effects of Fast Food. In the name of productivity, the Fast Life has changed our way of being and threatens our environment and our landscapes. (Slow Food 2004)

Slow Food describes itself as a champion of biodiversity and sustainable agriculture and development. It says about its logo the snail,

> The choice of this prehistoric-looking mollusk expressed the desire to reverse the passing of time, to counteract certain bad habits, both present and future. Among the causes of discontent was an obvious first target in the shape of shabby eating habits: fast food restaurants, meaning the reduction of food to consumption, of taste to hamburger, of thought to meatball. (Slow Food 2004)

The media portrays the stand taken by Slow Food as a head-to-head contest with fast food. For example in 2003, McDonald's sued slow food campaigner Eduardo Raspelli, for comparing its burgers to rubber and its fries to cardboard (BBC News World Edition 2003).

An example of Slow Food's political activity around food is provided in Leitch's paper on the social life of Lardo. She describes how Slow placed Lardo, which is cured pork fat from the Colonnata region in Italy, on its list of endangered foods, in response to the imposition of European Union Hygiene Legislation which would, she argues, diminish the economic viability of Lardo production for small-time artisan producers (Leitch 2000).

Slow's most visible presence operates at two levels: first, the locally based *convivia* in which members discuss aspects of slow food culture, and second, the website, which unites the global slow food community. It is a very postmodern organization in its use of up-to-date technologies to celebrate and rejuvenate time-honored and local foods and their traditions.

We turn now to a discussion of how slow and fast foods are exemplified in what we are calling car-centered diets, via a flavor of our fieldwork experiences of food and cars. Our fieldwork examples are commonly accepted illustrations of slow and fast food, used in Australian food discourses. Farmers' markets and specialist food providers employ the language of Slow Food to promote their wares. Thus we visited farmers' markets and Sydney Specialist Providores as widely accepted examples of Slow Food sites of exchange. While it verges on clichéd, we could not ignore McDonald's as an example of fast food. We also included a category that sits between slow and fast food, a business that produces and delivers heat-and-serve gourmet food. As we discuss later in this chapter, this business quite deliberately establishes itself as an intermediate category using the juxtaposition of Slow Food techniques and speedy consumption in its advertising material.

While there are other analyses that pit slow against fast food (Murdoch and Miele 2004), we concentrate in this chapter on the role of the car in shaping the operations of particular sites of food exchange. By doing this, a picture emerges of the centrality of the car to a range of culinary practices, so much so that we have coined the phrase *car-centered diets* to highlight what is happening.

Slow Food Sites of Exchange

We visited a number of slow food markets scattered up the east coast of Australia, some located in Sydney and small towns. They shared many characteristics, namely the sale of items produced by individuals or small, artisan businesses, which are sometimes subsidiaries of more mainstream farming activities. The Sydney market, described below, is the biggest market we visited and draws producers from the most distant locations, but in other ways it typifies smaller farmers' markets.

1. The Sydney Morning Herald Good Living Growers' Market

This market is situated at Pyrmont, across the road from the Star Casino and near the busy tourist destination, Darling Harbor. Held on the first Saturday of the month, it consists of approximately ninety-three stalls, with each producer paying $220 per stall (plus petrol and accommodation for some). Parking is scarce near the market. Many people park in the underground Casino car park, paying $15 for six hours instead of "cruising" for cheaper parking. People tend to drive their cars rather than take public transport, which is available nearby.

There is also limited car space for producers/stall holders, who use a service road for unloading but then must move their vehicles and find parking for the day. However, if they have goods that require refrigeration, there is a designated parking area near the market and their stall is set up close to the parked refrigeration vehicle (usually meat, cheese, and small-goods providers). Most producers drive a vehicle to bring their produce to the market. The greatest distances traveled by producers to this monthly market is 750 kilometers, while the shortest distance traveled by a producer was across town from Woolloomooloo, approximately five kilometers. Some of the more distant producers included:

- Gungel Farm Pork (Tenterfield)
  The producer travels 750 kilometers from Tenterfield in the northwest of NSW to visit the Sydney markets. Normally he would leave the farm gate at 5 P.M. and sleep overnight in Sydney. This weekend, though, he said he was late leaving Tenterfield with "too much to do" and so he drove through the night and "arrived at 2 A.M. and hung out at the Caltex station."
- Oyster Farm, Wooli (North Coffs Harbour)
  This business is also in northern New South Wales. The producer drives down during the week and the oysters are delivered by air the day before the market.
- Cowra Trout
  The producer travels about four hours to Sydney but stays overnight at Warick Farms on the outskirts. There is someone else selling Cowra Trout at the Warick Farm markets to make it worth the traveling and time.

This particular market sells a mix of fresh vegetables, herbs, fish, meat, cheese, bread, pastries, flowers, and durable or semi-durable small goods, smoked foods, olive oil, coffee, and tea. Most of the produce is not local to Sydney (see figure 14.1), but even so producers trade on their location. Each stall has a blackboard banner announcing their location, for example, *Eumundi Smokehouse; Mirrabooka Farms; Mandagery Creek Venison; Barrington Silver Perch; Ulladulla Oysters.* These names conjure visions of unspoiled rural settings, and customers agreed that one of the main attractions of the market is having access to all sorts of "farm" produce, in the city.

Most consumers arrive by car, with many embarrassed to admit to this: adding that on some occasions they had or would choose to travel by bus or light rail but for various reasons had not done so on this occasion (e.g., "the girls are going into town after the market and it's cheaper to leave the car parked at the casino"; or "we have visitors from Newcastle and we're going on elsewhere after the market").

The consumers we spoke to were all local Sydney-siders. Most confirmed that this market was not a substitute for their weekly/fortnightly grocery shop and that it was something special. They would still have to purchase food from their usual outlets.

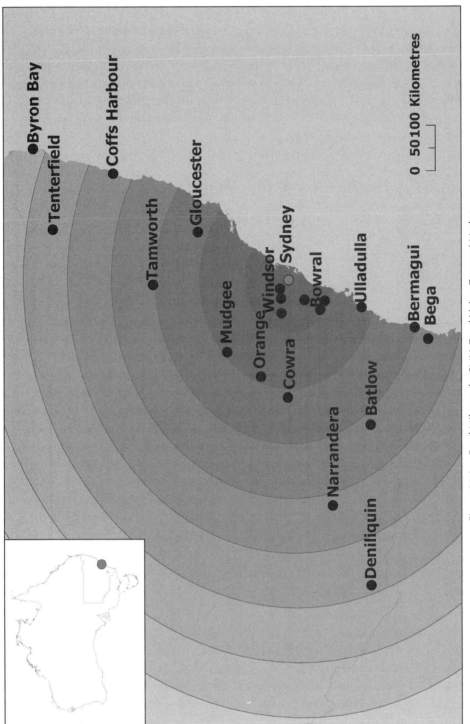

Figure 14.1. Food Miles to the SMH Good Living Growers' Market.

An alternative source of slow foods is the specialist merchants, some of whom originally catered to Australia's large immigrant population of Italians, Greeks, and other central Europeans. Many of the "delicatessens" in Australian cities stock some of the dry goods described below but are unlikely to sell such an array of fresh and refrigerated products. Some of these specialist merchants have attained a high profile in "foodie" circles and are described in newspaper articles (see the following) and food magazines.

2. A City Providore—Fratelli Fresh, Waterloo

This is a wholesaler/retailer market, situated in a light industrial area, fifteen minutes by car from the center of Sydney. It is open six days a week, 8–10 A.M. for the wholesale business and 10 A.M. until evening for the retail business. It is a very car-friendly outlet, because within the shell of a "chic" warehouse there is a drive-in, undercover car park accommodating about twenty cars. Up until 10 A.M., Fratelli operates as a wholesaler to Sydney's best restaurants, supplying small trucks with "larder" (durable and semi-durable items such as olive oil, balsamic vinegars, pasta, cheeses, riso, and chocolates) as well as fresh fruit, vegetables, and flowers. After 10 A.M. it is easy to find the car park although the entrance is a bit obscure. Car-space turnover takes about half an hour, so large numbers of consumers could not be accommodated on-site and the overflow would have to find a space in nearby warehouse car-parks or on the street. Still, once in the area, it would take no longer than five minutes to find a place to park. Consumers arrive mainly by car because there is no transport alternative and no surrounding housing to supply pedestrian consumers. Traffic congestion and ease of parking must influence how often shoppers would choose to return to Fratelli. Midmorning and midafternoon during weekdays are the best times to come in terms of traffic.

Fratelli's horticultural supplies are from the nearby Flemington Fresh Produce Market, and much of this comes from what is called the Sydney Basin with the remainder coming from interstate producers. The only imported "fresh" produce sighted at Fratelli are boxes of shallots from Holland, the world's epicenter for food distribution. The remaining products come from one country, Italy. These items have traveled considerable "food miles": much by ship and some as air freight. As one of the store's ads boasts: "air freighted Italian buffalo mozzarella—$7.45/125g."

The store has three sections. One is devoted to open boxes of fresh fruit and vegetables, such as the trays of white peaches and nectarines and ten different sorts of mushrooms giving off good aromas. These sit alongside odorless but glistening broccoli, carrots, and white asparagus. The see-into fridges comprise the second section—they line one wall and contain cheeses, butters, and ice cream, mainly from Italy. The third section consists of bulk and dry items such as crates of mineral waters, displays of different *risos* (Italian rice varieties), and chocolates. There is a mix of mass- and artisan-produced commodities. Consumers can buy dry goods in bulk and receive a discount, and buy fruit and vegetables for the coming days. Dinner party treats are also in evidence.

According to a glowing report in the *Sydney Morning Herald* newspaper, the shop owners keep the retail prices low because they cross-subsidize with the wholesale trade. Because Fratelli is in "an unusual location" (well away from public transport and surrounded by small warehouses and no other food stores), it has to be competitive on quality and price. It has adopted a by-line, "Great quality no longer has to be expensive."

While it offers on-site parking and value for money for high-quality produce, it does not offer everything you need for the week's shopping. Rather it augments the weekly supermarket shop. Fratelli's limited range of goods is nevertheless a bonus: the store's buyers have made the decisions about the day's freshest produce at the wholesale markets and they display items in an easy self-service manner. Thus, the shopper has few decisions and little distance to walk picking up items. This is the antithesis of today's supermarket shopping experience.

Fast Food Site of Exchange

Discourses of slow and fast food continually pit one form of consumption against another. The freshness, authenticity, and unique qualities of slow food are arrayed against the speed, convenience, and the safety of standardized pricing, product, and surroundings of fast food. We adhere to this convention by examining a McDonald's restaurant in suburban Canberra, once again focusing on the role of the car.

McDonald's, Dickson

This is a franchise of the global fast food retailer, situated in a suburban center within walking distance from nearby offices, a shopping center, and residential dwellings. It is located ten to fifteen minutes' drive from the center of Canberra, and ten to fifteen minutes to the highway leading north out of Canberra. Major bus stops are located nearby. As well as a shopping center, petrol stations, and businesses (including car parts and repair shops), there is a wide range of fast food outlets and restaurants within close proximity (see figure 14.2). The outlet is easily accessible by car, at the edge of a block with roads on three sides. There is free car parking for McDonald's customers located adjacent to two of the roads, on opposite sides of the restaurant, with drive-thru facilities next to one of those car parks.

Across the road from both McDonald's car parks is user-pays car parking. One is a large area close to Woolworths supermarket and the outdoor shopping center

Figure 14.2.   McDonald's at Dickson Shopping Center (marked with a cross) showing pedestrian crossings leading into McDonald's car parks.

(including bakeries, post office, newsagent, chemist, etc.), and the other car park is in front of the Dickson Trades Club and Northside Fitness Centre next door.

There are three entrances to the restaurant, one facing each of the car parks and another at the front facing the main road. Pedestrian crossings on this road provide easy access into two entrances of McDonald's, through an otherwise busy and car-dominated environment, almost funneling walkers into the restaurant. We saw both pedestrians and drivers accessing the McDonald's.

Unlike "slow food" providers, McDonald's advertises that it taps into a national rather than regional system of commodity chains. Statements such as "100% Aussie Beef" suggest Australia-wide sources as opposed to sources in the United States or elsewhere. It does on occasion name the locale of the produce: for example, their declared use of "Bega So-Light Cheese," from a small NSW coastal town, in their new healthy menu range.

When the burgers are combined with fries and a fizzy drink, they are discounted and sold as "value meal-deals." Recently, a product range was introduced to cater for those who prefer healthier, low-fat options. A vegetarian burger, chicken "wrap," and Caesar salad were introduced, along with low-fat fruit and nut yogurts, low-fat muffins, apples, bottles of water, and the like. The advertising campaigns encourage mothers and girlfriends to come to McDonald's, because they are now provided with healthier products while the men in their lives eat the usual burgers and fries. However, we saw few people eating these healthy options, and there is a waiting time (unlike for the other burgers) when you order the vegetarian burger.

We observed a large cross-section of people purchasing food at McDonald's, including mothers and their children, school groups, groups of tradesmen, single office workers, a "hippy," and groups of older people. Both men and women used the restaurant although few young women were seen inside the store and more women than men were seen using the drive-thru. Those who drove arrived in a range of cars including hatchbacks, utilities, station wagons, Holden Commodores, sports cars, and a BMW. Others arrived on foot, some entering through one door and continuing their journey via another exit.

On the day we visited the restaurant it was crowded, with many noisy children in evidence, our table was sticky, and rubbish wasn't cleared away. An employee was assisting two mothers with a high chair for one of their children but did not clear away the mounds of packaging, decorated with children's cartoon characters, that was on their table. The outdoor tables and children's playground were all busy. The patrons who remained at the restaurant to eat often lingered for as long as forty minutes. They were often in groups, such as the four tradesmen sharing their lunch break or the two mothers whose children played together on the playground. The turnover of the queue inside was fairly swift, as many people were leaving with their take-away food, perhaps returning to their nearby schools, workplaces, and homes by foot or car. A fairly constant stream of cars was observed filing through the drive-thru with most containing only a driver and no passengers. The few passengers we saw were usually children.

The displayed menu makes it clear that McDonald's products require no preparation by the consumer. The food is packaged to facilitate eating "on the run"—while walking or in the car. For example, the drinks (both hot and cold) have secure lids that prevent spillage, and the fries are packed tightly into the box in parallel making them easier to remove. Meals purchased in this way might be eaten in the car, on the way to the next destination, aided by cardboard drink holders and convenient packaging. Drive-thru offers a fast and convenient eating experience.

The Intermediate Site of Exchange
When looking for examples of fast and slow food, we considered a number of possibilities that constituted what appeared to be an intermediate category because they combined elements of both. We found Sizzle Bento, and other Japanese-style

sushi chains, to be an example of "intermediate food" because of the intermingling of discourses and images that evoke the centuries-old art of sushi making, drawing on specialist and fresh ingredients, with the swift, pre-packaged, and sometimes mechanical arrival of the products to the consumer. We have chosen to present the following example, Cuisine-to-go, because of its self-conscious juxtaposition of discourses and images drawn from both fast and slow foods. It is also "intermediate" in its use of artisanal and industrial cooking and storing technologies, and in its automobile-reliant delivery methods. While on the one hand, the producer of this cuisine states that he cannot use as much local and/or organic supplies as he would like because they are not "reliable" enough in their production and delivery, we found that he too has had problems with making regular deliveries, ironically because of an accident involving the delivery van.

Cuisine-to-go is a catering company located in an area zoned for light industry and retail businesses, fifteen minutes from the center of Canberra, which supplies slow food–style "meal replacements." The information collected about the company was based on an interview with Sven, who is the chef and the driving force behind this business. He gave permission to use the company's publicity because, as he said, any publicity is good publicity. We visited him at his office and kitchens, in Fyshwick, a light industrial and business suburb of Canberra. It is a district to which people drive to visit furniture storerooms and camping shops, to get their cars repaired, to visit a prostitute in a (legal) brothel, or to buy a pet from a large pet shop chain.

The business is located among a set of co-joined business sites, with a shared concrete forecourt offering easily accessible car parking. On this day the office is rather disorganized and cluttered. On the wall eight plates and certificates are proudly displayed as awards for catering and another wall displays photos of catered events and reviews from happy customers. There is a snapshot of the company catering for the prime minister's hand-picked cricket team, the "PM's Eleven." There is also a bookcase full of fifty to sixty cooking books, including those by famous Australian chefs such as Maggie Beer and Stephanie Alexander, and of course the very famous English chef Jamie Oliver. Two shelves are devoted to collections of cooking magazines such as *Vogue Entertaining*. Thus the company's cooking credentials are publicly displayed.

Despite a publicly stated commitment to "local" produce, the business uses mostly fresh fruit and vegetables obtained from a large vegetable wholesaler in Sydney because local, and in particular organic, suppliers are not considered reliable enough. A local butcher supplies the meat, although his supplies could come from anywhere. However, where practical, local produce is obtained. For example, the Canberra-based Poachers Pantry product range, consisting of smoked and cured game meats, is used. Most of the produce therefore probably travels the usual food miles that Australian food travels, sourced from anywhere up or down the east coast of Australia.

Cuisine-to-go sells a range of gourmet dishes, sometimes using European names such as "Beef Bourguignon." Its publicity explicitly links it with Slow Food but we found that it is prepared differently from traditional cooking techniques advocated by the Slow Food Movement. The chef grinds the spices and prepares the food and then sears the meat at high temperatures (300°C). All the food is then placed in nylon pouches and cooked under vacuum at 75°C for sixteen to seventeen hours. It is then rapidly chilled. This cooking process, called "sous vide," meaning under vacuum, was developed in France during the early 1970s by a French chef and a university food scientist as a method for improving the cooking and storing of foie gras. Because the food cooks slowly at low temperatures it is not damaged, the flavors are enhanced, and therefore it requires less seasoning and preservatives. The food is sold inside labeled cardboard boxes, with a see-through window showing the product encased in a plastic bag. Sven told us that consumers like to see what they are getting.

According to Sven, the typical consumer is middle aged, well-heeled, and often without children. There is a range, however: some are older single people who do not cook for themselves, but are "health" conscious. Others are busy professional couples, often in their forties and fifties, with reasonable incomes who do not have time to cook and want good quality food that they can buy on their way home from work. A smaller number are people who desire good quality food but do not have proper cooking facilities: campers, for example, who have a fridge and a hot plate in their car; or skiers, who want to eat in their hotel rooms rather than go out to dinner. The food is made for people who are essentially car travelers.

The company distributes the products through seven independent supermarkets all located within about five kilometers of the center of Canberra on major routes out of the city. These supermarkets are either in, or on the way to, comparatively high-income suburbs. This method of distribution was based on Sven's knowledge of Canberra and market research that identified Canberra as a car-reliant city, where people often drop into supermarkets on their way home from work. He wanted to reduce the risk of food spoiling on the way home by selling it in supermarkets close to the suburbs where he expected consumers to live. The company restocks each of the supermarkets once a week, and at the same time removes stock that has not sold. Company vans cover about two hundred kilometers a week.

Preparation by the consumer is quick and easy, as the instructions on the packet suggest. The food can either be heated in the pouch for twelve to fourteen minutes in boiling water, or it can be microwaved for two to three minutes. It comes in either one- or two-person servings, with detailed nutritional information on the package, describing the ingredients and the fat, carbohydrate, and caloric content.

As well as requiring rudimentary but rapid cooking, consuming this food, in contrast to fast food, requires at the bare minimum, eating utensils and a table. The advertising goes further, however, suggesting the food should be served with all the trappings of a ritualized meal, such as good quality tableware, and consumed with a bottle of good wine.

Unlike other cuisine courier businesses which are appearing in Australia's major capital cities, where the cooked meal is delivered to the door, Cuisine-to-go relies on a self-service customer, someone willing to use their own car to get to the supermarket and transport the food home. It could not survive without an extensive network of the archetypal car-dependent site of food exchange, supermarket chains.

Time-Space Compression and the Car-Centered Diet

A key feature of car-centered diets is the presence of sites of exchange that allow the consumer to access food at almost any point in time and space. Our research has revealed that the car-centered diet has different manifestations. We can identify both the car-centered fast food diet (CCFFD); its counterpoint, the car-centered slow food diet (CCSFD); and a hybrid, the slow food, fast car-centered diet. The automobile contributes to structuring each of these diets. The essential role of the car in different forms of Australia's culinary culture gives rise to two extreme possibilities for how much time and space exists between the site of exchange and point of consumption:

1. The ability to purchase food, transport it large distances, and delay consumption for days or months. This feature underpins the home-cooking based form of the CCSFD, which involves gathering produce from farmers' markets, farm-gate outlets, and inner-city specialist merchants.
2. The ability to purchase food and consume it instantaneously on the spot (or, in the car) where practices revolve around solitary eating by the person-on-the-go, grazing or snacking "24/7," and continuous novelty in products that are, more often than not, the outcome of industrial food technologies.

However, our research reveals that the car has played a part, along with food technology, in spawning a hybrid, Cuisine-to-go. This is food prepared from traditional ingredients, using novel cooking techniques, to heat and serve at home. It is purchased and prepared quickly, and transported short distances, but it is slow in its original production. We think that there are numerous car-centered mixes and matches, bricolages of food that could be combinations of fast food slow, or slow food fast.

Like a number of other authors in this book we question the utility of the concept of Fast Food and Slow Food as oppositional categories. Even the McDonald's shop at Dickson confounds the proposition that all fast food is car dependent. While consumers use the drive-in service, pedestrians buy the food to eat in the restaurant. The numerous doors in and out facilitate easy pedestrian access. Fast food outlets typically focus on speed (Shelton 1990), but we observed that as well as those who ate quickly, others sat and read newspapers, or watched children climb on the play equipment. We suspect that fast food chains, in an attempt to broaden their appeal and shore up their profits, are doing more than just adding a few healthy alternatives to their menus. Fast food chains are capitalizing on pedestrian customers, rather than relying on drivers alone. Some critics may consider their products to be pedestrian, but they are certainly pedestrian friendly.

Furthermore, as the concept of slow food becomes more widespread, it is being elaborated, expressed, and commercialized in numerous ways. We chose to study Cuisine-to-go as an example of slow food and rapidly found that it was an intermediate category that uses some of the discourse and practices of Slow Food for production and marketing purposes, but uses Fast for its delivery practices. We expect that there are many more examples to be found. The following sections suggest other ways in which the Fast/Slow categories are being destabilized.

Globalization of Slow Food and Nationally (Re)Presented Fast Food

The concepts and marketing strategies of Fast Food are often cited as a leading example of the globalizing forces of modernization. Slow Food, on the other hand, promotes itself as a protector of local and regional products. And yet, through its sophisticated networking and use of its website it is an international movement. Furthermore, our fieldwork with the providers of Sydney reveals that the distribution of slow food products is as much about global, as well as local, production and distribution networks. We do not know how complex these are but suspect that Bestor's comments apply. Writing about the international trade in bluefin tuna, he states that:

> Production and distribution [of bluefin tuna] are even more a function of time and space than in the past. Global food production and distribution revolves around complex co-ordination not only of single-stranded relationships between producers and markets (point to point) but of multi-lateral trade relationships. (Bestor 2001)

It is not our intention here to describe the complex flows of commodities, culture, capital, and people (Bestor 2001) involved in the air freighting of, for example, Italian buffalo mozzarella to Sydney. We note however that the demand for imported mozzarella can be seen as part of a trend first identified by Belasco in the 1970s, as gourmets or the affluent and well-educated turned to ethnic foods. He comments that "haute cuisine turned anthropological, celebrating the endangered regional cooking of provincial Europe, Asia, and North America" (Belasco 1987). Now multicultural cuisine is an important part of "global popular culture" (Bestor 2001).

Our examples show that slow foodways have much that is global about them, and that fast foodways contain national components. For example, McDonald's specifically advertises its "Aussie" ingredients and as elsewhere, it uses country-specific language, symbols, and products on its website to effectively locate itself within national cultures (Rowley 2004).

Ritzer too unsettles the distinctions between fast-global and slow-local. He describes a continuum of which the extreme points are the global distribution of products with no distinctive content and local and highly distinctive products. He notes there are many points along this continuum (Ritzer 2003). And it is along these intermediate points that our examples of fast and slow foods seem to fit. Farmers' markets are, in Ritzer's view, an example of what he calls "glocalisation," because although an international phenomenon, they are locally conceived and controlled, selling local products.

Yet another perspective on the intermingling of international and local foods and forces can be observed by taking "a longer historical perspective [which] shows, that there have been many different periods of globalization in world history" (Wilk 2002:68). For example, changes in Belizean foodways since colonization illustrate how different ethnic and social groups have mixed, adapted, changed, and replaced foods over time. We also think that Cuisine-to-go might be seen as a more recent example of what Wilk calls creolization, with its combination of imported cooking practices and recipes, regional ingredients, and local marketing.

The Fast/Slow terms are constantly evolving as well. The Slow Food–authorized buffalo mozzarella, imported into Australia from Italy, travels a huge distance, physically and symbolically, from the slow food of David and Gerda Foster (2001). These Australian authors, in their book *A Year of Slow Food*, out-slow others when they describe a dish cooked with home-grown eggs, milk, and spinach. "Preparation time: pullet to point of lay (say four or five months) dairy cow to first lactation (say two and a half years) sprouts at this late stage, about 8 months" (Foster and Foster 2001). Thus in this example, slow food lives up to its name because it is slowly produced by those who consume it. Other authors adopt the same approach. Gary Nabhan produces his own food or eats local wild produce, often following the example of Indians who live in his region of Arizona (Nabhan 2002). Local food movements offer an overtly political repudiation of global food production (Norberg-Hodge et al. 2002), basing their case on the pursuit of human and ecological health and sustainability.

Slow Food Is Possibly More Car-Reliant Than Fast Food

Contrary to the ambiences of slow food discourses, slow food is particularly car-dependent in car-reliant societies and societies that have long been industrial feeders (Symons 1982). Some slow food ingredients need to be almost instantly transported to retain their freshness and cars are needed to cope with their frequently bulky nature, their lack of portability, and the dispersed, and sometimes obscure, locations from which they are sold, be they farmers' markets or providers. The artisan producers of slow food travel large distances to bring their food to market, and slow food purchasers travel long distances by car to access the produce markets.

These same purchasers can cross a city as big as Sydney to visit a specialist merchant whose shelves are stocked with imported produce, both artisan and mass-produced. One could even argue that car-reliance has spawned this growing part of the food services sector. And yet only a few passing references have been made to the role of the car in slow food. Leitch notes that "the popularity of food festivals in post-war years [in Italy] can be traced to a complex mixture of the growth of domestic tourism from the 1950s when people began to travel in new acquired cars and motorbikes" (Leitch 2000). The Fosters, describing the three cars they own, say "but we can't do without our Landrover. We have to have a four–wheel drive to pull the livestock float. No slow vehicle, no slow food" (Foster and Foster 2001:222). Even Nabhan records long car trips in search of local wild foods and along the way he brings home the road kill for the dinner pot (Nabhan 2002).

The Poor Environmental Record of Slow Foods in the Australian Context

In a country like Australia that is evolving as a polyethnic culinary culture, far from the sites of production of so many ingredients, the distribution of slow food ingredients is dependent on all the available forms of mechanized mobility: the ship, plane, train, truck, and delivery van. The considerable distances traveled by some artisan products from overseas to Australia may be as great or greater than those traveled by mass-produced supermarket products (for example, see Boge's [1995] article on the well-traveled yogurt pot). Even locally produced fresh produce is transported by road often hundreds of kilometers to farmers' markets dotted around cities, regional centers, and country towns. And without consumer access to cars for the purpose of shopping, it seems the farmers' markets could not exist. In a car-reliant society there are unacknowledged social, financial, and environmental externalities associated with the distribution of slow food and its accessibility by consumers. We see an unfortunate contradiction between Slow's admirable adherence to the principles of sustainable agriculture and the maintenance of biodiversity, and the destructive environmental implications of transporting bulky produce to and from the markets and providers. And yet this is not so much Slow's problem, but one that we drew attention to at the outset of this chapter. Australia has few alternatives to car travel, such as trams, trains, and buses, because these have withered through lack of government support and funding. The anticipated impacts of greenhouse gases, global warming, and other environmental disasters may have more impact on food transport systems than influence of local food systems or food miles.

Inequalities and Delocalized Diets

Car-centered diets have social implications as well. Researchers in England argue that "car ownership is the principal determinant of major variations in shopping behavior for groceries and DIY products," and they note that "lack of a car is associated with social disadvantage such as unemployment, old age, lower levels of home-ownership and single parent families" (Bromley and Thomas 1993). In other words, the disadvantaged who do not own cars are further disadvantaged because the cheaper, bulk purchase food outlets, including farmers' markets, often located on urban fringes, are otherwise inaccessible to them.

Our fieldwork indicates that some fast food outlets, because of their pedestrian-friendly nature, are more accessible than slow food outlets. Furthermore, Australian research shows that fast food outlets are often concentrated, perhaps cynically, in the vicinity of poorer suburbs (Reidpath et al. 2002). Car-reliance is encouraging a bifurcated food system. The middle classes are able to add the slow food part of the system, such as localized fresh ingredients and regionally identified specialty products, to their consumption patterns. Those without cars are restricted to the mass processed and usually delocalized, although often nationally sourced, component of the system. We believe that further fieldwork would reveal that a delocalized diet is currently cheaper than the local one, because the former is part of mass industrialization and the latter is the output of a craft system.

Addressing Inequality and Environmental Sustainability through Relocalized Food Systems

In his social history of food, Fernandez-Armesto (2001) highlights how fast food has been a feature of culinary cultures for centuries. What is new is who is producing and distributing the fast foods: rather than being the output of artisans and small businesses, they come to market by virtue of often global food processing conglomerates and are traded not by small owner-operators but by giant supermarket and fast food company chains. Most consumers justify their consumption of fast foods on the basis of thrift and convenience. But food histories also reveal how convenient and cheap local, slow foods can be. Less than fifty years ago in Australia, large numbers of suburban and rural dwellers produced vegetables, fruit, and eggs in their backyards (Dixon 2002; Symons 1982). This is the cheapest food sourcing option we know. Delivery vans would ply the suburban streets daily, selling bread, fish, and vegetables (Kingston 1994) and this is, after wandering into the back-yard to gather produce, the second most convenient possible provisioning strategy. Ironically, today's traffic density precludes such meandering vans. The delivery van was supplemented by walks to the local, suburban center consisting of perhaps a dozen shops supplying in the main fresh foods sourced mainly from city wholesale markets and numerous bakeries. As in other countries, Australia's strip shops have disappeared due to the commercial tactics employed by the supermarket oligopoly in this country and due to urban design, which has made cars, and not pedestrians, the king of the road.

However, just as we are witnessing diminished slow food sites of exchange, there is a small renaissance in slow food possibilities. Most Australian capital cities now have community food gardens, attached either to public high-rise buildings, schools, or local government-run allotments. These are readily accessible to nearby residents and offer cheap produce in return for the labor and other inputs of the participants. They are the logical replacement to the backyard garden given that many inner and outer suburban dwellings now have little space in which to cultivate anything. They recall the centuries-old food allotments dotted across England in high-density neighborhoods.

Equally, the authors have all at one point in their busy lives made use of food cooperatives, where we pay money for a weekly delivery of fresh produce from a small group of local producers. This is not necessarily a cheap option, particularly if the suppliers are organic, but it is certainly convenient when the box of produce is waiting in the carport. It even obviates the need for a car to visit the farmers' market, and in this way cuts into the aggregate food miles traveled by individual consumers.

Thus, while the use of cars is widely accepted because they offer convenient solutions to numerous problems, including food provisioning, nothing could be more convenient than food supplies being located in backyards or neighborhood allotments, or food traders plying their wares to our front doors. The message of healthy convenience so beloved by today's consumers (Dixon 2004) could easily be appropriated by these alternative, local slow foodways in their promotional material. However, they require sufficient buyers and producers who know how to produce and appreciate home cooking. And this, as increasing evidence testifies, is itself in short supply (Lang et al. 2001; Santich 1995).

Conclusion

This chapter discusses two rapidly co-evolving commodities, food and cars. We suspect that the perceived need to access slow food, as well as mass food outlets, encourages the ownership of at least one or more cars. One of our female relatives calls her car her "shopping trolley." She bought this particular car because its size makes it easy to park in shopping center car parks and it is convenient to load large amounts of produce through the hatchback boot. It is now common for Australian families to own more than one car and for the purchase of cars to be linked to specific needs and tasks, such as shopping, traveling, off-road camping, or taking groups of children to sports games. Do specialist shopping trips, visits to providers, farmers' markets, and farm gate outlets, require a specialist car? We don't know yet, but we suspect that car manufacturers would like to think that they do. We argue that fast food is designed to mesh with a car-reliant society, and that in a car-reliant society, it is almost impossible for slow food to escape from this reliance. But more than this we show, as do many authors in this book, that simplistic dichotomies, such as fast and slow food, when subjected to the vagaries of time and place are much more complex than we originally thought.

Note

Acknowledgments. We thank Gerard Wilson and Susie Berger for assistance with slow food research, Ivan Hanigan for his map work, and Olivia Harkin and Colin McCulloch for technical assistance.

References

Australian Bureau of Statistics. 2000. People and the environment—Use of resources: transport choices and the environment [on-line]. Vol. 2003: Australian Bureau of Statistics.
———. 2002. Transport special article—Australia's motor vehicle fleet since the 1920s [on-line]. Vol. 2003: Australian Bureau of Statistics.
———. 2003. Driving to Pluto and back: Australians drive 190 billion kilometers (Media Release Cat. No. 9208.0). Vol. 2003: Australian Bureau of Statistics.
Austroads. 2000. Road Facts 2000. Sydney: Austroads Incorporated.
BBC News World Edition. 2003. McDonald Sues "Slow Food" Critic. May 30 [on-line].
Beckmann, Jorg. 2001. Automobility—A Social Problem and Theoretical Concept. Environment and Planning D: Society and Space 19:593–607.
Belasco, Warren. 1987. Ethnic Fast Foods: The Corporate Melting Pot. Food and Foodways 2:1–30.
Bestor, Theodore. 2001. Supply-Side Sushi: Commodity, Market and the Global City. American Anthropologist 103(1):76–95.

Boge, Stefanie. 1995. The Well-Travelled Yoghurt Pot: Lessons for New Freight Transport Policies and Regional Production. World Transport Policy and Practice 1(1):7–11.

Bromley, Rosemary, and Colin Thomas. 1993. The Retail Revolution, the Carless Shopper, and Disadvantage. Transactions of the Institute of British Geographers 18(2):222–36.

Commonwealth Treasurer. 2004. Transcript The Hon Peter Costello MP, Treasurer. Doorstop Interview: Wednesday, 21 January 2004 12.15 pm. In Patterson Cheney Holden Ringwood. http://www.treasurer.gov.au/tsr/content/transcripts/2004/005.asp Melbourne.

Dixon, Jane. 2002. The Changing Chicken: Chooks, Cooks and Culinary Culture. Sydney: UNSW Press. Dowling, Robyn.

Dowling, R. 2000. Cultures of Mothering and Car Use in Suburban Sydney: A Preliminary Investigation. Geoforum 31:345–53.

Fernandez-Armesto, Felipe. 2001. Food: A History. London: Pan Books.

Foster, David, and Gerda Foster. 2001. A Year of Slow Food. Sydney: Duffy and Snellgrove.

Garvey, Pauline. 2001. Driving, Drinking and Daring in Norway. In Car Cultures. Daniel Miller, ed. Oxford: Berg.

Harris, Marvin. 1985. Good to Eat: Riddles of Food and Culture. Baltimore: Simon and Schuster.

Hinde, Sarah, and Jane Dixon. 2005. Changing the "Obesogenic Environment": Insights From a Cultural Economy of Car-Reliance. Transportation Research, Part D 10:31–53.

Jakle, John, and Keith Sculle. 1999. Fast Food, Roadside Restaurants in the Automobile Age. Baltimore: Johns Hopkins University Press.

Kingston, B. 1994. Basket, Bag and Trolley: A History of Shopping in Australia. Melbourne: Oxford University Press.

Laird, Philip, with Peter Newman, Mark Bachels, and J. Kenworthy. 2001. Back on Track: Rethinking Transport Policy in Australia and New Zealand. Sydney: UNSW Press.

Lang, Tim, with David Barling, and Martin Caraher. 2001. Food, Social Policy and the Environment: Towards a New Food Model. Social Policy and Administration 35(5):538–58.

Leitch, Alison. 2000. The Social Life of Lardo. The Asia Pacific Journal of Anthropology 1(1):103–118.

Murdoch, Jonathon, and Mara Miele. 2004. Cultural Networks and Cultural Connections: A Conventions Perspective. In The Blackwell Cultural Economy Reader. A. Amin and N. Thrift, eds. Oxford: Blackwell Publishing.

Nabhan, George. 2002. Coming Home to Eat. New York: W. W. Norton.

Noguchi, Paul. 1994. Savor Slowly: Ekiben—the Fast Food of High-Speed Japan. Ethnology 33(4):317–30.

Norberg-Hodge, Helena, with Todd Merrifield, and Steve Gorelick. 2002. Bringing the Food Economy Home: Local Alternatives to Global Agribusiness. London: Zed Books.

O'Dell, Tom. 2001. Raggare and the Panic of Mobility. In Car Cultures. Daniel Miller, ed. Oxford: Berg.

Reidpath, Daniel, with Cate Burns, Jan Garrard, Mary Mahoney, and Mardie Townsend. 2002. An Ecological Study of the Relationship Between Social and Environmental Determinants of Obesity. Health and Place 8(2):141–45.

Ritzer, George. 2003. Globalization of Nothing. SAIS Review Summer-Fall 23(2):189–200.

Rowley, Jennifer. 2004. Online Branding: The Case of McDonald's. British Food Journal 106(3):228–38.

Santich, Barbara. 1995. "It's a Chore!" Women's Attitudes Towards Cooking. Australian Journal of Nutrition and Dietetics 52(1):11–13.

Shelton, A. 1990. A Theater for Eating, Looking and Thinking: The Restaurant as Symbolic Space. Sociological Spectrum 10:507–526.

Slow Food Website. 2004. All About Slow Food. Our Philosophy, Vol. 2004 [on-line].

Symons, Michael. 1982. One Continuous Picnic: A History of Eating in Australia. Adelaide: Duck Press.

Urmetzer, Peter, with Donald Blake and Neil Guppy. 1999. Individualized Solutions to Environmental Problems: The Case of Automobile Pollution. Canadian Public Policy 25:345–59.

Wilk, Richard. 2002. Food and Nationalism: The Origins of "Belizean Food." In Food Nations: Selling Taste in Consumer Societies. W. Belasco and P. Scranton, eds. Pp. 67–89. New York and London: Routledge.

Just Java: Roasting Fair Trade Coffee   15

SARAH LYON

IN 2003 CLOSE TO NINETEEN MILLION pounds of fair trade coffee were sold in the United States, a 91 percent growth rate from 2002 market sales (TransFair USA 2004). Despite the fact that coffee's inherent production limitations as a tropical commodity preclude its regionalization or localization, the North American specialty coffee market's emphasis on artisanal, high-quality products and sustainable production parallels the goals of slow food advocates. Fair trade advocates maintain that its true counterhegemonic power results from the ability to link northern consumers and southern producers within transnational commodity networks, thereby re-embedding their relationships and creating modes of connectivity. In short, fair trade represents one attempt to counteract the anonymity characterizing transnational, agro-industrial food chains through the decommodification of products such as coffee and the transformation of abstract trade relations into social reality.

However, the success of this attempt to replicate, across vast distances, the regular social interactions that characterize local food systems ironically rests on roasters' abilities to attract increasing numbers of consumers through the marketing and commodification of fair trade coffee as both a personally and culturally significant product. This chapter builds upon fieldwork conducted between 2001 and 2003 and employs information and quotes from interviews conducted by the author with over thirty specialty coffee roasters and their employees. All interviews were conducted confidentially, and the names of interviewees are withheld by mutual agreement. The chapter explores the contradictions resulting from the commodification and mass marketing of fair trade certified coffee. I briefly sketch the recent history of fair trade coffee certification and the primary reasons for its ready adoption among specialty coffee roasters, such as the market's historical coupling of quality and sustainability, specialty roasters' desires to identify themselves in opposition to conventional, corporate coffee roasters, and their searches for certified and secure relationships with producers. Fair trade coffee provides specialty roasters with a simple and subtle way to signal their social responsibility to the growing number of ethical shoppers. The coupling of fair trade marketing and corporate social responsibility by high-profile specialty roasters, such as Starbucks and Green Mountain Coffee Roasters, raises ethical issues as skeptics increasingly assert that the fair trade seal is losing its integrity (see figure 15.1). However, the commodification of fair trade coffee and its appearance in unexpected places, such as Exxon/Mobil gas stations, counteracts the elitist tendencies of alternative

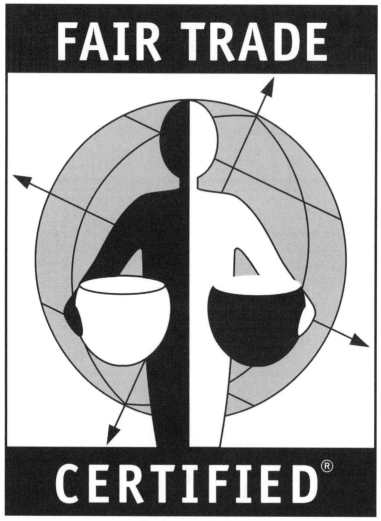

Figure 15.1.   The fair trade seal.

markets while simultaneously expanding its consumption, thereby increasing the remunerative benefits for the previously disenfranchised coffee farmers the market purportedly aims to help. This complex interplay between ideology and market growth is helping to transform fair trade coffee into a "food at moderate speed" (Mintz this volume); however, time will tell if the market is able to successfully balance the competing demands for respect of place, locality, distinctiveness, *and* profitability.

Fair Trade Certification

The fair trade coffee market is part of a growing body of alternative trade systems attempting to challenge historically unequal international market relations by transforming North-South trade relations from a vehicle of social exploitation into an avenue of producer empowerment (Raynolds et al. 2004). Fair trade advocates claim the market presents a viable alternative to traditionally inequitable global trade relations and international development programs operating in less developed nations through "trade not aid." While still small, international fair trade products, including coffee, handicrafts, bananas, cocoa, and tea, claim a growing market share, and there are currently over eight hundred producer organizations located in forty-five countries registered with FLO International (Fair Trade Labeling Organizations). In the United States, the fair trade seal was first introduced in 1999 with the formation of the certifying agency TransFair USA, which focused its initial efforts on expanding the fair trade coffee market.

There are four commonly cited requirements coffee importers must meet in order to use the fair trade label. First, they must buy their coffee directly from small coffee farmers organized in democratic associations. Second, they must offer these farmers long-term contracts that extend at least beyond one annual harvest. Third, they must pay a price premium of $1.26 per pound and an additional $.15 per pound premium for organic fair trade coffee. Finally, they must offer the farmer organizations pre-financing covering at least 60 percent of the annual contract. Similarly, there are three commonly cited requirements for participating coffee producers. First, they must be small, family farmers. Second, they must be organized into independent, democratic associations. And, third, they must pursue loosely defined ecological goals.

Targeting the Specialty Coffee Market

TransFair USA initially identified roasters as the critical components of the more equitable coffee consumer-producer relationships they hoped to foster through fair trade labeling (Raynolds 2002). With the help of the San Francisco–based NGO,

Global Exchange, TransFair initiated an ultimately successful consumer campaign to lobby the specialty coffee industry. Similar to many industrial agricultural food markets, the international coffee market consists of buyer-driven commodity chains propelled by the product specifications and supply networks of roasters, distributors, and their brands. This is particularly the case within the specialty coffee market (Ponte 2002). While buyer-driven commodity chains tend to be more flexible and mutable, they also contribute to an industry's vulnerability as brands and corporate image become integral components of perceived value within the marketplace. Due to its high profile as a heavily branded and publicly traded corporation, Starbucks became the first, and most influential, target of fair trade advocates. The fact that Starbucks primarily markets its coffee to urban, middle-class consumers who are thought to be more sympathetic to social justice causes also made the corporation an attractive target.

In response to fair trade protestors at Starbucks's 2000 general stockholders' meeting, the corporation announced a one-time shipment of seventy-five thousand pounds, which Global Exchange promptly labeled a mere "Drop in the cup." In April 2000, Starbucks agreed to offer fair trade coffee in each of its outlets three days before Global Exchange planned to launch a large-scale consumer boycott. During an interview, Starbucks' vice president of corporate social responsibility recalled how one fair trade campaign leader told her, "You're not public enemy number one but your customers care about these types of issues." As an indisputable industry leader, Starbucks's entry into the fair trade market became an influential factor in the decisions made by many smaller specialty roasters to follow suit. One coffee roaster stated simply during an interview, "I feel strongly that fair trade would not be where it is today if it weren't for Global Exchange taking Starbucks to the mat" (Author interview with coffee roaster, April 1, 2003).

Some within the industry decried the targeting of specialty coffee roasters by fair trade activists, complaining that conventional coffee market giants, who represent the bulk of all coffees bought and sold in the United States, were not threatened with bad publicity and decreased sales. For example, writing in *Tea and Coffee Trade Journal*, Schoenholt argues, "If the fair traders actually mean what they say, how come all the pressure was applied in the place it would affect the fewest number of green coffee bags purchased?" (2001). Despite specialty coffee's growing market share, the U.S. coffee market remains a near oligopoly dominated by supermarket "can" coffees. In 1979, there were only forty specialty roasters in the United States. By 1989 this number had risen to 385 and today there are more than 1,200 roaster retailers operating across the country. Similarly, specialty coffee sales rose from $750 million in 1979, to $1.5 billion in 1989 and $5.4 billion in 1999 (Talbot 2004:201). Despite this rapid growth, specialty coffee roasters still sell considerably less coffee than the four canned coffee giants (Folgers owned by Procter & Gamble,

Maxwell House owned by Kraft, Nescafe owned by Nestle, and Real Coffee owned by Sara Lee). As a result, like many commodity markets, the U.S. coffee market is bifurcated between a handful of high-volume corporate giants and a large number of specialty roasters. Brand consolidation, centralized roasting and processing, and the growing use of inexpensive and inferior coffee blends all contribute to and help maintain the dominant market share of these corporate giants.

As a result of their large size and standardization, conventional coffee roasters are slow to adapt to emerging market trends. In contrast, small, specialty coffee roasters are models of flexible accumulation, sourcing small amounts of coffee from diverse locales around the world and quickly adapting to market demands through efficient organizational decision-making and operational execution. Furthermore, specialty roasters have steadily increased their market share by redefining coffee as a specialty foods product in contrast to its historic status as a "boring bulk commodity" (Raynolds 2002). The industry has historically defined itself in opposition to the larger roasters since its fledgling days when specialty coffee enthusiasts chose to associate with the National Association for the Specialty Food Trade instead of the can coffee–dominated National Coffee Association (Pendergrast 1999:326). These progressive roots are echoed in contemporary rhetoric. For example, Paul Katzeff, president of Thanksgiving Coffee, names the specialty industry the "caring part" of the coffee industry: "The difference between them and us is a caring component of sustainability and social responsibility" (Easson 2000). After years of demarcating the boundaries between quality coffee and inferior canned varieties, many specialty roasters welcomed the opportunity to further distinguish themselves from the conventional coffee market by introducing fair trade coffees to their product lines, which often already included coffees differentiated by origin and quality.

Sustainability and Quality

The first Sustainable Coffee Conference was held in 1996 and a second one followed in 1998, both consisting of active and often contentious debate over what exactly sustainability meant to the industry. Writing in the industry publication, *Tea and Coffee Trade Journal*, one attendee reported, "Even though the word 'sustainable' was spoken in most every speech, the term still proved elusive. Maybe it was because there were so many presenters, all giving a particular definition based on their perspective" (Brown 1998). Two short years later, in 2000, the Specialty Coffee Asssociation of America named the corporate social responsibility guru, Paul Hawken, its keynote speaker. He began his speech by stating, "I want to honor you as an industry. You are the first economic sector in the world to come out and commit to the principles of sustainability" (Hawken 2000). Since the industry's early years, many specialty coffee roasters have strategically worked to position specialty coffee as a sustainable alternative to the conventional coffee market, making it difficult for the industry to dismiss wholesale the more recent demands of fair trade advocates.

The proliferation of articles focusing on sustainability within specialty coffee publications over the course of the last ten years demonstrates an increasing interest in the links between economic success, social well-being, and environmental stewardship. Over the past decade, as the specialty coffee market in the United States expanded and more firmly established itself, it consciously began to model itself on the wine appellation system—one that pays close attention to the details of origin and flavor characteristics. As the sophistication of the North American specialty coffee palette increased, growing numbers of roasters began to routinely visit coffee producers in order to expand their coffee knowledge and identify higher quality coffees. Because of the rapid growth of the specialty coffee industry, a number of smaller roasters recalled during interviews how they entered the market propelled by a simple entrepreneurial spirit, not necessarily a deep passion for coffee. For these relative coffee novices, trips to origin can prove enlightening. One stated, "Well, personally, when I came into coffee, I didn't know how coffee was grown, and who does know that it comes from a tree? I think generally everybody is just blown away by all the labor involved" (Author interview with coffee roaster, April 2, 2003).

This increasing popularity of estate and origin coffees within the specialty market encouraged a heightened awareness among roasters of the cultural, economic, and environmental contexts of coffee production; this awareness was channeled by a segment of industry leaders into a focus on sustainability. Several interviewed roasters recalled that in the past they focused on buying the best quality coffee at the lowest price. They claimed that visiting coffee farmers, especially small farmer cooperatives, caused them to rethink this business strategy. For example, during an interview one roaster maintained, "There are a number of issues morally there. Number one, we don't do that with any other supplier . . . our copy paper? Here's our core product [coffee] that we've seen and know and we've seen how people live and can we feel good about doing that [paying low prices]? I don't think so" (Author interview with coffee roaster, April 1, 2003). Today, the specialty coffee industry's second largest roaster, Green Mountain Coffee Roasters, annually sends groups of employees to Guatemala and Costa Rica to visit the farmers who grow the company's coffee. Approximately a year after her visit to a small coffee cooperative in Guatemala, one Green Mountain employee explained during an interview, "Just seeing in a small isolated community what a commitment like it [fair trade] can do, the pride that those people took—it was almost spiritual. I remember him [the president of the cooperative] saying, 'What you've done is not just for our families it's for our grandchildren and our future generations'" (Author interview with Green Mountain employee, April 2, 2003). During three of these trips in Guatemala and follow-up interviews conducted in Vermont, multiple employees shared their belief that these visits to coffee-producing regions form the foundation of the strong commitment to fair trade and organic coffees within the corporation. This finding parallels the recent argument made by Lewin et al. that the emergence of differentiated coffee products has begun to shift the locus of power within the coffee industry and that the most progressive firms are "staking claims with better producers in many countries and strengthening those relationships" (2004:98). Similarly, Franz Vander Hoff maintains that fair trade coffee is passing into a new and distinct phase, requiring new marketing approaches and forms of cooperation between producers and buyers (Giovannucci 2003:39; Vander Hoff 2002).

Although interviewed coffee roasters were quick to laud the merits of fair trade and organic coffees, they also repeatedly stressed that social justice principles must be backed up by consistently high-quality coffee. However, I found little evidence to support Giovannucci's argument that the specialty industry has clearly indicated that consistency and quality are *more* important for value and premiums in the marketplace than sustainability principles (2003). While specialty roasters may claim they maintain consistent quality standards, quality is always a socially constructed concept and the way it is measured and signified is constantly subject to change and adaptation. For example, some specialty coffee roasters may enjoy the slight wine flavor that results from the overfermentation of coffee cherries during wet processing, whereas others may consider this a serious flaw. Furthermore, unlike fair trade certification, there is no independent monitoring system or set of collective standards defining quality coffee. Finally, the publicity generated by fair trade advocates and the media creates a ready demand for fair trade–certified coffees among some consumer market segments. On the other hand, the increased use of lower-quality robusta coffees in blends and the growing market share of flavored coffees indicate that American consumers may not overwhelmingly share specialty coffee roasters' passions for high-quality, flawless coffee. Therefore, far from competing with vague quality standards for price premiums, fair trade certification actually contributes to the very definition of high-quality specialty coffee for many specialty roasters.

Certified and Secure Fair Trade Relationships

Fair trade–certified cooperatives are especially attractive to roasters seeking to establish relationships with coffee producers because the outside certification lends them an air of legitimacy, permanency, and business acumen that other cooperatives and larger producers may lack. The fair trade model is useful for some smaller roasters who have neither the time nor financial resources to establish and nurture relationships with widely dispersed producers in order to maintain consistent quality and supply in their retail offerings. The independent monitoring and certification ensured by the fair trade label provides a ready-made way for roasters to mark their social responsibility, saving them the difficulty of explaining the terms and conditions of their "self-certified" coffees (such as the case for noncertified "relationship" coffees). For example, one roaster explained during an interview, "The fact is to explain what fair trade is on the supermarket shelf is complicated. If we have our own program that's not even tied into a seal on the front of the bag that people can research, how are our customers going to learn about it?" (Author interview with coffee roaster, April 1, 2003). Furthermore, fair trade certification can save smaller roasters the hassles of developing and monitoring their own independent criteria. This point was made by a Green Mountain employee during an interview. She explained, "We've tried home-grown criteria for years. You get into 'How is it that we check it off?' We would want a good benchmark, but in the end, we're just not the ones with the skills" (Author interview with Green Mountain employee, April 1, 2003).

As a result of the current world coffee market crisis and historically low prices, many interviewed roasters suggested it will become increasingly difficult to find high-quality coffee sources in the future and therefore it makes good business sense to nurture long-term relationships with producers in order to ensure future stocks. In the contemporary world many individuals associate the conditions of globalization with a deep sense of political fatalism and chronic insecurity in that the sheer scale of contemporary social and economic change appears to outstrip the capacity of national governments or citizens to control, contest, or resist that change (Held et al. 1999:1; Beck 1992). Reflecting this analysis, a number of interviewed roasters directly linked their adoption of fair trade coffee to their belief that global poverty contributes to perceived threats to our national security and way of life. For example, one interviewed roaster contextualized his business decisions within larger security concerns, stating, "Politically, I think it's important for the stability of the region. . . . If you have economic stability, you don't have revolutionaries and you don't have problems" (Author interview with coffee roaster, October 2, 2002). However, their statements also reflected a belief in the power of individual action, thereby refuting the fatalism some scholars believe is endemic to contemporary times. These concerns reflect the framing of fair trade coffee as an individual action-oriented alternative to the exploitive economic relationships characterizing international trade. In the same way that consumers are urged to link their own morality and consumption to global understandings of humanity and justice, some roasters reflect on their individual role within the global marketplace of commodities and ideas and reason that their economic activities may contribute to our collective well-being.

Marketing the Fair Trade Commodity

Those specialty roasters who do offer fair trade coffees employ a variety of marketing tools in order to translate the equitable, yet intangible, trade relationships linking fair trade consumers and producers into pithy descriptions on packages and in print advertisements, thereby commodifying both the product and the market relationships. Today's consumer market is characterized by product standardization, meaning products now *require* signs, such as brand names or certification seals, that add value to them (Goldman and Papson 1996:3). Communicating product attributes other than use-value has long been the goal of advertising (Tinic 1997), however, during the recent years of post-Fordist flexible production and increasing levels of consumption, advertising and sign values have become constitutive features of products, not simply descriptors of them. Marketing fair trade coffee presents a strategic challenge—how does one communicate to customers what exactly makes this coffee different, and why they should care? The framing of the fair trade market by advocates and the media as an alternative to the perceived negative consequences of economic globalization provides some assistance to marketers. The recent market expansion proves that once the fair trade premise is understood by consumers it is relatively easily absorbed into the educated, liberal-leaning middle-class habitus. However, it nonetheless is difficult to distill the modes of connectivity linking dispersed fair trade market participants into sign values that both inform and entice consumers.

Many specialty coffee companies built their image and definition of quality around taste combined with environmental responsibility or social justice issues. This strategic coupling of ideology and more conventional product attributes was reflected in the statements of many interviewed roasters, such as one who explained, "It's not necessarily just promoting your product, but promoting a cause and then also your product." This ideological marketing has also been noted by industry experts, such as Kimberly Easson, who writes, "Their [roasters'] success has been based on making quality coffees 'with a conscience' more accessible to consumers, and then educating consumers about these issues" (2000). Similarly, in an article published in *The International Journal of Retail and Distribution Management*, Nicholls argues that fair trade products need to be supported by marketing communications that allow the individual consumer to feel a sense of "making a difference" (2002).

While ideological appeals to consumers' beliefs in social and environmental justice can serve as powerful marketing tools, they also run the risk of tarnishing the image of the product by repeatedly associating it with poverty, exploitation, and deforestation. While some roasters readily acknowledged the fact that fair trade coffee makes for good advertising copy, others claimed promoting fair trade coffee to consumers poses a distinct challenge, especially in light of the widespread tragedies resulting from the contemporary coffee crisis. However, the framing of fair trade as an alternative to globalization resting on individual choice and action provides a direct means of combating these negative associations. For example, during an interview the director of marketing at one specialty coffee company recalled, "The copywriter said, 'Oh it's just so tragic.' She didn't want to put a tragic message out there. So how do you take a tragic situation and flip it so it's more embraceable? What we try and do is say 'The coffee you buy can make a difference,' and the tag line we use with fair trade is 'The taste of a different world' " (Author interview, April 2, 2003).

The growing popularity of specialty coffees in the United States is a direct result of widespread and diligent consumer education. Across the country, coffee drinkers have been taught to eschew the watered-down inferior brews of their grandparents in favor of high-quality *and* high-cost specialty coffees. Many roasters relish their role as teachers of taste and have expanded their consumer pedagogy to include lessons in coffee origins and the processing factors that influence quality and flavor. Roaster trips to coffee-producing regions, during which they purchase coffee and attempt to nurture relationships based on proximate contact with producers, are readily shared with consumers who daydream of similar exotic travel experiences. A powerful way for retailers to market this vicarious travel is through the prominent display of the photos and profiles of the farmers who supply the coffee they serve.

Educating consumers about the lives of the people who grow the coffee their consumers drink has proven for many roasters to be a logical next step *and* an added marketing tool. In January 2003, the CEO and employees of Green Mountain Coffee Roasters traveled to a fair trade coffee cooperative located on the shores of Lake Atitlan in Guatemala. The group also included a film crew from the PBS show *Frontline* and the trip coincided with the launch of the Green Mountain and Newman's Own co-branded (meaning both company logos are displayed on the label) fair trade and organic coffee blends. Nell Newman also traveled with the group in order to interact with the producers growing the coffee that bore her family's name. *Frontline* filmed the whole visit to include in a piece on the coffee crisis, which aired in the spring of 2003. The resulting *Frontline* piece was educational, emotionally moving, and provided free publicity for Green Mountain, Newman's Own, and the cooperative. However, this combination of marketing and education can prove risky. Green Mountain's marketing director relayed during an interview, "What we're struggling with is the words and what's the right tone. And it's a tricky thing, especially when you want to convey your social and environmental initiatives. You really don't want it to sound like you're puffing your chest and patting yourself on the back. You'd like it to be more of a discovery, that someone discovers you do this as a company" (Author interview, April 2, 2003).

While none of the interviewed roasters directly mentioned it, an analysis of the advertising materials distributed by specialty roasters demonstrates that emotional

branding has become a significant marketing tool for them. The emotional branding strategy effectively counteracts the inherent problem of communicating the fair
trade message without relying on tragedy to sell the product. In his recent book,
Emotional Branding (2001), Gobè outlines the "ten commandments" of emotional
branding, advising marketers to transform their offering from a service into a relationship through the creation of perceived emotional connections with consumers.
Fair trade coffee is an ideal candidate for emotional branding as it is not so much
the intrinsic features of the product, for example its flavor or quality, that distinguishes it from other specialty coffees, but instead the trust consumers place in
its symbolic values of fairness and sustainability. This emotional branding of fair
trade coffee is experienced by consumers as a commodified substitute for the regular
social interactions characterizing local food systems. For example, much fair trade
marketing includes representations of smiling, grateful farmers and their families
accompanying brief quotes testifying to the importance of fair trade within their
community. These images evoke the trustworthy advertising personas of an earlier
era, such as Aunt Jemima, Quaker Oats, and the Jolly Green Giant.

Fair Trade's Detractors

While the fair trade coffee market has enjoyed a degree of success almost unpar-
alleled within the North American sphere of ethical consumption, it remains a
hotly debated topic within the specialty industry. Some roasters steadfastly refuse
to purchase fair trade coffee because they do not fully trust the certification process
or because they do not think they need an independent seal to help them create relationships with producers. Several smaller roasters explained their reluctance to offer
fair trade–certified coffees by arguing that TransFair's system lacks transparency and
the organization's management collects overly remunerative salaries. For example,
one interviewed roaster called fair trade a "joke," maintaining, "You've got all these
people trying to start this fair trade thing up and you ask them what their wages
are and what their overhead is. Why do we have people that are making $80,000 or
$100,000 a year? How can that be fair trade?" (Author interview with coffee roaster,
November 1, 2002). Another argued, "I think that the fair trade certification people
have made a purposeful intent to drive up the need for those certifications so that
their organization can get funded. They say they're a NGO that doesn't make any
profit and yet they have employees living in San Francisco, driving Lexuses" (Author
interview with coffee roaster, November 8, 2002). These allegations have also been
publicly made in the print media. For example, in an article published in the *Tea
and Coffee Trade Journal*, Schoenholt poses the question of whether "TransFair USA
may have more of an interest in seeing revenues from licensing fees than an interest
in seeing the coffee reach a wider audience" (2001).

Undoubtedly, TransFair has placed itself in a delicate position of simultaneously trying to grow the fair trade market and strengthen the organization itself. To avoid similar problems, in 2003 the Fair Trade Labeling Organization International, responsible for certifying producer organizations, split into two legal entities: FLO Certification Ltd. is responsible for certification, inspection, and trade auditing, while the charitable side of FLO regulates all other activities. TransFair is supported by the licensing and certification fees paid by roasters and they are therefore correct to demand accountability. Currently, TransFair and similar certifying agencies are the only participants in the fair trade supply chain who do not submit to routine external oversight. However, full transparency on behalf of all involved parties should be a prerequisite for the just and equitable international trade relationships arguably fostered through fair trade.

While more than two-thirds of specialty coffee roasters reportedly believe that independent certification systems (such as fair trade, organic, and shade grown) will be important to their business in the future (Giovannucci 2002), some have chosen to eschew TransFair's label in favor of self-certification or independent auditing. For example, one smaller roaster stated during an interview, "I like to tell people when they ask if our stuff is certified that we're self-certified. I have direct relationships, you want to go down and meet the farmers? I can arrange that" (Author interview with coffee roaster, October 2, 2002). He continued to explain,

> We want to find some small importers who have direct relations with farmers and work into the fair trade angle without necessarily going through TransFair, which I support and think is a wonderful thing for companies that don't want to do the relationship part on their own. In essence you're paying someone else to have the relationships; we want to have that relationship ourselves. (Author interview with coffee roaster, October 2, 2002)

This desire to forge meaningful relationships with coffee producers may represent an attempt made on behalf of small roasters to extend the embedded, social relationships of local food systems across transnational boundaries. However, in our current age of consumer skepticism, selling self-certified coffees may be interpreted as an act of greenwashing, a publicity stunt with little actual substance. For example, Allegro Coffee Company, which supplies Whole Foods Markets with roasted coffee, eschews fair trade certification. Instead, the company claims to focus their social responsibility efforts on improving the long-term quality of the coffees they supply while allowing Ernst & Young LLP to independently monitor their business and accounts. A recent *Wall Street Journal* article detailed Whole Foods' "High Five for Farmers" program, which donates 5 percent of the sales from select coffees directly back to the farmers. However, the author pointed out, this 5 percent is not from the retail price, but instead from the lower wholesale price (Stecklow 2004). This article generated ongoing debate on several fair trade coffee list-servs as participants questioned the company's good intentions. Instead of a percentage of the wholesale or retail price, fair trade certification ensures farmers are paid a documented price premium.

The Murky World of Corporate Social Responsibility

Selling fair trade–certified coffees can be a straightforward way for companies to signal their standing as a responsible corporate citizen to consumers, attract publicity, and reap the resulting financial rewards. During an interview, Green Mountain's public relations director stated that fair trade coffee is "the biggest story the company has ever had public-relations wise and it's all been positive. We're a publicly traded company and it's gotten the attention of socially responsible investors." The company's reputation as a socially responsible corporation has undeniably contributed to its rapid growth. In 2004 Green Mountain was ranked eighth on *Business Ethics* magazine's list of the one hundred best corporate citizens and named to *Forbes* magazine's list of the top two hundred best small companies in America for the fifth consecutive year. The president and CEO of Green Mountain, Robert Stiller, stated in a press release, "While the ranking emphasizes financial performance, I believe much of our success is a direct result of our commitment to operating the business in a socially responsible way. This ranking affirms our belief that we can do well by doing good" (Business Editors 2004a).

That same year, Green Mountain formed a team of three executives to enhance the company's focus on corporate social responsibility and environmental affairs. The team included Liam Brody, the former manager of Oxfam's global coffee crisis awareness campaign during the past four years (Business Editors 2004b). Similarly, in October 2004, Starbucks announced that by 2007 close to 60 percent of its coffee will be sourced according to their own code of conduct. The corporate executive Orin Smith's comment at the time, "If you are tapped as a bad corporate citizen, the penalty is large" (Groom 2004), reveals that this business plan emerged as much from strategic image protection as from corporate altruism. The following month, Starbucks was ranked forty-second out of fifty companies by Sustain Ability (a U.K.-based CSR consulting firm) and the UN Environment Program for its 2003 Corporate Social Responsibility Annual Report, titled "Living Our Values" (Business Editors 2004c).

Specialty coffee companies are far from unique in celebrating their models of corporate social responsibility. Ben and Jerry's, Patagonia, The Body Shop, and Stonyfield Farms are all examples of multi-million dollar corporations that built their brand image around professed allegiance to the principles of sustainable development. As Ruggie explains (2002), beginning in the 1990s, there has been a "sharp escalation in social expectations about the role of corporations in society." The advertised strength of Green Mountain's and Starbucks's corporate social responsibility programs combined with their financial successes support the claim that corporate social responsibility enhances business performance (made by Balabanis et al. 1998 in Nicholls 2002).

However, this strategic use of the fair trade seal to enhance the corporate image of larger specialty roasters is leading some smaller roasters to question the integrity of the certification. For example, several small, yet respected and influential roasters, who were early proponents of fair trade, recently announced their withdrawal from the fair trade coffee market, reportedly claiming "that the large firms which buy only a small percentage of fair trade beans are turning it into a marketing ploy rather than an effort to help farmers" (Rogers 2004). Dean Cycon, founder of the Massachusetts-based Dean's Beans Organic Coffee Company, publicly targeted Green Mountain Coffee Roasters (Dean's Beans' major regional competitor), questioning its commitment to fair trade. In a print advertisement, he asked Newman's Own Organics, "How can you partner with a company whose meager percentage of fair trade smacks more of marketing than sincere commitment when farmers and their families are literally being starved off their land?" (Walker 2004). Socially committed roasters such as Cycon believe anything less than a one hundred percent commitment to fair trade is greenwashing or inexpensive advertising. Questions regarding the role of large players in the fair trade market are not limited to the realm of consumption. There have been some attempts to extend fair trade certification to large coffee plantations. At the 2003 Specialty Coffee Association meetings in Boston, one session on fair trade was labeled "a heavy-weight title bout" (Inman 2003) by a participant due to the heated debates over the relative merits of expanding the fair trade label to include plantation-grown coffee.

Smaller roasters who have built their brand identity around social and environmental concerns may find their market share diminishing as mainstream companies recognize fair trade and organic coffees to be more of a sound economic strategy rather than a counterculture alternative movement. Their concerns echo those of scholars such as Jaffee, who argues, "The marketness of Fair trade is a contested arena, one in which the powerful forces of transnational capital are struggling against civil society in an attempt to neutralize the movement's potential to meaningfully transform market relations" (2004). However, Paul Rice, the CEO of TransFair, recently counteracted these arguments, telling a reporter that, "If a corporate giant roasts a million pounds of fair trade coffee in one year, they are still doing far more than some of the smaller 100 percent roasters will in their entire history" (Rogers 2004).

Conclusion

Expanding the ethical products marketplace is the biggest challenge facing alternative trade advocates in the twenty-first century. The tensions explored here reflect

the larger question of whether fair trade fosters market access or market reform, whether it is working within or against the market. Larger specialty coffee companies, such as Green Mountain and Starbucks, have introduced fair trade coffees to a broader and more diverse base of consumers, thereby enabling their participation in alternative trade networks. For example, beginning in 2000, the Exxon/Mobil "On the Run" convenience stores have sold relatively inexpensive cups of brewed Green Mountain fair trade and organic coffees (see figure 15.2). This retail outlet

Figure 15.2.   Green Mountain Coffee Roasters' fair trade coffee for sale at an Exxon/Mobil gas station in rural Vermont.

effectively expands the fair trade consumer market beyond its previous confines of educated, middle-class, ethical shoppers. In growing the fair trade market in the north, these larger roasters are also increasing the size of the market for southern producers, potentially enabling more producers to reap the benefits of fair trade. Elsewhere I demonstrate (Lyon 2005) that fair trade provides previously excluded small farmers with an unprecedented degree of market access and contributes to their long-term sustainability. This achievement represents a practical and structural form of market reform in coffee's historical relations of production. In light of these documented benefits, it is shortsighted to automatically associate the growth of the fair trade coffee market with a loss of integrity. The commodification and market expansion of alternative food products, whether organic, fair trade, regional, or slow, raises complex ethical concerns that cannot be reduced to simple binaries of morally infused markets versus corporate greed. A more nuanced analysis demonstrates that emerging alternative markets, such as fair trade coffee, represent the successful combination of both the oppositional characteristics of slow food and the market-driven strategies of fast food.

Note

Acknowledgments. Thanks to the participants at the 2004 SEA meetings for their helpful questions and suggestions. I am especially grateful to Richard Wilk for his editorial comments on an earlier version of this chapter. This research was generously supported by the Wenner-Gren Foundation and Fulbright-Hays. Thanks to Green Mountain Coffee Roasters, the Specialty Coffee Association of America, Elan Organic Coffees, the Northwest Sustainable Coffee Campaign, and the many coffee roasters, advocates, and producers who participated in this research.

References

Balabanis, G., H. Phillips, and J. Lyall. 1998. Corporate Social Responsibility and Economic Performance in the Top British Companies: Are They Linked? European Business Review 98(1):25–44.

Beck, Ulrich. 1992. Risk Society: Towards a New Modernity. London: Sage.

Brown, Suzanne J. 1998. Sustaining the Sustainable Coffee Conference. Tea and Coffee Trade Journal 170(8):100.

Business Editors. 2004a. Green Mountain Coffee Roasters, Inc. Named to Forbes' 200 Best Small Companies in America List 5 Years Running. Business Wire, October 15.

———. 2004b. Corporate Social Responsibility Reaches New Levels at Green Mountain Coffee. Business Wire, July 20.

———. 2004c. Starbucks Recognized as Global Leader in Corporate Social Responsibility Reporting. Business Wire, November 5.

Easson, Kimberly. 2000. The Revolution of Quality. Tea and Coffee Trade Journal 172(2):33.

Giovannucci, Danielle. 2002. Volume, Value and Trends for Sustainable Coffees. Tea and Coffee Trade Journal 174(2):37.

———. 2003. The State of Sustainable Coffee: A Study of Twelve Major Markets. Colombia: Cenicafe.

Gobè, Marc. 2001. Emotional Branding: The New Paradigm for Connecting Brands to People. New York: Allworth Press.

Goldman, Robert, and Stephen Papson. 1996. Sign Wars. New York: Guilford.

Groom, Nichola. 2004. Starbucks Seeks More Socially Responsible Coffee. Reuters News Service, October 29: Los Angeles.

Hawken, Paul. 2000. Keynote Speaker: Reframing Sustainability. Annual Specialty Coffee Association of America Conference, April 16, San Francisco, CA.

Held, David, Anthony McGrew, David Goldblatt, and Jonathan Perraton. 1999. Global Transformations: Politics, Economics and Culture. Palo Alto: Stanford University Press.

Ilbery, B., and M. Kneasfey. 2000. Producer Constructions of Quality in Regional Specialty Food Production: A Case Study from South West England. Journal of Rural Studies 167:217–30.

Inman, Mark. 2003. The Debate over Fair-Trade Expansion. Fresh Cup Magazine, July:56.

Jaffee, Dan, Jack R. Kloppenburg Jr., and Mario B. Monroy. 2004. Bring the "Moral Charge" Home: Fair Trade within the North and within the South. Rural Sociology 69(2):169–96.

Lewin, Bryan, Daniele Giovannucci, and Panos Varangis. 2004. Coffee Markets: New Paradigms in Global Supply and Demand. Agriculture and Rural Development Discussion Paper 3. Electronic document. http://lnweb18.worldbank.org/ESSD/ardext.nsf/11ByDocName/PublicationsCoffeeMarket.

Lyon, Sarah. 2005. Maya Coffee Farmers and the Fair Trade Commodity Chain. PhD dissertation, Department of Anthropology, Emory University.

Nicholls, Alexander James. 2002. Strategic Options in Fair Trade Retailing. International Journal of Retail and Distribution Management 30(1):6–18.

Pendergrast, Mark. 1999. Uncommon Grounds: The History of Coffee and How It Transformed Our World. New York: Basic Books.

Ponte, Stefano. 2002. The "Latte Revolution"? Regulation, Markets and Consumption in the Global Coffee Chain World Development 30(7):1099–307.

Raynolds, Laura T. 2002. Consumer/Producer Links in Fair Trade Coffee Networks. Sociologia Ruralis 42(4):404–24.

Raynolds, Laura T., Douglas Murray, and Peter Taylor. 2004. Fair Trade Coffee: Building Producer Capacity via Global Networks. Journal of International Development 16(8):1109-121.

Rogers, Tim. 2004. Small Coffee Brewers Try to Redefine Fair Trade. Christian Science Monitor, April 13.

Ruggie, John. 2002. The New World of Corporate Responsibility. Financial Times, October 25.

Schoenholt, Donald N. 2001. The Fair Trade Ideal: The Ultimate Answer for Sustainability. Tea and Coffee Trade Journal 173(12):39.

Silver, Sara. 2003. Coffee's Crisis Stirs Traders to Take Action. Financial Times, May 14.

Stecklow, Steve, and Erin White. 2004. How Fair Is Fair Trade? Wall Street Journal, June 8.

Talbot, John. 2004. Grounds for Agreement: The Political Economy of the Coffee Commodity Chain. Lanham, MD: Rowman & Littlefield.

Tinic, Serra A. 1997. United Colors and United Meanings: Benetton and the Commodification of Social Issues. Journal of Communication 47(3):3–26.

TransFair USA. 2004. Fair Trade Market Achieves Record Growth in 2003. TransFair USA Press, March 29. Electronic document. www.transfairusa.org/content/about/pr_040329.php.

Vander Hoff Boersma, Franz. 2002. Poverty Alleviation through Participation in Fair Trade Coffee Networks: The Case of UCIRI, Oaxaca, Mexico. Fort Collins, CO: Fair Trade Research Working Group.

Walker, Rob. 2004. The Joys and Perils of Attack Marketing. Inc:April 29.

Winter, Michael. 2003. Embeddedness, the New Food Economy and Defensive Localism. Journal of Rural Studies 19(23–32).

Index

A City Providore, 226–27
agribusiness, 18, 20, 22, 163, 211
Agri-Mark, 203, 210
agri-tourism, 211
agrotourism, 174
alternative food systems, 163–65
—immigrant populations and, 163
—New York City's Chinatown as, 164–65,
    176; development of, 165–67; role of
    trust in, 168–69, 171, 173; social
    networks in, 171, 173, 177. *See also*
    Chinese farmers
—*See also* Community Supported Agriculture
alternative trade systems, 243. *See also* fair
    trade
Ark of Taste, 75, 79. *See also* Slow Food
artisanal beer, 14
artisanal cheese, 23, 201–14; cultural capital
    of, 203, 207, 213; elite producers of,
    205; similarities to wine industry, 205,
    210–11
automobility, 219–23, 229–33; gendered
    self-expression and, 221. *See also*
    car-reliance

Belasco, Warren, 77
Belize, 16–17, 234
Bell, Glen, 73. *See also* Taco Bell
Bestor, Theodore, 233
Big Mac, 73, 76, 150. *See also* McDonalds
bottled water, 20
Bové, José, 69, 74, 79
Burger King, 13

Cabot cheese, 202–3. *See also* Agri-Mark
capitalism, 5, 19–20, 22, 69; fast food and,
    145
capitalisms, 19
car-reliance, 219–20, 235, 238
—Australian infrastructure and, 220, 236
—defined, 220
—dietary patterns and, 219; social
    implications of, 236; time-space
    compression and, 232
—environmental externalities and, 235. *See
    also* automobility
Chefs Collaborative, 10. *See also* Slow Food
Chez Panisse. *See* Waters, Alice
Chinese farmers, 166–76
Chinese immigration to United States, 166,
    168, 175
Chipotle, 74–75
Chowking, 152–53, 155–56
class, 10, 77–78, 202, 210, 236; food
    systems and, 165
commodity chains, 15, 93–94, 116, 228;
    analysis of, 58; coffee market, 244;
    definition of, 83; indigenization of, 65;
    Malian, 51, 59, 62. *See also* subsector
    analysis
commodity flows. *See* commodity chains
Community Supported Agriculture (CSA),
    181–97
—class and, 189–90, 196
—costs of, 198n3
—defined, 181–82
—expansion of, 195

259

—government support for, 194
—grower-member relations, *190*, 190–93,
    196–97
—history of, 182
—ideological differences in, 184, 188,
    192–93, 196–97; "pragmatists" versus
    "visionaries," 189–90, *190*
—in Japan, 182
—leaders in, 187–89
—member retention in, 183, 187, 197–98
—in New Mexico, 184–96
—*See also* farmers' markets
consumers, 19, 142
consumption, 7, 19, 202; state regulation of, 4
corporate social responsibility, 253–54.
    See also fair trade
creolization, 234
CSA. *See* Community Supported Agriculture
cuisine: defined, 5–6; future of, 6, 10;
    industrialization of, 117–18. *See also*
    Italian cuisine
Cuisine-to-go. *See* intermediate food
Culinary tourism, 98–99, 107–8. *See also*
    Russia, food travel in

De Certeau, 19
domestic sector. *See* informal sector
Douglas, Mary, 18
dual economy, 17

economic anthropology, 17, 24
economic rationality, 202
economics, 17–18; culture as productive of,
    210
economies of sentiment, 202, 213–15
Emotional Branding, 250–51
environment, 8, 10
ethical consumption, 251, 256. *See also*
    Community Supported Agriculture; fair
    trade
Exxon/Mobil, 242, *255*

fair trade, 23, 250
—certification of, 243, 247–48; seal, *242*,
    254; self-certification, 248, 252

—class and, 249, 256
—criticisms of, 251–54
—ethics of, 242, 246, 254, 256
fair trade coffee, 22, 241–56
—commodification of, 241, 256
—national security and, 248
—quality of, 247
—slow food, parallels with, 241
—specialty coffee market and, 242–46;
    marketing tools of, 245, 249–51
—*See also* Exxon/Mobil; food of moderate
    speed; Starbucks; Green Mountain Coffee
    Roasters
farmers' markets, 13–14, 22, 181–82, 204,
    211; car-reliance and, 223–26, 235;
    contrasted to McDonalds, 14; endurance
    of, 21; in New Mexico, 185; Slow Food
    language and, 223; in Sydney, 223–27.
    See also Community Supported
    Agriculture
farmstead cheese. *See* artisanal cheese
fast food, 10, 13, 99, 116–17, 127, 177;
    automobile and, 221, 233, 238;
    definition, changes in, 233–34; endurance
    of, 21; history of, 236; in Japan, 116–17,
    127–28n2, 131; less developed countries
    and, 146–47, 156; literature on, 145–46;
    localization of, 20, 147, 157; in Mali, 51;
    middle-class and, 74; national
    components in, 234; pedestrians and,
    233; production of, 146; restaurants,
    145, 147; in Yap, 45. *See also* fast
    food/slow food dichotomy, challenge to;
    Chowking; Jollibee; McDonalds; Taco
    Bell
Fast Food Nation, 13
fast food/slow food dichotomy, challenge to,
    10, 15–16, 142, 238; alternative markets
    and, 256; destabilization of categories
    and, 232–34; globalization and, 69. *See
    also* food of moderate speed; intermediate
    food
Federated States of Micronesia (FSM), 34.
    See also Yap
food

—activism and, 21–22, 234
—body of the nation and, 105
—boutique, 22
—commodification of, 21. *See also* fair trade
   coffee
—consumption of, 7–8; affluence and global
   patterns of change in, 8
—decommodification of, 20–21
—ethical production and, 10. *See also*
   economies of sentiment; fair trade
—gendered production of. *See* Yap; Mali
—history of, 3–5, 234, 237;
   industrialization and, 21; mileposts
   in, 5
—hybrid, 15, 49
—local, 7, 13; loss of, 13–14. *See also*
   Community Supported Agriculture
—processed, 15
—safety of, 15, 58, 127
—seasons and, 6, 9, 53
—social role of, 8; status marker, as, 94, 202,
   205, 213
—Southeast Asian, 83, 85, 154; as culinary
   area, 86
—symbolic role of, 21, 142–3
—taste of, 7
—technological innovations in preparation
   of, 6–7
—world distribution of, 4
—*See also* fast food; slow food
food culture, 18; Fordist, 118
food economy, 14, 18, 20
food industry, 19, 22; regulation in, 19, 23;
   technologies of, 117–18, 120
food of moderate speed, 10, 15, 21, 65, 215;
   fair trade coffee as, 243. *See also* fast
   food/slow food dichotomy, challenge
   to
food systems, 15–16, 31
—changes in, 13
—industrial, 163; alternatives to, 163, 188,
   237; policy and, 15. *See also* Community
   Supported Agriculture
Fordism, 118, 124–25. *See also* post-Fordist
   flexible production

Formaggio Kitchen. *See* Gurdal, Ihsan
Frontline, 250
FSM. *See* Federated States of Micronesia
Fuerman, Anne. *See* U.S. Secretary of
   Agriculture

geogastronomia, 100–104
global agriculture, 169–70, 172;
   employment in, 5
Global Exchange. *See* TransFair
globalization, 14, 94, 163, 248; alternatives
   to, 176, 250; food and, 15, 69; in
   Lao PDR, 85, 90; in Mali, 49, 57;
   Mexican food and, 73; studies of,
   99
glocalisation, 234
Golden Arches East, 74
Green Mountain Coffee Roasters, 242,
   246–48, 250, 253–55; criticism of, 254.
   See also fair trade coffee
Greenpeace, 76
Gross Domestic Product, 18, 32
Grupo Maseca, 70–71, 76, 78. *See also*
   multinational corporations
Gurdal, Ihsan, 204–6, 208

Hannerz, Ulf, 108
Hawken, Paul, 245
heritage foods, 105. *See also* Lao PDR: hunger
   foods in
home-cooked meals, 21
hunter-gatherers, 15

identity, 45
industrial food systems. *See* food systems:
   industrial
Industrial Revolution, 5
informal sector, 17; in Mali, 55; in
   Philippines, 149
intermediate food, 223, 229–32;
   Cuisine-to-go, 230–34; Sizzle Bento,
   229–30; *See also* fast food; slow food; food
   at moderate speeds
international food trade, 5
Italian cuisine, 70

Japan, 115–27; fast food in, 116–17, 127–28n2, 131; food culture of, 116, 118; globalization in, 127; "Gross National Cool" of, 121, 127; mass production and food culture of, 118; retail environment of, 115, 118, 123; history of sushi in, 116; technological innovations and sushi in, 120–21. *See also* Community Supported Agriculture; *kaiten-zushi; konbini*
Jasper Hill Farm, 208–11, 214
Jollibee, 153–56

kaipen. See khai pen
kaiten-zushi, 119–22, 124–27; chains, 112, 114, 128n4; chefs and, 122; criticism of, 125–26; history of, 119–20; popularity of, 121, 125; restaurants, 115, *119*; restaurants outside Japan, 121
Kearney, Michael, 78
khai pen, 83, 91–94
khai kiep, 83, 91, 93–94
konbini, 122–7, 137, 141; criticism of, 125–26; food in, 123, 131; franchising, 124l; history of, 122, 134; number of, 122; services of, 122–23; use of information technology, 124. *See also* 7-Eleven; Lawson; *Onigiri*
konbini onigiri, 141–42
Kraft cheese, 74

Lao PDR, 83–94
—bioprospecting and, 90–91
—development in, 87, 89
—ethnic groups in, 86
—food insecurity in, 83–85
—food system in, 86–87; colonialism and, 88
—fish in, 87–88
—hunger foods in, 83, 92–94; export as heritage foods, 83, 92–93
—per capita income in, 84
—poverty in, 85
—rice in, 84–87, 89–90, 92–93
—trade in food, 84
—wild foods in, 83, 87, 89–90

—*See also khai pen; khai kiep*
Lawson, 134, 137–38, 143n5, 144n7; *Onigiri-ya* campaign, 138–40. *See also Onigiri*
Linger, Daniel, 104–5

Mali, 49–65
—consumer spending in, 51
—cotton production in, 60, 63, 66n7
—food in: export production of, 59–60, 63; external dependence and, 56; French colonialism and, 49, 52, 54; gendered production of, 59, 61–62; government regulation of, 58–59; grain, 52–53, 63, 66n5; intermediaries and, 58–59, 61; local versus imported, 52–53; peanuts, 60–62; powdered milk, 56 (*See also* Nestle); price of imported, 57; processing and, 56–59, rural diet, 52–53; self-sufficiency, 58–59. *See also* fast food
—foreign aid and, 50, 63
—groceries in, 55–56
—history of, 49–50
—map of, *50*
—middle-class in, 49, 51–52, 57; composition of, 51; diet of, 49, 52–54, 59, 61–63; invisibility of, 51, 63
—political economy in, 49
—retail market system in, 54–55, 57, 60–61; gender in, 55, 60; traditions of, 56
—structural adjustment and, 50–51, 60
—subsector analysis in, 49, 63
Mankekar, Purnima, 104
market forces, 4; global capital and, 69; in Yap, 46
McDonaldization, 20, 74
McDonalds, 13, 18; in Australia, 227–29; contrasted to farmers' markets, 14; French cuisine and, 74; healthy options at, 228–29; national food sources and, 228; pedestrians and, 228, 232–33; in Philippines, 147, 150–52, 154–56; protests against, 75–76, 222; in Russia, 97, 102; Taco Bell and, 73. *See also* fast food; Slow Food; Mcjobs

McJobs, 73. *See also* McDonalds
Mexico, 69–79; agricultural subsidies in, 72; cuisine, modernization of, 70–72; developed world organizations and, 75; indigenous exploitation in, 77; labor migration from, 76; *masa harina (see* Mexico, tortillas); middle-class in, 70, 75; migrant remittances to, 76–77; revolutionary tradition, 69, 75; tortillas, 70–72, 76; tourism in, 70, 77. *See also* Grupo Maseca; Taco Bell
Mintz, Sidney, 13–14, 117, 126–27. *See also* food of moderate speed
mitmit. See Yap: gifting in
modernization, 6–7, 14; social change and, 9
moral economies, 214. *See also* economies of sentiment
Multinational corporations, 78; in Mali, 56–57. See also Grupo Maseca
Mussolini, Benito, 79

Nabhan, Gary, 234–35
NAFTA. *See* North American Free Trade Agreement
Neighborly farms, 212–14
Nestle, 56–57, 65
Newman's Own, 250, 254
North American Free Trade Agreement (NAFTA), 75, 79

Obesity, 15, 32
Onigiri, 131–42, 143n1; commodification of, 132; history of, 132, 135; moral discourse on, 141; sales of, 131–32, 134, 139; school lunches and, 132–33; social role of, 134–35, 141; symbolic role of, 133–35. *See also* Japan: fast food in; *Konbini*
Ott, Sandra, 207

Petrini, Carlo, 14, 79, 99, 105, 222
Philippines, 147–57
—fast food growth in, 156
—local tastes in 154, 157
—middle class in, 156–57
—national palate of, 154

—San Fernando city, 148; commerce in, 148–49, 155–56; ethnic Chinese in, 148, 155
—*See also* McDonalds: in Philippines
post-Fordist flexible production, 249

Ritzer, George, 19, 73, 234
Roadside Restaurants in the Automobile Age, 221
Ruski, 104
Russia, 97–108
—culinary magazines in, 101–2, 105
—desire for travel by citizens of, 97–98, 107; promotions and, 102
—food travel in, 97, 100–4, 107
—foreign restaurants in, 107
—nostalgia cuisine, 98, 104–5, 107; compared to Slow Food, 106. *See also* Russia, theme restaurants in
—theme restaurants in, 103, 106, 109n15, 110n16

Schlosser, Eric. *See Fast Food Nation*
7-Eleven, 124, 128n5
—in Japan, 132, 143n2; expansion of, 134–35; marketing strategy of, 134–37. *See also Onigiri*
—just-in-time system, 124, 137
—*See also* Fordism, *Konbini*
Sizzle Bento. *See* intermediate food
slow food, 10–11; artisanal cheese as, 203; car-centered diets and, 223–27, 235–36, 238; Chinatown and, 165; class and, 22, 77; international quality of, 233–34; new directions for, 237; Sydney and, 223, 226. *See also* intermediate food; fast food/slow food dichotomy, challenge to; Slow Food
Slow Food, 9, 10, 77–8, 99–100; artisanal cheese and, 209; car-reliance and, 223–27, 235; changes in meaning of, 234; criticisms of, 22, 78, 201–2, 233–35; history of, 69–70, 75, 204; Italian Communist Party and, 69; McDonalds and, 222; nostalgia and, 10, 105, 109n12. *See also* Petrini, Carlo; slow food

spices, 4
"squat and gobble," 14
Starbucks, 242, 244, 255; code of conduct, 253; protests against, 244. *See also* fair trade coffee
subsector analysis, 52. *See also* commodity chain; Mali: subsector analysis in
subsistence, 33–34
subsistence economy, 45
Subway, 16
sugar, 4
supermarkets, 18. *See also* Mali: groceries in
supply chains, 123–24. *See also* commodity chains
sustainability, 79, 210; agricultural practices and, 174, 181; coffee production and, 245–46; corporate social responsibility and, 253; local level and, 8. *See also* Community Supported Agriculture
Sustainable Coffee Conference, 245
Sutton, David, 100
Sydney Morning Herald Good Living Growers' Market, 223–26; distance traveled to, *225*
synesthesia. *See* Sutton, David

Taco Bell, 13, 70; history of, 73–74; in Mexico, 70, 73–74
Taylorization, 73
Tea, 4
Tea and Coffee Trade Journal, 245, 251
terroir, 94, 210–11
Tía Tana, 75, 77
tradition, 16–17; fluidity of, 45
TransFair, 244, 251–52, 254
Tsukiji wholesale fish market, 116, 120

U.S. Secretary of Agriculture, 194

Vermont, 203–14; agricultural regulations in, 204; dairy production in, 203–4; need for agricultural development in, 208
Vermont Cheese Council, 201, 204
Vermont Shepherd, 201, 206–8, 211, 214; cheese-making guild and, 208–9

Wal-Mart, 23, 195
Waters, Alice, 204
Watson, James. *See Golden Arches East*
Whole Foods, 195, 201, 212, 252
Wilk, Richard, 65

Yap, 31–46
—access to electricity in, 38, 41
—cash crops in, 32
—culinary categories in, 39, 41
—*def. See* Yap: household in
—dietary choice in, 40, 46
—food consumption: hierarchy and, 38–39, 44; social role of, 33, 36, 43
—food imports in, 32, 34, 40, 42; economic consequences of, 32, 39; indigenization of, 39–40; perceptions of cultural loss and, 32
—food transfers in, 40–44. *See also* Yap: sharing of food resources in
—*ggaan. See* Yap: culinary categories in
—gifting in, 41, 43
—household in, 33–38, 42, 44; defined, 35; division of labor by age in, 38; division of labor by gender in, 37–38; hours of food production and, 37; life cycle of, 37, 41, 44; linkages between, 40–41, 44
—history of, 34
—land in, 35–36
—local foods in, 31, 45; decline of production in, 31; gendered production of, 31–32, 37; level of production, 40; monetized sale of, 42
—modernity in, 45–47
—political economy of, 32
—sharing of food resources in, 32–33, 40, 43–44
—*tabinaw* in, 35, 39, 44
—*thumag. See* Yap: culinary categories in
—United States subsidies to, 34; wage economy and, 40

Zapata, Emiliano, 69
Zapatistas, 75. *See also* Mexico: revolutionary tradition in

About the Contributors

Cathy Banwell is an anthropologist of risky consumption. She works at the National Centre for Epidemiology and Population Health at the Australian National University.

Theodore C. Bestor is a professor of anthropology at Harvard University. His writings include *Neighborhood Tokyo* (1989), *Doing Fieldwork in Japan* (2003), and *Tsukiji: The Fish Market at the Center of the World* (2004). He is continuing his research on global food systems and is also studying skyscrapers in Tokyo.

Michael L. Burton is professor of anthropology at the University of California, Irvine. His main research focus is on social processes within families and households, including economic anthropology of the household, gender division of labor, and cross-cultural human development.

Melissa L. Caldwell is assistant professor of anthropology at University of California, Santa Cruz. She writes on changing food practices and food welfare programs in postsocialist societies. She is the author of *Not by Bread Alone: Social Support in the New Russia* and co-editor with James L. Watson of *The Cultural Politics of Food and Eating*.

Jane Dixon is a food sociologist. She works at the National Centre for Epidemiology and Population Health at the Australian National University.

James A. Egan is a lecturer in anthropology at the University of California, Irvine. A chapter based on his research on the Yapese cultural topography of wealth was published in a previous SEA volume. He did the primary ethnography for the chapter in this book and supervised the survey data collection.

Sarah Hinde is working on a PhD on car-reliance. She works at the National Centre for Epidemiology and Population Health at the Australian National University.

Valerie Imbruce is a doctoral candidate at the Graduate Center of the City University of New York and the New York Botanical Garden. Her current work focuses on the changing nature of markets for agricultural products and how small farmers deal with opportunity and loss.

Dolores Koenig is professor of anthropology at American University in Washington, DC. She has focused on the anthropology of development in French-speaking West Africa, with special emphasis on the ways in which households respond to the changing political economy. She is a co-author of *Innovation and Individuality in African Development* and has published articles in the *Journal of Political Ecology, Urban Anthropology and Studies of Cultural Systems and World Economic Development*, and elsewhere.

Sarah Lyon is an assistant professor of anthropology at the University of Kentucky. She completed her dissertation, *Maya Coffee Farmers and the Fair Trade Commodity Chain*, and received her PhD from Emory University in 2005. Currently she is researching the impact of alternative markets and corporate social responsibility in Guatemalan communities.

Ty Matejowsky is an assistant professor of anthropology at the University of Central Florida. He received his PhD in anthropology from Texas A&M University in 2001. His research focuses on fast food and retail globalization in the Philippines.

Heather McIntyre is interested in farmer's markets. She works at the National Centre for Epidemiology and Population Health at the Australian National University.

Sidney Mintz, research professor of anthropology at Johns Hopkins University, has authored, co-authored, and edited fifteen books and three hundred articles during nearly sixty years of teaching and research. Mintz studies Caribbean social history and the anthropology of food. His recent work focuses on the importance of food in material and symbolic life. Mintz's *Sweetness and Power* (1985) looks at the history of sugar as a tool for studying the rise of consumer economies, and sugar's role in linking tropical colonies to Europe. In *Tasting Food, Tasting Freedom* (1996), Mintz looked at food behavior anthropologically, to ask what *cuisine* really means when applied to societies such as the United States. He is currently conducting research on soybeans and soy foods in world economy and diet.

Karen L. Nero is professor and director of Macmillan Brown Centre for Pacific Studies at the University of Canterbury. An anthropologist, she investigates intersections between indigenous knowledge and practices. She was field director of the UCI study of the Social Relations of Contemporary Food Systems in Four Micronesian Societies.

Heather Paxson teaches anthropology at the Massachusetts Institute of Technology. Her current study of American artisanal cheesemakers and cheeses reflects a wider interest in socio-ethical relationships that connect bodies, selves, and communities. She is the author of *Making Modern Mothers: Ethics and Family Planning in Urban Greece.*

Jeffrey M. Pilcher, associate professor of history at the University of Minnesota, is the author of *¡Que vivan los tamales! Food and the Making of Mexican Identity* (1998) and *Food in World History* (2005). The chapter in this volume comes from his current research on the globalization of Mexican cuisine.

Lois Stanford is an agricultural anthropologist at New Mexico State University, Las Cruces. Her research focuses on local-level responses to the transformation of agricultural systems, studying how farmer organizations and cooperatives defend market interests, identify niches, and maintain local food systems. In Mexico, she documented the social organization of the avocado industry and is writing a book on the bi-national integration of Michoacán's and California's avocado industry. She also researches alternative agricultural organizations in the U.S. Southwest and the preservation of local food systems and foodways.

Penny Van Esterik is professor of anthropology at York University, Toronto. She teaches nutritional anthropology, advocacy anthropology, and feminist theory, and works primarily in Southeast Asia. Past publications include *Materializing Thailand* (on cultural interpretations of gender in Thailand), *Taking Refuge: Lao Buddhists in North America* (on the reintroduction of Buddhism by Lao refugees to North America), and *Food and Culture: A Reader,* edited with Carole Counihan (currently being revised). She has recently been on research leave in Lao PDR, assisting the National University of Laos in the development of research capacity in the area of food security, resource management, and poverty reduction.

Gavin Hamilton Whitelaw is a doctoral student in Yale University's department of anthropology. With the assistance of a Fulbright doctoral dissertation research fellowship, his fieldwork includes ongoing participant observation as a store clerk in a downtown Tokyo *konbini.* Gavin is presently affiliated with Waseda University. His other research projects include Japan–North American soy distribution and concerns over genetically modified foods.

Richard Wilk is professor of anthropology and gender studies at Indiana University. He has conducted fieldwork in Belize over a span of more than thirty years, and has also worked in West Africa and the United States. His most recent book is *Home Cooking in the Global Village* (2006); he is also author of *Household Ecology* (1991) and *Economies and Cultures* (1996), and has edited or co-edited seven other volumes on topics as diverse as household archaeology, the anthropology of media, and beauty pageants.